Protecting, Isolating, and Controlling Behavior
Population And Resource Control Measures in Counterinsurgency Campaigns

A Thesis Presented to the Faculty of the US Army
Command and General Staff College
by
Mark E. Battjes, Major, US Army
M.S., University of Maryland University College
B.S., University of Southern California

Fort Leavenworth, Kansas
2011

The cover photo courtesy of the Library of Congress is that of General Dwight Eisenhower giving orders to American paratroopers in England.

Published by Books Express Publishing
Copyright © Books Express, 2012
ISBN 978-1-78039-803-7

Books Express publications are available from all good retail and online booksellers. For publishing proposals and direct ordering please contact us at: info@books-express.com

Abstract

Protecting, Isolating, and Controlling Behavior

Population and Resource Control Measures in Counterinsurgency Campaigns, By Major Mark E. Battjes

The classical counterinsurgency theorists emphasize that it is necessary for the government to gain and maintain control of the population in order to defeat the insurgency. They describe population and resource control measures as a means of doing so. However, some contemporary writers have questioned the legitimacy of such tactics and doubt that they can be employed effectively in modern campaigns. Four case studies from three different campaigns: the Philippines, Vietnam, and Iraq, examine how population and resource control measures can be employed effectively and legitimately by the counterinsurgent force. The case studies reveal that protecting and isolating the population is the most critical component of any such measures, without this condition the measures will not achieve their desired effect. The case studies also reveal that once the protection and isolation are in place, the government can focus on controlling the behavior of the population. That is, it can prevent behavior that supports the insurgency while enabling behavior that supports the government or is neutral. This denies the insurgency its means of support and facilitates the destruction of its armed and subversive elements by the counterinsurgent forces.

Objectives of the Art of War Scholars Program

The Art of War Scholars Program is a laboratory for critical thinking. It offers a select group of students a range of accelerated, academically rigorous graduate level courses that promote analysis, stimulate the desire for life-long learning, and reinforce academic research skills. Art of War graduates will not be satisfied with facile arguments; they understand the complexities inherent in almost any endeavor and develop the tools and fortitude to confront such complexities, analyze challenges, and independently seek nuanced solutions in the face of those who would opt for cruder alternatives. Through the pursuit of these outcomes, the Art of War Scholars Program seeks to improve and deepen professional military education.

The Art of War Program places contemporary operations (such as those in Iraq and Afghanistan) in a historical framework by examining earlier military campaigns. Case studies and readings have been selected to show the consistent level of complexity posed by military campaigns throughout the modern era. Coursework emphasizes the importance of understanding previous engagements in order to formulate policy and doctrinal response to current and future campaigns.

One unintended consequence of military history education is the phenomenon of commanders and policy makers "cherry picking" history—that is, pointing to isolated examples from past campaigns to bolster a particular position in a debate, without a comprehensive understanding of the context in which such incidents occurred. This trend of oversimplification leaves many historians wary of introducing these topics into broader, more general discussion. The Art of War program seeks to avoid this pitfall by a thorough examination of context. As one former student stated: "The insights gained have left me with more questions than answers but have increased my ability to understand greater complexities of war rather than the rhetorical narrative that accompanies cursory study of any topic."

Professor Michael Howard, writing "The Use and Abuse of Military History" in 1961, proposed a framework for educating military officers in the art of war that remains unmatched in its clarity, simplicity, and totality. The Art of War program endeavors to model his plan:

> Three general rules of study must therefore be borne in mind by the officer who studies military history as a guide to his profession and who wishes to avoid pitfalls. First, he must study in **width**. He must observe the way in which warfare has developed over a long historical period. Only by seeing what does change can one deduce

what does not; and as much as can be learnt from the great discontinuities of military history as from the apparent similarities of the techniques employed by the great captains through the ages....Next he must study in **depth**. He should take a single campaign and explore it thoroughly, not simply from official histories, but from memoirs, letters, diaries... until the tidy outlines dissolve and he catches a glimpse of the confusion and horror of real experience... and, lastly, he must study in **context**. Campaigns and battles are not like games of chess or football matches, conducted in total detachment from their environment according to strictly defined rules. Wars are not tactical exercises writ large. They are...conflicts of societies, and they can be fully understood only if one understands the nature of the society fighting them. The roots of victory and defeat often have to be sought far from the battlefield, in political, social, and economic factors which explain why armies are constituted as they are, and why their leaders conduct them in the way they do....

It must not be forgotten that the true use of history, military or civil... is not to make men clever for the next time; it is to make them wise forever.

Gordon B. Davis, Jr.
Brigadier General, US Army
Deputy Commanding General
CAC LD&E

Daniel Marston
DPhil (Oxon) FRHistS
Ike Skelton Distinguished Chair in
  the Art of War
US Army Command & General
  Staff College

Acknowledgments

This thesis and the research behind it were only possible as a result of the tremendous support provided by so many people. Thanks are due to the faculty and staff of the Command and General Staff College who supported the 2011 Art of War Scholars Program. Many individuals, units, and institutions across the United States and the United Kingdom generously provided us with their time, facilities, and assistance and we owe them a debt of gratitude. Special thanks to Dr. Marston and Dr. Hull for their guidance, support, and encouragement.

Sincerest thanks to my Art of War colleagues of Nathan Springer, Dustin Mitchell, Benjamin Boardman, Richard Johnson, Robert Green, Aaron Kaufman, and Thomas Walton for all of their assistance and camaraderie during the course and throughout our research. A big thanks to my family and friends for their support along the way.

Finally, thanks to Maggie for enduring lengthy, one-sided, animated discussions about historical campaigns, carefully editing countless pages of text, and for sacrificing time that rightfully belonged to her.

Table Of Contents

Abstract iii
Objectives iv
Acknowledgments vi
Table of Contents vii
Acronyms viii
    Chapter 1: Introduction 1
    Chapter 2: Insurgency, Counterinsurgency, and Control of the
        Population 7
    Chapter 3: The Philippines, 1899-1935 53
    Chapter 4: Vietnam, 1954-1963 89
    Chapter 5: Vietnam, 1966-1970 129
    Chapter 6: Iraq, 2003–2011 191
    Chapter 7: Conclusions And Recommendations 245
Further Research 257
Bibliography 259

Acronyms

1AD	1st Armored Division
1ID	1st Infantry Division
101 ABN	101st Airborne Division (Air Assault)
25ID	25th Infantry Division
3ACR	3d Armored Cavalry Regiment
3ID	3d Infantry Division
4ID	4th Infantry Division
82ABN	82d Airborne Division
AAR	After Action Report
APC	Accelerated Pacification Campaign
AQI	Al Qaeda in Iraq
ARVN	Army of the Republic of Vietnam
BCT	Brigade Combat Team
CGSC	Command and General Staff College
CIA	Central Intelligence Agency
CENTCOM	US Central Command
COIN	Counterinsurgency
COP	Combat Outpost
CORDS	Civil Operations and Revolutionary Development Support
CPA	Coalition Provisional Authority
CTZ	Corps Tactical Zone
DRV	Democratic Republic of Vietnam
EFP	Explosively Formed Penetrator
FM	Field Manual
FWMAF	Free World Military Armed Forces
G.O.	General Orders
GOI	Government of Iraq
GVN	Government of Vietnam
HI	Harassment and Interdiction

IA	Iraqi Army
IED	Improvised Explosive Device
IIFFORCEV	II Field Force, Vietnam
IIG	Interim Iraqi Government
IP	Iraqi Police
ISF	Iraqi Security Forces
JAM	*Jaysh-al-Mahdi*
LOC	Line of Communication
MACV	Military Assistance Command, Vietnam
MEDCAPS	Medical Civic Action Programs
MEF	Marine Expeditionary Force
MNC-I	Multi-National Corps Iraq
MND-B	Multi-National Division Baghdad
MNF-I	Multi-National Force Iraq
NLF	National Liberation Front
NVA	North Vietnamese Army
OMS	Office of the *Martyr Sadr*
ORLL	Operations Report–Lessons Learned
PAVN	People's Army of Vietnam
PIRA	Provisional Irish Republican Army
PROVN	Program for the Pacification and Long-Term Development of South Vietnam
RD	Revolutionary Development
RVN	Republic of Vietnam
RVNAF	Republic of Vietnam Armed Forces
TAL	Transitional Administrative Law
TAOI	Tactical Area of Operational Interest
TAOR	Tactical Area of Responsibility
TNA	Transitional National Assembly
UNSC	United Nations Security Council
USAID	United States Agency for International

	Development
USMC	United States Marine Corps
USOM	United States Operations Mission
VBIED	Vehicle Borne Improvise Explosive Device
VC	Viet Cong

Chapter 1
Introduction

Controlling the Population

Population and resource control measures have been employed to one degree or another in every modern counterinsurgency campaign. They have ranged from the extremely coercive, such as the reconcentration of the population by the US Army in the Philippines, to the relatively benign, such as registering cars in Iraq. They are also an essential part of how Western, liberal, democratic states secure their populations and the symbols and mechanisms of their government from violence.

Modern states supply their populations with identification cards, require them to register cars, conduct censuses, restrict the ability of the population to purchase certain commodities, and deny them freedom of movement when security demands it. If the President of the United States is arriving in town, it is best to avoid driving anywhere remotely near where he will be. Moreover, they do so, generally, without the explicit endorsement of the population. All of this notwithstanding, population and resource control measures are often viewed negatively.

During the course of the research for this paper, a number of US and UK military officers became visibly uncomfortable when asked about their employment of them. One US Army Brigade Combat Team (BCT) commander did not even want to use the term, preferring to say that what he was doing was creating a "controlled environment."[1] Yet, as one senior British Army officer noted, "you do have to be hard headed in COIN [counterinsurgency] because you are facing one of the most dangerous threats to governance."[2]

This highlights the primary difficulty associated with the employment of population and resource control measures. They are an essential tool in a counterinsurgency campaign but how can they be employed effectively so that the most severe restrictions can be lifted quickly? How can they be enacted and enforced legitimately so that they do not alienate the population from the government? Can they be utilized in a manner that prevents only behavior that supports the insurgents?

Research Questions

This thesis seeks to answer the following generic research question. How can the government and its counterinsurgent forces employ population and resource control measures as part of a comprehensive campaign to defeat an insurgency? To answer this question, this thesis will address several supporting questions.

1. What does the historic application of such measures tell us about employing them in the contemporary operating environment?

2. How can population and resource control measures be employed legitimately? Are there key conditions or outcomes that make their employment more or less legitimate?

3. Can the measures be targeted so that they prevent behavior that supports the insurgent and enable behavior that supports the government?

4. As population and resource control measures are essentially legal actions, is it necessary for them to be employed within a holistic control mechanism established by the state?

Methodology

This study is based primarily on the close examination of historical case studies. While population and resource control measures have been employed in every modern counterinsurgency campaign, it was necessary to focus the research on a few case studies in order to examine the employment of such measures with sufficient depth. Population and resource control measures closely reflect the form of the threatened government, respond to the nature of the insurgency, and are shaped by the type of counterinsurgent forces that employ them. Therefore, only a thorough understanding of the entire campaign allows any valid conclusions to be drawn.

In Chapter 2, the thesis considers the nature of war, insurgency, and counterinsurgency by reviewing the work of the highly regarded classical and modern theorists of war and counterinsurgency. It also briefly examines the nature of control in war and why it is such a critical element. The review also examines current US Army doctrine regarding the employment of population and resource control measures. The second chapter concludes with the establishment of a population and resource control measures construct whose validity will be tested through the four case studies.

Beginning with Chapter 3, the thesis considers four case studies drawn from three campaigns. Each of the case studies has unique characteristics that enable the population and resource control measures employed to be considered in light of those characteristics. The four case studies also benefit from an abundance of primary source material concerning the employment of such measures. This is critical as an understanding of how the measures were actually employed and what their effects were on the insurgency can only be obtained through a close reading of the primary sources.

The US campaign in the Philippines from 1898 to1935 composes the first case study. This campaign is unique as it is the only one in which US forces are the colonial power. It is also a campaign in which the US used both military and civil law to establish its control over territory. Furthermore, it highlights the difficulty of determining the legitimacy of any given population and resource control measure. The tactic of reconcentrating the population horrified the US public but it was also very effective and does not seem to have been considered illegitimate by ordinary Filipinos.

The second case study considers the employment of population and resource control measures by the regime of Premier Ngo Dinh Diem in South Vietnam from 1954 to1963. This presents an opportunity to research the use of such measures by a regime that is allied with and supported by the US but without a significant level of US military participation. Moreover, it presents an opportunity to reconsider the Strategic Hamlet Program. This program has generally been written off as an utter failure but as US military and Vietnamese Communist documents have been declassified in recent years it is obvious that the truth is much more nuanced.

The next case study also occurs in Vietnam but examines how US ground forces supported the Government of Vietnam's pacification efforts with population and resource control measures using the example of the 25th Infantry Division's operations from 1966 to1970. The notable feature of this case study is the battle with Communist main force units and their effect on the counterinsurgency effort. It also affords a chance to examine how well US forces, operating completely outside of the control mechanism of the Vietnamese state, performed in support of that mechanism.

The final case study looks at the as yet unfinished US campaign in Iraq. Operation Iraqi Freedom has been lengthy, has involved nearly every active brigade-size unit in the US Army, and has evolved significantly over time. The campaign is also unique in that the US and its Iraqi partners confronted multiple insurgent groups within the same geographical area.[3] Moreover, during 2006 and 2007 in Baghdad, the insurgencies fought each other for control, producing a situation more akin to a civil war than a true insurgency. Thus, studying the Iraq campaign, though not yet complete, enables a rich analysis of the employment of population and resource control measures in the contemporary operating environment.

Summary of Results

The historical record indicates that the employment of population and resource control measures almost always produces short-term tactical success. However, in order for that success to be sustained over time and across the entire theater of war, they must be employed within a holistic control mechanism that enables them to be synchronized and mutually reinforcing. Protection and isolation of the population are the most important objective of any population and resource control measure regime. If the protection and isolation components break down, all other elements will fail. Moreover, it is primarily the security afforded to the population through their protection and isolation that makes such measures legitimate.

Notes

1. BH020, BCT Commander, Interview by Mark Battjes, Ben Boardman, Robert Green, Richard Johnson, Aaron Kaufman, Dustin Mitchell, Nathan Springer, and Thomas Walton, 21 March 2011, Washington, DC.

2. BI010, Senior British Officer, Interview by Mark Battjes, Benjamin Boardman, Robert Green, Richard Johnson, Aaron Kaufman, Dustin Mitchell, and Nathan Springer, 29 March 2011, United Kingdom.

3. Although the US confronted several distinct insurgencies in the different islands of the Philippine archipelago, they did not occur in the same geographical space. Moreover, the insurgencies on the outlying islands did not threaten US control of the archipelago as significantly as did the Tagalog insurgency on the main island of Luzon.

Chapter 2
Insurgency, Counterinsurgency, and Control of the Population

> Undoubtedly some of my readers will accuse me of ignoring the deeper causes of revolutionary wars. They will cite poverty, exploitations, imperialism, poor administration, and so forth. I plead guilty to these charges. I recognize that such conditions breed revolutionary wars. The governing authorities should detect and eliminate them early because revolutionaries will exploit them to create popular support for their cause. Nevertheless, experience indicates that often governing authorities do not recognize the danger in time and allow a revolutionary movement to spawn. By this time, mere reforms will not only be ineffective but will be thwarted by the revolutionaries who want only to oust the old regime. Much more important, however, will be the fact that often the Free World cannot allow the country to pass under the control of Communist-supported revolutionaries. In such a situation, we cannot predicate our actions on what might have been. We must accept the situation as it is and win.
>
> —John J. McCuen, *The Art of Counter-Revolutionary War*

As the quote above indicates, it is useless to focus on actions that a government may have taken to prevent an insurgency from occurring once it has begun. Rather, the government must recognize the circumstances that confront it and take all necessary action to defeat the insurgency. This chapter will examine the nature of war and, within that context, insurgency and counterinsurgency. It will discuss why controlling the population is necessary for governments, particularly when combating an insurgency, and a mechanism that governments and their counterinsurgent forces may employ to maintain control where they have it and to regain control where they have lost it.

Insurgency and Counterinsurgency

The US Army's current understanding of insurgency and counterinsurgency is informed by its experience and the writings of many historians, theorists, and practitioners. These writers have presented insurgency and counterinsurgency in many different ways, complicating their study. This section will examine the nature of war and use the observations of historians, theorists and practitioners to derive characteristics of insurgency and counterinsurgency and establish definitions for them.

War

Before insurgency and counterinsurgency can be studied, it is necessary to examine the nature of war itself. One of the seminal writers on this subject is the Prussian military officer, Carl Von Clausewitz. Clausewitz' writing is an excellent starting point for understanding war, as it is studied by the US and other Western armies. Another prominent writer on the subject, the Chinese general Sun Tzu, has much to say on the specifics of waging war but does not, as Clausewitz does, establish what war is at a fundamental level.

Clausewitz defined war in two different ways. At the beginning of his first chapter, his definition stated, *"war is thus an act of force to compel our enemy to do our will."*[1] He then noted that:

> Force–that is, physical force, for moral force has no existence save as expressed in the state and the law–is thus the *means* of war; to impose our will on the enemy is its *object*. To secure that object we must render the enemy powerless; and that, in theory, is the true aim of warfare. That aim takes the place of the object, discarding it as something not actually part of war itself.[2]

For Clausewitz this is the central nature of war. It is force, in all of its manifestations, employed to render the enemy completely unable to resist. Thus, will the enemy capitulate and victory be achieved.

Regarding the use of force, Clausewitz observed that "kind-hearted people might of course think there was some ingenious way to disarm or defeat an enemy without too much bloodshed and might imagine this is the true goal of the art of war."[3] However, Clausewitz viewed this as a dangerous fallacy. He noted that "it would be futile–even wrong–to try and shut one's eyes to what war really is from sheer distress at its brutality."[4] In Clausewitz' view, war is fundamentally violent and both sides must be prepared to use all of the force at their disposal to completely disarm and defeat the other.

He clarified this point by stating, "if the enemy is to be coerced you must put him in a situation that is even more unpleasant than the sacrifice you call on him to make. The hardships of that situation must not of course be merely transient, at least not in appearance. Otherwise the enemy would not give in but would wait for things to improve."[5] If the enemy does not capitulate he is still a threat because "so long as I have not overthrown my opponent I am bound to fear he may overthrow me. Thus I am not in control. He dictates to me as much as I dictate to him."[6]

Clausewitz' initial definition of war logically leads to these observations. As war is a contest between opponents who both seek forcefully to impose their will on the other, it is necessary that one be completely disarmed in order for the other to win. Thus, each opponent must employ all of the elements of power available to them to win. If they do not, they risk giving the enemy an opportunity to exploit through a greater exertion of force. This was Clausewitz' conception of absolute war: both sides applying every means available to them to win. It was not a vision of war that he believed would come to pass but an idealized version of war that could never be achieved.[7]

The use of force is modified, however, by the reason for fighting the war, which is the political objective. In Clausewitz' initial discussion surrounding the use of force in war the political objective was overshadowed. However, he later noted that:

> If it is all calculation of probabilities based on given individuals and conditions the *political object*, which was the *original motive*, must become an essential factor in the equation. The smaller the penalty you demand from your opponent, the less you can expect him to try and deny it to you; the smaller the effort he makes, the less you need make yourself. Moreover, the more modest your own political aim, the less importance you attach to it and the less reluctantly you will abandon it if you must.[8]

That is, the nature of war might be absolute, but the men and states fighting it would necessarily limit the means they used to achieve their objective.[9] Nonetheless, Clausewitz stated that the military commander must understand the absolute ideal of war and approximate it *"when he can* or *when he must."*[10]

It is the political objective which dictates the military goals to be achieved and the overall effort made by the state to accomplish it. This observation led to the conclusion that "war is no pastime . . . It is a serious means to a serious end."[11] Moreover, "when whole communities go to war–whole peoples, and especially civilized people–the reason always lies in some political situation, and the occasion is always due to some political object. War, therefore, is an act of policy."[12] Clausewitz referred to this as a more precise definition of war.

He further identified that :

> We see, therefore, that war is not merely an act of policy but a true political instrument, a continuation of political intercourse, carried on by other means. What remains peculiar to war is simply the peculiar nature of its means. War in general, and the commander in any specific instance,

is entitled to require that the trend and designs of policy shall not be inconsistent with these means. That, of course, is no small demand; but however much it may affect political aims in a given case, it will never do more than modify them. The political object is the goal, war is the means of reaching it, and means can never be considered in isolation from their purpose.[13]

Thus, in Clausewitz' conception war could only be understood in relation to the reason it was being waged, the political objective. This objective and the importance of the objective to the state seeking to accomplish it would dictate the conduct of the war, particularly the use of force. Moreover, as states fundamentally changed their natures so then would their policies, and thus their wars, change.[14] Clausewitz summarized:

> *First*, therefore, it is clear that war should never be thought of as *something autonomous* but always as an *instrument of policy*; otherwise the entire history of war would contradict us. Only this approach will enable us to penetrate the problem intelligently. *Second*, this way of looking at it will show us how wars must vary with the nature of their motives and of the situations which give rise to them.[15]

Clausewitz was also indicating the need for the state, and the commander, to possess a strategy to win the war. He dismissed the definition posited by Heinrich von Bülow that differentiated strategy and tactics by the distance of marches.[16] Rather, Clausewitz stated that strategy was "the use of engagement for the purpose of war."[17] He noted that the strategist had to "define an aim for the entire operational side of the war that will be in accordance with its purpose. In other words, he will draft the plan of the war, and the aim will determine the series of actions intended to achieve it."[18]

This framework provided a way of understanding war and how it was to be waged. Most particularly, war cannot be divorced from the political objective and causes that are driving it. Clausewitz cautioned practitioners that "the first, the supreme, the most far-reaching act of judgment that the statesman and commander have to make is to establish by that test the kind of war on which they are embarking; neither mistaking it for, nor trying to turn it into, something that is alien to its nature."[19] Once they have made this judgment, they must determine a strategy that will employ the means available to the state and army to accomplish the political objectives. This would, in most cases, lead to a limited war but the statesman and the commander both had to be prepared to commit all of the state's resources if it became necessary, approximating an absolute war.

Clausewitz' definition of war is crucial to understand in order to properly study insurgency and counterinsurgency. Insurgency and counterinsurgency are war, and like all wars, they require particular means to accomplish a very specific objective. If they are considered to be something other than war, their fundamental nature is denied and inappropriate solutions to the problems that they pose may be implemented with disastrous consequences. The state and its leaders must understand what is at stake in the war and employ all the means necessary to win it.

Observations of Insurgency and Counterinsurgency

If insurgency and counterinsurgency are wars with specific objectives and particular means of accomplishing those objectives it is important to identify them to understand the nature of insurgency and counterinsurgency. Many practitioners, theorists, and historians have recorded their observations of insurgency and counterinsurgency campaigns. Examining and comparing these observations, made from the perspective of both the insurgent and the counterinsurgent and different cultural backgrounds, can yield a description of the particular objectives and means of these conflicts. These fundamental characteristics can then be used to derive an accurate definition for insurgency and counterinsurgency.

The Insurgent Experience

Chinese Communist leader Mao Zedong waged a protracted insurgency campaign that culminated in his assumption of total control over China. He recognized this war as total and noted, "because ours is the resistance of a semi colonial country against imperialism, our hostilities must have a clearly defined political goal."[20] He further articulated this objective as the "complete emancipation of the Chinese people."[21] In emancipating the Chinese people, he also intended to establish a new, Communist regime. This new regime would be a major shift in the political governance of China. Echoing Clausewitz, Mao noted that this war could not be divorced from what he considered China's national policy.[22]

Mao understood that accomplishing his objective would require the complete mobilization of the Chinese population and the employment of every means available to defeat his enemies. He articulated his strategy[23] as:

1. Arousing and organizing the people.
2. Achieving internal unification politically.

3. Establishing bases.

4. Equipping forces.

5. Recovering national strength.

6. Destroying enemy's national strength.

7. Regaining lost territories.[24]

This strategy required his army to engage in political operations as their first and most essential task, because the war required the support of the population.[25] Gaining and then leveraging the support of the population is the essence of the first four steps listed above. Mao's army had to politically indoctrinate the masses, control them, and use that control to establish bases from which to develop a disciplined and well equipped guerrilla force. This force would then attack the enemy where they were weak to build up the strength of Mao's army and weaken the enemy's.

Mao instructed his guerrilla bands to seek out the enemy where they were weak to attack, exhaust, and ultimately annihilate them.[26] The guerrilla bands destroyed critical infrastructure such as railroad tracks and depots to hamper the enemy. They also employed printing presses, paper, and brushes to conduct propaganda to subvert the governing authority outside of their areas of control.[27] Such political subversion enabled his forces to increase the amount of the population under his control and increase the size of his guerrilla forces. While these actions did weaken the enemy, Mao did not believe that guerrilla warfare alone was sufficient to accomplish his objective.

Instead, the weakening of the enemy allowed the war to progress from guerrilla warfare to maneuver warfare. He stated that "our fundamental strategical form must be the war of movement. If we deny this, we cannot arrive at the victorious solution of the war."[28] Mao knew that to win he had to completely destroy the ability of his enemy to wage war, which would then allow him to gain control over the entire country and complete the accomplishment of his political objective.

Mao's writing greatly influenced the Vietnamese military leader Vo Nguyen Giap. Giap modified Mao's ideas to match the specific conditions within Vietnam itself and constructed a campaign to force the French to relinquish political control over Vietnam. He identified that the objective of the war against the French was "to win back the independence and unity of the country, to bring land to the peasants, and to defend the achievements of the August Revolution."[29] The August Revolution removed the feudal governmental structure in existence under the French and prior to their rule, so, similar to Mao's objective, his aim was not just liberation, but a fundamental change to the political structure of Vietnam.

Giap recognized that his enemy's forces, the French, were vastly superior to his at the outset of the war. As a result, he determined that:

> It was necessary to adopt a strategy of long-term resistance in order to maintain and gradually augment our forces, while nibbling at and progressively destroying those of the enemy. It was necessary to accumulate thousands of small victories and to turn them into one great success, gradually altering the balance of forces, transforming our weakness into power, and carrying off final victory.[30]

His strategy was based on a gradual, but steady, alteration of the balance of power in his favor. To accomplish this required the use of every means available. Thus, the war against the French was a total war.[31] It involved all elements of power–political, civil, and military–in support of the objectives of the campaign. It combined the political work of the party to subvert the French-led government and indoctrinate the population with attacks by guerrilla forces on the French-led armed forces and terror attacks against landholders to gain control of the country side.[32]

Once his forces began to alter the balance of power, Giap, as with Mao, transitioned from guerrilla warfare to maneuver warfare. He noted that:

> As the resistance war went on, the strategic role of mobile warfare became more important with every passing day. Its task was to annihilate a bigger and bigger number of the enemy in order to develop our own strength. . . . Only by annihilating the enemy's manpower could we smash his big offensives, safeguard our bases and rear areas, and win the initiative. By wiping out more and more of the enemy, by liberating larger and larger localities one after the other, we could eventually destroy the whole enemy force and liberate our country.[33]

Giap understood that only by destroying the enemy's means and will to fight could he accomplish his political objective.

Mao and Giap believed that the insurgencies that they led were wars. These wars were total, requiring the mobilization of the entire population to accomplish the objective of seizing political power and changing the political regime within the country. Controlling the population was a necessary subordinate objective to facilitate the mobilization of the population. Once mobilization occurred, they could leverage the manpower, material, and information support provided to alter the balance of power between their forces and the government's forces. After achieving near parity, they could use their forces to destroy the enemy's will and means to fight and achieve victory.

The French Experience

Roger Trinquier was an officer in the French Army during its counterinsurgency campaigns in Indochina and Algeria. Trinquier's participation in these operations and their ultimate outcomes led him to write about insurgency and counterinsurgency, which he characterized as modern warfare.[34] He stated that the objective of modern warfare was the *"overthrow of the established authority in a country and its replacement by another regime."*[35] In this statement, Trinquier indicates his adherence to the French theory of *guerre revolutionnaire* which was developed by officers whose service in Indochina confronting Giap's army had led them to formulate a new theory of counterinsurgency.[36]

The *guerre revolutionnaire* theorists recognized the insurgent's objective as the capture of political power and therefore concluded that the war could not be won through negotiation.[37] They also believed that the insurgents were either Communists, inspired by Communists, or irresponsible nationalists who could easily be exploited by the Communist bloc.[38] Thus, the West was under permanent assault from the Communist bloc and that required a response from all of society which was total. Moreover, as negotiations could not resolve the conflict, the war could "end only with the effective–if not the total–defeat of the enemy."[39]

The total nature of guerre revolutionnaire can be seen in Trinquier's writing regarding the need to gain the support of the population. Trinquier asserted that "the *sine qua non* of victory in *modern warfare* is the unconditional support of a population."[40] In this, he and the other adherents of guerre revolutionnaire recognized that the insurgent's combination of military and political warfare was not a weakness but an essential strength.[41] He then identified that if such support did not exist for the insurgents, they would seek to secure it through any possible means, but especially terrorism.[42] Moreover, he warned that in countering the insurgents:

> it is essential to realize that in *modern warfare* we are not up against just a few armed bands spread across a given territory but rather against an *armed clandestine organization* whose essential role is to impose its will upon the population. Victory will be obtained only through the complete destruction of that organization.[43]

In other words, in accordance with *guerre revolutionnaire* theory, counterinsurgency was a total war and it required the state to mobilize all of its power to wage it. Specifically, Trinquier, restating the theory, noted that "control of the masses through a tight organization, often through several organizations, is the master weapon of *modern warfare*."[44] If the insurgents exercised this control they could compel the populace to participate in the conflict by providing supplies, intelligence, and shelter.[45]

However, if the government controlled the population through a counter-organization, by registering each family with a designated agent and tying all of those agents into the government, for example, it could deny support to the insurgents by restricting the ownership and use of food, livestock, and resources, as well as the movement of the population itself.[46] These mechanisms enabled the government to isolate and suffocate the insurgents, while simultaneously protecting the population. Moreover, if the government controlled the population it could use this as a prelude to persuading them to provide it their unconditional support, Trinquier's necessary precondition for victory. However, the population could only provide this support if they were certain that the government would protect them and do everything possible to defeat the insurgents. Once the government obtained their support it could use the power generated to completely destroy the enemy's armed clandestine organization and win the war.

David Galula was also a French military officer and he served in Algeria from 1956-1958. He identified insurgency as a struggle for a series of intermediate objectives that lead ultimately to a change in the political structure of the country.[47] He believed that the conflict inherent in an insurgency was the result of the insurgent side's attempt to seize political power.[48] Echoing Clausewitz' definition of war, he stated that an insurgency was the "pursuit of the policy of a party . . . by every means."[49]

Galula believed that the population was the battleground in an insurgency.[50] He noted that the exercise of political power, the ultimate objective of insurgency, rested on "the tacit or explicit agreement of the population or, at worst, on its submissiveness."[51] Therefore, if the insurgents could physically control and gain the support of the population they would win.[52] Therefore, to successfully counter the insurgency, it was necessary for the government to control the population.[53]

Galula's control mechanism is much less holistic than Trinquier's counter-organization, however. He believed that the government could control the population using measures such as a census, curfew, and movement restrictions to isolate them from the insurgency.[54] These measures also protected the population, allowing them to support the government without fear of reprisal. The government could then destroy the insurgent's political organization, build local political parties, and form governments. These local governments would then be used as the base of a national party to exercise political power, and therefore control, throughout the country.[55]

Galula's battle for control of the population did not rely solely on military or police forces but was part of a larger political operation.[56] He noted that the government had to apply all of its sources of power to the war. This included the administrative system, economic resources, the media, and the security forces.[57] The government's total power had to be utilized to achieve victory. He stated that "victory is not the destruction in a given area of the insurgent's forces and his political organization. . . . Victory is that plus the permanent isolation of the insurgent from the population, isolation not enforced upon the population but maintained by and with the population."[58] Thus, the government's control of the population was merely the means to achieving their support and destroying the power and capability of the insurgents to wage war.

Both Trinquier and Galula recognized insurgency and counterinsurgency as war. They believed that the conflict was waged to exercise political power; the insurgents seeking to seize it, the government seeking to retain it. The insurgent and counterinsurgent fight for control of the population because they are the source of political power and their unconditional support is the weapon by which either side can destroy the other's capability and will to fight. Without such support, and the power it provides, victory is unattainable. Therefore, every means available must be employed to control the population and gain its support.

The British Experience

British colonial administrator Sir Robert Thompson served as the Permanent Secretary of Defense during the Malay Emergency and provided advice to the South Vietnamese government under President Diem in the early 1960s. He wrote extensively about insurgency following his experiences in these counterinsurgency campaigns.

Thompson identified that an insurgency has two strategic aims, one political and one military. He stated, "the political aim is to gain control of the population, starting in the rural areas, and to destroy the government's prestige and authority. The military aim is to neutralize the government's armed forces and render them powerless to save the country."[59] Thus, the insurgency seeks to destroy the government's ability to fight the war, which will ultimately lead to victory. Moreover, the government cannot focus solely on defeating the military threat, because the "political and subversive struggle will go on and can still win."[60]

Thompson believed that to defeat an insurgency, the government had to fight the insurgents for control of the population. He noted that "an insurgent movement is a war for the people. It stands to reason that government measures must be directed to restoring government authority and law and order throughout the country so that control over the population can be regained and its support won."[61] If the government does not regain control of the population, the insurgents could use their control over them to pressure the government into negotiating and conceding political victory.[62]

Gaining control over the population was so important to the government that Thompson advocated a range of harsh measures to do so, including resettlement of the population into strategic hamlets, movement restrictions, curfews, and physical barriers.[63] He responded to critics of such measures, stating that:

There are many who will criticize the harshness of the measures which may have to be used. This is a mistaken attitude. What the peasant wants to know is: Does the government mean to win the war? Because if not, he will have to support the insurgent. The government must show it is determined to win. Only in that way will it instil (sic) the confidence that it is going to win.[64]

However, he noted any such measure must always be employed legally, legitimately, and with the aim of protecting the population.[65] If the government demonstrated its ability to protect the population and its determination to totally defeat the insurgency, it could then receive the support of the population that would enable it to fully accomplish its objective. If it did not, the war would continue until one side triumphed.

Thompson's conclusions are echoed by the British Army officer and theorist, Lieutenant General Sir Frank Kitson. Kitson combated insurgents in Kenya, Malaya, Cyprus, and Northern Ireland. He identified that the "ultimate aim of an insurgent organization is to overthrow a government, or force it to do something it does not want to do."[66] Moreover, he believed that the subversive element of an insurgency, not the armed fighters, was more dangerous to the government because of the essentially political nature of the conflict.[67] Although this is true, it is not unique, as insurgency is a form of war and all war is political in nature as identified by Clausewitz.

The political nature of the conflict led Kitson to conclude that it was essential for the insurgent to have the support of the population to force the government to capitulate.[68] The insurgents must implement a program consisting of military, political, psychological, and economic measures that target the population.[69] He believed that the insurgents targeted the population to first control them and then persuade or coerce them to support the insurgency. He went on to state that the government must not underestimate the ability of a small group of men to control and extract support from the population using threats.[70]

As a result of this observation, Kitson concluded that the government must also control the population.[71] He stated, "the aim of the government is to regain if necessary and then retain the allegiance of the population, and for this purpose it must eliminate those involved in subversion but in order to eliminate the subversive party and its unarmed and armed supporters, it must gain control of the population."[72] As suggested above, government control begins by securing the population from the threats of the insurgents. Only if the population is secure will they be able to support the government. Once secure, the population can be counter-organized so that the government can make its case to them through action, rather than mere propaganda.[73] In order to be successful, however, "it must base its campaign on a determination to destroy the subversive movement utterly, and it must make this fact plain to its people."[74] Only by doing so, would the population provide its full support to the government.

To accomplish its objective of destroying the subversive movement, the government must decide exactly how much force to use and when. Kitson did not shy away from the use of force but did believe that only the minimum amount of force necessary should be applied.[75] The police must maintain law and order and confront the subversive organization as long as they could do so. The military should be used only as required to defeat the guerrilla elements and to impose control over areas of the country that had been subverted. He argued that all operations, whether political or military, must be conducted in accordance with the law.[76]

The law is not static, however. Kitson noted that the government may modify the law in order to provide it additional powers to combat the insurgency.[77] Moreover, once an insurgency begins the government may implement and enforce the law differently. Thus, the government acknowledges that insurgency and counterinsurgency are not ordinary affairs, but are in fact war and it must take extraordinary actions to win.

The British theorists identified insurgency as a phenomenon that seeks to subvert and destroy the governing authority within a country.

To accomplish its objective the insurgency had to gain control of the population to extract support. The government must recognize the danger that insurgency poses, understand what is at stake, and provide itself with the powers and tools necessary to control the population. Then, the government had to gain control of the population and completely destroy the insurgency's means and will to fight.

The American Experience

US Army officer John McCuen was a close observer of the British and French campaigns in Southeast Asia and North Africa and the developing American campaign in South Vietnam. He classified insurgency as revolutionary war and noted that it "obviously has political objectives."[78] The political objectives require the insurgency to gain support from the population and therefore, the insurgency would seek to control the population using terrorism, intimidation, coercion, and force.[79] By controlling the population, the insurgency ensured that no one was truly uncommitted; that is, even if they were not actively supporting the insurgency they were not providing support to the government.

McCuen's counterinsurgency strategy mirrors the strategy of the insurgents, and therefore he believed that the government must organize and control the population to break the insurgency's hold over it.[80] By securing, organizing, and if necessary, coercing the population through force and sanctions, the government could deny the insurgents the support they had previously extracted. He noted that this requirement to control the population through any means placed the government in

The first great dilemma of counter-revolutionary warfare–if they use intimidation, sanctions, and dislocation to separate the revolutionaries from the population, they will antagonize and lose the vital support of the people; and if they do not use these pressures, they find that the population reacts to the dictates of the more feared revolutionary terrorism, which they do not have the means to stop.[81] Moreover, he cautioned that the government usually facilitated the spreading of the insurgency "by always underestimating the problem, making too small an effort, and staying mentally one step behind the revolutionaries–reacting rather than initiating."[82]

The threat the insurgency posed was so great that McCuen concluded that "force and sanction–not torture and terror–may be the quickest and most humane methods of neutralizing fear of the terrorists, breaking the rebel organization, destroying revolutionary control and isolating the population from further pressure."[83] Once the rebel organization was neutralized or destroyed and the population isolated, the government could mobilize the population to support it. However, if this was not accomplished, the population would never support the government.[84]

McCuen believed that the government had to commit itself fully to defeating the insurgency or it would not win. He noted that "inherent in this process is early recognition of the nature of the revolutionary threat and application of maximum psycho-politico-military effort in time to seize the initiative."[85] Moreover, winning "will take massive organization, dedication, sacrifice, and time. The government must decide early if it is willing to pay the price. Half-measures lead only to protracted, costly defeats."[86] Therefore, it was necessary for the government to employ all of its power to destroy the insurgency's means and will to fight.

Modern Theorists and Historians

Trinquier, Galula, Thompson, Kitson, and McCuen are generally referred to as the classical counterinsurgency theorists. They wrote and practiced at a time when Mao's theory of protracted popular war was believed to be the preeminent form of insurgency. This was not in fact the case, as each conflict, and thus each insurgency, is unique and shaped by the state and the environment in which it occurs. However, Maoist insurgency clearly dominates the writing of the classical theorists and the belief in its preeminence colored their views as they defined and identified the characteristics of insurgency and counterinsurgency. Modern theorists have noted that Maoism is no longer predominant but their writing identifies many of the same fundamental characteristics of insurgency and counterinsurgency found in the work of the classical theorists.

John Mackinlay served as a British Army officer and is now an academic and writer on modern insurgency. Mackinlay uses Maoist insurgency to frame his ideas about contemporary insurgency. He characterizes Maoist insurgency as holistic, consisting of military, subversive, and psychological activities deployed across the operational spectrum.[87] He identifies that ideology and the ability to exploit the grievances of the population are central to the success of a Maoist insurgency. Moreover, he notes that Mao believed the population to be the primary asset of an insurgency.[88]

However, despite the above characteristics, Mackinlay does not classify Maoist insurgency as war. He asserts that only Mao's first phase is insurgency and that it consists of "political activism, infiltration, propaganda, subversion and the selective use of terror and assassination."[89] He classifies these activities as politics and not war, stating that they cannot be used to defeat armies or seize territory.[90] Meanwhile, he only acknowledges Mao's third phase as war.[91]

This is a strange distinction to make considering Mackinlay's assertion that Mao's campaign was holistic and Mao's own belief that his campaign was a total war. Mackinlay lists violent activities, such as terrorism and assassination, as means of the insurgent. While terrorism and assassination may not be the same as armies confronting one another in open combat, the classical theorists believed that they posed a threat to the state's ability to control the population, thus threatening the existence of the state itself. Furthermore, it seems artificial to draw a line between the phases of Maoist insurgency and declare some to be war and others not. Mao believed that all phases might be underway at any one time in different portions of the country and that the campaign could go backwards from one phase to another if the insurgents did not achieve success.

Mackinlay believes that modern insurgencies are evolutionary successors of the Maoist model and are essentially political and not forms of warfare.[92] Insurgency "is the option of the weaker side whose towering political ambitions are not matched with the commensurate power to translate them into reality."[93] He notes that the Cold War proxy insurgencies and the ability of modern insurgents to gain control of resources within weakly governed states has the potential to reduce the need of both insurgents and the government to gain the support of the population but nonetheless maintains that the support of the population is critical.[94]

Mackinlay notes that isolating and controlling the population from the insurgency is still necessary to achieve its support but believes that this can no longer be done through direct methods.[95] That is, he thinks that the coercive measures cited by the classical theorists are not feasible in today's environment. Rather, he believes that the government and counterinsurgent forces must confront the insurgency in the informational and social dimensions and remove the desire of the population to support the insurgency.[96] This differs from the classicists' views because it focuses on changing the population's attitude towards the insurgency rather than on destroying the insurgency's capability and will to fight.

Australian writer Mark O'Neill has studied insurgency through the lens of his country's long involvement in this type of conflict. He defines insurgency as "an organised, violent, and politically motivated activity conducted by non-state actors and sustained over a protracted period that typically utilizes a number of methods such as subversion, guerrilla warfare, and terrorism, in an attempt to achieve change within a state."[97] Moreover, he believes that the intersection of politics and the population are at the center of all insurgencies.[98] This intersection requires the counterinsurgent force to think strategically and not focus on the tactical and operational components of the military campaign.

In O'Neill's understanding, insurgency and counterinsurgency are a battle for control. He envisions the government controlling its borders, the movement of goods across those borders, the information generated within the state about the war, and the actions of the population itself.[99] However, control is only a first step. He states that "pacification is not an end in itself but a means by which the state can create the necessary permissive environment, free of major insurgent influence, to enable the implementation of comprehensive measures addressing the issues raised by the insurgency."[100] Moreover, security, which is often the objective of the military campaign, is necessary but not sufficient to defeat the insurgency.[101]

O'Neill notes that control of the population is best achieved with the cooperation of the population.[102] In other words, the government should persuade the population to support it by employing an approach that encompasses all of society. However, if the government cannot achieve control through cooperation, it must achieve it somehow. In this way, he is reinforcing the classical theorists' notion of control as coercive.[103] In contrast to Mackinlay, he stresses that insurgency and counterinsurgency are war and so such measures are justified because the government must control the population to win.[104]

Mackinlay and O'Neill's characterizations of insurgency and counterinsurgency differ only modestly from those of the classical theorists. Other modern writers, however, diverge much more sharply. In his critique of the US Army and Marine Corps' field manual on counterinsurgency, Frank Hoffman condemns an over reliance on classical theory. He believes that the classical theorists failed to understand how unique the Maoist phenomenon actually was and that they would be shocked by the complexity of the campaigns in Iraq and Afghanistan.[105] He also disputes some of the characteristics of insurgency that have been articulated above.

Citing the work of another modern writer, Australian Army Officer and an adviser to General David Petraeus, David Kilcullen, Hoffman argues that some modern insurgents do not seek a political objective or the change of a political regime, and that they may only seek political paralysis.[106] This is to some extent a mischaracterization of Kilcullen's writing. Kilcullen does note that some insurgent movements may pursue political objectives that are unlikely to be achieved or may not include the seizure of political power.[107] However, creating political paralysis is a political objective and is akin to seizing power since it prevents the state from exercising power. It is a de facto seizure of power because the political vacuum that results benefits the insurgent. Moreover, although many insurgencies do seek the overthrow of an entire state, others merely try to gain autonomy for a given region.[108]

Hoffman also disputes the classicists' contention, particularly Galula's, that the insurgents must seek support from the undecided mass of the population. He contends that massive urbanization has changed the dynamics of insurgent support since insurgent movements can now gain material support from a variety of sources that are not located within the state where the insurgency is active.[109] While this assertion is valid to a point, it is unsupported by recent history. It may have appeared that Al Qaeda in Iraq did not need the support of the population in Anbar province but when it lost such support it became nearly impossible for the group to exist.

His criticisms notwithstanding, Hoffman does acknowledge that the classical theorists have a role to play in understanding modern insurgency. He is primarily disputing the lack of emphasis the new manual gives to some characteristics of the current operational environment. However, Steven Metz disputes both the idea that modern insurgencies bear a resemblance to those studied by the classical theorists and the idea that they are wars in the Clausewitzian sense.[110] He does not deny that insurgencies seek political objectives but contends that these are no longer the primary motivation for insurgents. Rather, he argues that insurgencies are actually competitions in a violent market place and that they satisfy economic and psychological needs rather than seek political objectives.[111]

In Metz' assessment, insurgencies are really about providing economic power and a feeling of self worth to the combatants.[112] The contest between the government and the insurgent organization may be violent but this armed conflict does not rise to the level of war. This is a fine line to draw. If an insurgency can only provide economic power and a feeling of worth to its members by actively challenging the power of the state, then the state no longer has a monopoly on the use of violence. Therefore, it can no longer be said to be in control and, as noted above, the absence of state control is just as much a political objective as the positive control sought by classical insurgencies. In order to regain control, the state will have to

23

embark on a campaign combining military, political, and civil measures. This would appear to be a war that Clausewitz would recognize.

Metz' counterinsurgency strategy goes beyond those espoused by the classicist's in one significant way. Metz contends that to successfully resolve an insurgency requires a fundamental change of society brought about through social re-engineering.[113] The social re-engineering project envisions a wholesale alteration of how the society functions and what its values are. In essence, his strategy is the ultimate form of population control. It seeks to change the behavior of the population in every fundamental way, not merely as it relates to supporting the insurgency or the government.

The modern theorists and writers are not in as much agreement on the nature of insurgency as are the classical theorists. There are some common themes, however. Though the centrality of a political objective is doubted by Hoffman, his notion of destabilizing the state rather than destroying it is a political objective. Metz' assertion that insurgents are seeking economic and psychological satisfaction is also a political objective. Mackinlay and O'Neill both define insurgency as political. Mackinlay and Metz dispute the characterization of insurgency as a war but both identify that all elements of power will be employed to achieve a political objective. Hoffman questions the necessity of gaining support from the population but O'Neill and Mackinlay assert that the population is still at the center of any insurgency. Metz envisions controlling the population through a fundamental re-ordering of society.

Characteristics of Insurgency and Counterinsurgency

The above descriptions lead to the conclusion that insurgency and counterinsurgency have several defining characteristics. First, the insurgent and counterinsurgent both seek a political objective, the exercise of political power within a given territory. The counterinsurgent must achieve the positive exercise of power. In classical insurgencies the insurgent also seeks this objective. However, in some modern insurgencies, the insurgent side may only seek to deny the state the ability to govern. Regardless, the insurgent seeks political power to gain an advantage vis-a-vis the state.

Because the insurgent is seeking political power within a given territory of a state, the insurgency must be conducted within a state. This is not to say that the insurgency cannot take any action outside of the targeted state but the majority of the campaign will be waged within the confines of that state. An insurgency could seek political power in multiple states but it would still have to wage separate campaigns against each state that it is contending with. Similarly, the counterinsurgent may take action against the insurgency outside of the state's borders. However, this will not likely end the insurgency as the government must exercise positive political power within the state. Therefore, the counterinsurgent's fight will also be primarily within the state.

As the insurgent must seize political power from the state, it cannot by definition be a member of that state. This distinguishes insurgency from other violent regime change paradigms such as the coup d'etat, which is undertaken by elements within the state's power structure. The non-state actor that wages an insurgency is weaker than or disadvantaged by the state, which is why it is seeking political power in the first place. Conversely, it is states that wage counterinsurgency. Counterinsurgency only exists in relation to insurgency and if the insurgent is the non-state actor then the counterinsurgent must be a state actor.

The population is the ultimate source of political power and their support is necessary for either the insurgent or the counterinsurgent to be successful. Before garnering the support of the population it is necessary for both the insurgent and the counterinsurgent to control the population. If the insurgent controls the population it can extract support from them and overcome its weakness in comparison to the state. When the counterinsurgent controls the population, it denies the insurgency the support it requires and uses the separation generated to win their support.

Populations outside of the affected state may have a stake in the outcome of the campaign. Diaspora populations and populations of intervening states may provide material, financial, moral, or legal support to either the insurgency or the counterinsurgency. However, it is unlikely that this support will be decisive to the campaign. The counterinsurgent must retain political power and the insurgent must seize it, so it is the state's population whose support is decisive.

Insurgency and counterinsurgency involve all instruments of power: political, military, civil, economic, legal, and psychological. In order to control the population and counter the power of the state, the insurgency cannot rely solely on military means. It must employ political subversion and organization, civic action to address grievances, and wage a psychological warfare campaign to ensure support for its political objective. Similarly, if the state wages counterinsurgency solely as a military campaign it is likely to lose. Many of the insurgent's actions cannot be countered by the military and must be addressed using the other instruments of power.

Here the state has an advantage because it has access to political, legal, economic, and psychological resources that the insurgent does not.

Employing all of the instruments of power simultaneously will not guarantee success. Insurgency and counterinsurgency campaigns must be synchronized between the different instruments of power and coordinated across the levels of government from the local to the national level. Military force used inappropriately may alienate the population and disrupt economic or political measures. The campaigns in each locality may be unique for both sides, but all must operate in support of the national campaign.

Lastly, insurgency and counterinsurgency are war. Fundamentally, both sides are employing force in order to accomplish a political objective, a policy, and must destroy the military capability of the other side to compel them to consider and agree to a political solution. Kitson identified this when he stated that:

> The first thing that must be apparent when contemplating the sort of action which a government facing insurgency should take, is that there can be no such thing as a purely military solution because insurgency is not primarily a military activity. At the same time there is no such thing as a wholly political solution either, short of surrender, because the very fact that a state of insurgency exists implies that violence is involved which will have to be countered to some extent at least by the use of lethal force.[114]

It could even be asserted that insurgency and counterinsurgency are the ultimate form of Clausewitzian war because it is a battle for the ultimate political objective–exercise of political power. In comparison, many so called conventional wars had very limited political objectives. The objectives of the US and its allies during the Persian Gulf War of 1991, those of the British during the Falklands war, Germany's objectives in the Franco-Prussian war, or the British and French objectives during the Crimean war were all limited when compared to the objective of an insurgency.

Moreover, a characterization of insurgency and counterinsurgency as something other than war leads to a dangerous underestimation of the threat posed by insurgency. If insurgency is considered to be a political campaign as Mackinlay says or a market competition as Metz asserts it could lead the state to attempt to counter it with very limited means. This might escalate the conflict and result in a more protracted and bloodier struggle. The insurgent has no doubt about the nature of his campaign, the state should not either. It is a violent contest for political power that must be won.

Definitions of Insurgency and Counterinsurgency

The above discussion allows a definition for insurgency to be created which will be used throughout this study. Insurgency is a war waged within a state by a non-state actor through a combination of military, political, economic, civil, legal, and psychological means to control the population and gain its support to destroy or subvert the government's instruments of power and seize political power.

Counterinsurgency only exists as a form of warfare because of its reciprocal relationship with insurgency. Therefore, counterinsurgency is a war waged within a state by a government and its allies, which may include intervening states, using the instruments of state power in a combination of military, political, economic, civil, legal, and psychological means to maintain control over and support of the population and defeat an insurgency to prevent the seizure of political power by a non-state actor.

Population and Resource Control Measures

Many of the modern and classical theorists discussed above assert that both the insurgent and the counterinsurgent must control the population to be successful in their respective campaigns. However, it is not always clear why such control is necessary. What is it about control of the population that makes it so essential and how can that control be established and maintained by the government and counterinsurgent forces? This section will establish why control of the population is necessary, examine the population and resource control measure construct derived from the classical counterinsurgency theorists and articulated in current doctrine, discuss the misconceptions and limitations of this construct, and postulate an alternative construct.

Why Control?

Controlling the behavior of their populations is fundamentally what governments do. This is particularly true where the employment of violence is concerned. The sociological theorist Max Weber believed "that a state is a human community that [successfully] claims the *monopoly of the legitimate use of physical force* within a given territory."[115] Moreover,

> the right to use physical force is ascribed to other institutions or to individuals only to the extent to which the state permits it. The state is considered the sole source of the 'right' to use violence. Hence, 'politics' for us means striving to share power or striving to influence the distribution of power, either among states or among groups within a state.[116]

Weber believed that the state's very existence depended on its ability to control the use of violence. He further identified that this required the state's subjects to obey the authority of the government. If the state lost control of the use of violence, the state could no longer claim to govern.[117] Thus, control is all important, and it extends not just to the actual use of violence, but also to "those material goods which in a given case are necessary for the use of physical violence."[118]

Weber's conclusions are echoed by the classical counterinsurgency theorists who indicate that control of the population is necessary for both the insurgent and the counterinsurgent. Specifically, they identified that control was a necessary precursor to achieving the support of the population but if security can be achieved then why is control necessary? What if the counterinsurgent can exercise control through a third party? Can the counterinsurgent skip establishing control by using non-lethal means such as economic development and government reforms to gain the population's support? On their face these shortcuts make logical sense, but they are dangerous to pursue.

Security is not an Indication of Control

The most obvious manifestation of an insurgency is the ongoing violence that highlights the government's inability to control the use of violence and affects the security of the population, the government, and the counterinsurgent forces. It would make sense to use the amount of security of these three elements as an indicator that the government is in control of the population and defeating the insurgency. However, security without control can be misleading.[119]

One of the major difficulties of assessing the security situation is to determine the actual level of violence. The most obvious way to do so is to record the number of attacks against the population and counterinsurgent forces. Unfortunately, this is not a good measure of how secure the population actually is. The population will only report acts of violence against it if they can be certain that the security forces will be able to take action to detain the perpetrators and prevent violent acts in the future. Thus, many acts of intimidation against the population will go unreported in areas where the government does not have control. Moreover, attacks against the counterinsurgent forces are an even worse measure because violent groups may choose not to attack them to maintain the illusion that the area is secure.

Two recent examples demonstrate that security is not a good indicator of control. Following the uprising in Sadr City in the late summer and early fall of 2004, the 1st Cavalry Division agreed to a cease-fire with the leaders of the Office of the Martyr Sadr (OMS) political party and their *Jaysh al-Mahdi* (JAM) militia.[120] As a result of the agreement, attacks in Sadr City fell precipitously during the remainder of 2004 and remained low throughout 2005.[121] However, the Iraqi government, the Iraqi Security Forces (ISF), and the US Army did not have control over the neighborhood; it resided with OMS and JAM. As a result, after the bombing of the Golden Mosque in 2006 violence increased in Sadr City and a major battle using conventional military forces, including Abrams tanks and Bradley fighting vehicles, was waged against JAM to reassert control over the neighborhood in early 2008.[122] Sadr City appeared to be secure but the government did not have control.

Northern Ireland provides another example. The British Army deployed to Northern Ireland in 1969 in order to protect the Catholic population following riots by Protestant mobs.[123] However, by mid-1970, Catholics felt that they were under siege from both the mobs and the British Army which led to an increase in recruiting for the newly formed Provisional Irish Republican Army (PIRA).[124] During the intervening time period, PIRA established "no-go" areas in Catholic residential neighborhoods by emplacing barricades.[125] Neither the British Army nor the Royal Ulster Constabulary could patrol in those areas and PIRA controlled the population.[126] After control had been established and the Catholic population had been radicalized, PIRA attacked British forces and the first British soldier was killed in February 1971.[127] PIRA's campaign accelerated and 1972 was the worst year of violence during the insurgency.[128] The security situation appeared positive, especially for the counterinsurgent forces of the British Army in 1969 and 1970, but PIRA's control of the population allowed it to radicalize them and initiate a more violent campaign.

Third Party Control

If the government and counterinsurgent forces are not in control of the population, someone else will be. Power abhors a vacuum and if the counterinsurgent does not maintain control and tries to pass that control to a third party, then it is possible that control will be seized by the insurgent. This is not to say that a third party can never exercise control. However, it must be able to defend its territory from the insurgency and its interests must align with the government and counterinsurgent forces. If the former is not true the insurgency can attack and defeat the third party to gain control, if the latter is not true the third party may take action that is inimical to the government's interests.

Two examples from the campaign in Iraq highlight these points. Following the first Battle of Fallujah in the spring of 2004, US forces transferred control of the city to a group of elders and their local security forces, the Fallujah Brigade.[129] This arrangement appeared to allow the government of Iraq and US forces to exert control over the city through a third party but this was an illusion. The elders of Fallujah and their security forces could not secure the city and the insurgency scattered the Fallujah Brigade and dominated the populace.[130] In late 2004, US and Iraqi forces mounted an assault to recapture the city.[131] Once the coalition had re-established control, residents reported that they no longer believed insurgent success was inevitable.[132]

The British experience in Basra, Iraq, illustrates the other problem. During 2006, the British Army determined that they had to conclude the campaign in southern Iraq quickly and entered into an "accommodation" with the leaders of OMS and JAM in Basra.[133] After JAM leaders had proven their ability to halt attacks against British forces, the British Army withdrew from Basra, ceased operations in the city, and released JAM members they held in custody.[134] Once these concessions were complete, JAM resumed attacks on the British Army and battled the Iraqi Army for control of the city. In order to prevent the total loss of Basra, the Iraqi government mounted Operation Charge of the Knights to retake the city using ISF supported by British and American forces.[135] While the British assumed that they had passed control over to a responsible partner, this was not the case.[136] JAM and OMS wanted total control over Basra to use its lucrative port operations to support their insurgency in the rest of Iraq, a goal inimical to those of the Iraqi government.[137]

<u>Gaining the Support of the Population without Control</u>

Control of the population is very difficult to achieve and requires a large commitment of security forces to maintain. Therefore, it might make sense to skip establishing control over the population and gain their support by improving their material well being. The thought being is that improving the population's material circumstances will lead them to support the government and not the insurgency.

This logic is highlighted in much of the recent writing about counterinsurgency, particularly that concerning so called "hearts and minds" strategies. In a RAND Corporation report issued in 2008, such strategies were summarized as beginning from the idea that "if the government can provide the population with the things they want, a bond will form and the population will shun the insurgents. This is the logic of appropriateness. The population comes to identify with the government."[138] There are many problems with this assertion but the most glaring is that it ignores the possibility that the insurgents will use violence to gain benefits for the population under their control and thus undermine the government's control. It further assumes that the government can determine what it is the population requires for it to abandon supporting the insurgency.

This logic had great appeal in Iraq and was tried throughout the country to various degrees. As part of the cease-fire agreement in Sadr City discussed above, the US government spent hundreds of millions of dollars upgrading critical infrastructure.[139] This was desperately needed but it did not connect the population to the government and may have solidified OMS and JAM's control. American Army officer Colonel Craig Collier, who served as a battalion commander in Baghdad in 2007-2008, asserts that no effort was made to test the validity of the theory that improving material well-being would lead to an appreciable weakening of the insurgency.[140] Certainly the violence in Sadr City in 2008 demonstrates that it did not in that particular case.

Another major difficulty of attempting such as a strategy is the need to accurately assess what the population wants in return for abandoning its support of the insurgency. One writer has noted that it is often difficult for insurgent leaders to understand what the populations they are seeking to control want to gain from the insurgency.[141] Therefore, it is no great surprise that counterinsurgents suffer from the same difficulty. Mackinlay believes that the British achieved success in Northern Ireland because they raised much of the population into the middle class through economic development and education.[142] However, it could be asserted that the insurgency in Northern Ireland that began in 1969 was not caused by relative economic poverty but rather by systematic governmental anti-Catholic discrimination coupled with Protestant violence.[143] If the British had addressed these causes directly in the 1970s, then there would have been no need for economic development. Nor can it be demonstrated conclusively that it was economic improvements as opposed to changes in the political structure and a backlash against violence that ended the insurgency.

The last major difficulty with trying to gain support without asserting control is inherent in the way people think about their behavior and the control they have over it. The Theory of Planned Behavior is a construct used by psychologists to predict whether an individual will engage in a specific behavior by examining three key factors: attitude toward the behavior, subjective norms about the behavior, and perceived behavior control.[144] The Theory of Planned Behavior establishes that all three of these factors combine to yield intentions and that this will produce a reasonably accurate prediction of behavior.[145] Actual behavior control is assumed because without it the individual could not engage in the behavior. In other words, if it can be determined what a person thinks about a behavior, how his or her social group feels about the behavior, and whether or not the person believes he or she can engage in the behavior, this will indicate whether or not he or she will actually engage in the behavior.

The government and counterinsurgent forces, especially intervening forces, have a very difficult time ascertaining the population's attitude towards a specific behavior or the subjective norms regarding it. Even if they could determine that the population was favorably disposed to act against them, it is difficult to design information operations campaigns that can change attitudes and group norms rapidly. However, the government and counterinsurgent forces can change the population's perceived behavior control by enforcing restrictions on the behaviors that support the insurgents. Thus, the population no longer believes that it can engage in such support and therefore will not. This idea is reinforced by the Theory of Planned Behavior which demonstrates that if a person believes that he or she cannot perform a certain behavior then he or she will not engage in that behavior.[146] Certain restrictions may remove actual behavior control as well.

A simple example will illustrate this idea. Imagine that a member of the population wants to support the insurgency. Also suppose that the social group this person belongs to does not view aiding the insurgency negatively. Then, if he or she has access to some resource that would be beneficial to the insurgents and a means of providing it to them–that is, actual and perceived behavior control–then he or she will provide support to the insurgents. However, if the government and counterinsurgent have control over the population they can impose restrictions that remove the person's perceived behavior control and thus prevent him or her from supporting the insurgency.

Therefore, a focus on behavior, as opposed to intentions, allows the government and counterinsurgent forces to direct their efforts at controlling behaviors they can observe and restrict. It is true that insurgency and counterinsurgency are ultimately a battle for men's minds.[147] However, control gives the government and counterinsurgent forces time, space, and a mechanism to destroy the insurgency. Then they can employ strategies to gain the support of the population who is now free of intimidation and coercion.

Current Population and Resource Control Construct

The current construct for population and resource control measures will be considered, revised, and then evaluated through examination of historical case studies. These case studies will demonstrate that control of the population is necessary if the counterinsurgent is going to defeat the insurgency and that population and resource control measures can be employed to gain and maintain that control. Shortcuts involving security, transfer of control to seemingly responsible parties, and gaining support through improved material well being provide only the illusion of control, however. If this illusion of control is allowed to persist, the counterinsurgent may have to expend greater effort later to regain control, because the insurgency will have greater material, manpower, and intelligence support and a measure of control over the population that must be broken.

To gain and maintain control of the population the counterinsurgent can apply population and resource controls. By applying such controls the government asserts its authority over the population and breaks the insurgent's domination of them. Further, such controls allow the counterinsurgent to protect the population, isolate them from the insurgency, prevent behavior which supports the insurgency, enable behavior that supports the government, and target the armed and subversive components of the insurgency to eliminate them. Thus, these measures aim at coercing the population into not supporting the insurgent. Moreover, it enables the pro-government portion of the population to provide support to the counterinsurgent forces. Once the government's control has been reestablished it can then set about the task of persuading the population to voluntarily support it.

The classical theorists identified how the government could employ population and resource controls to coerce the population to end their support for the insurgency. They articulated a wide variety of specific measures such as curfews, census operations, movement restrictions, resettlement of the population, and food and resource controls, and provided examples of their use. Their ideas have been collected and codified into a population and resource control construct that is articulated in the US Army's Field Manual (FM) 3-24.2, *Tactics in Counterinsurgency*.

However, population and resource control measures cause discomfort for many current writers and practitioners. This results from a number of misconceptions about the nature of population and resource control measures. First, since they are a precursor to gaining the support of the population then they should be viewed as providing incentives or disincentives to the population. Second, that they are coercive, only applied in areas where the population supports the insurgent, and therefore are collective punishment. Third, that those measures used in previous campaigns can no longer be employed, especially by an intervening power, because they will not be viewed as legitimate.

These misconceptions have arisen for a variety of reasons: an incomplete understanding of how population and resource control measures were used in previous campaigns, classifying insurgency and counterinsurgency as something other than war, and a misunderstanding of why population and resource control measures are employed. By examining historical campaigns and specifying why population and resource control measures are used, these misconceptions can be altered.

Theorists and Population Control

All of the classical theorists discussed controlling the population in similar terms. They believed that controlling the population allowed the government to protect them, to isolate them from the insurgents, to reduce the supplies they provide the insurgents, to gather intelligence from them, and use that intelligence to target the insurgents, especially the subversive element. The major difference is that Trinquier viewed control as an end in itself, while Galula, Thompson, Kitson, and McCuen viewed it as a precursor to gaining the support of the population.

Trinquier believed that population control measures should remain in place across the entire country until the war had been won.[148] Galula did not address the lifting of the control measures specifically, but did indicate that once the subversive element was destroyed, the counterinsurgent should begin improving the life of the population.[149] This is similar to Thompson who stated that once the government had full control of an area, and that area was no longer under threat from the insurgency, that all restrictions could be removed. Then the government could focus on producing a stable community.[150]

Kitson focused on the destruction of the subversive element as the purpose of population control. However, he viewed this as part of the government's overall plan, which included economic, civil, and political measures to rectify grievances and attract popular support.[151] Therefore, Kitson believed that control preceded persuasion. McCuen's ideas were similar. He identified that convincing the population to support the government through persuasion is the best option. However, he believed that coercion, in the form of population and resource controls, might have to precede persuasion.

Current Doctrine on Population and Resource Control

Population and resource controls are discussed minimally in the Army's capstone counterinsurgency manual, FM 3-24. There are only four paragraphs dedicated to the topic and these paragraphs provide only an outline of what they are and how they can be utilized.[152] However, the companion manual to FM 3-24, FM 3-24.2, *Tactics in Counterinsurgency*, has a much larger section on their employment.

The section in FM 3-24.2 begins by providing the following definition:

Populace and resource control (PRC) operations are government actions to protect the populace and its materiel resources from insurgents, to deny insurgents access to the populace and material resources and to identify and eliminate the insurgents, their organization, their activities, and influence while doing so.[153]

This is very similar to the concepts of the classical theorists. The manual goes on to state that "the objective of populace and resources control is to assist in preserving or reestablishing a state of law [and] order within an area or entire nation."[154]

The list of available populace and resource controls provided in the manual is similar to the techniques described by the theorists. It includes curfews, movement restrictions, identification cards, rationing of food and other essential items, and the organization of the population.[155] Resettlement of the population is not included in the list of population control measures and is instead categorized as a protective measure.[156] The manual also addresses intelligence, surveillance, and security operations as part of its population and resource control construct.

Misconceptions Surrounding the Use of Population and Resource Controls

There are three major misconceptions about the use of population and resource control: they are incentives and disincentives to support the government, they are collective punishment, and they are not legitimate. These misconceptions arise for a variety of reasons and each will be discussed in detail.

The idea that controlling the population is a necessary precursor to gaining its support is a powerful one. However, the conclusion that they are incentives and disincentives is a mischaracterization. In the capstone report for the RAND Corporation's counterinsurgency study, authors David Gompert and John Gordon refer to population and resource control measures as "carrot-and-stick strategies" which seek to employ the logic of punishment and reward to the population in order to get them to support the government.[157] The use of food control by the British in Malaya is used as the primary example of this strategy. The authors, citing the analysis of the retired military officer and writer, John Nagl, state that food control "created a powerful motivation to support the government, while establishing negative incentives for insurgents and their supporters–a classical carrot-and-stick approach."[158] Unfortunately, this analysis is based on a shallow reading of the history of the Malaya campaign.

It is hard to imagine that restricting how, when, and where the population can cook its own food would lead to an increase in government support. Furthermore, it is difficult to understand how this constitutes a negative incentive for the insurgents and their supporters as averred by Gompert and Gordon. The food control policy in Malaya was intended to prevent the Chinese population from giving food, particularly rice, to the insurgents, without which their morale and well being would severely suffer.[159] It also prevented the insurgents from forcing unsupportive Chinese and Malays to provide them food. As a result, the insurgents either had to grow food in the jungle, which could be spotted by aerial reconnaissance, or come into the open areas surrounding the villages to get food, both of which exposed them to targeting by security forces.

When viewed in this manner it is clear that the food controls used by the British were primarily intended to control the behavior of the population, not provide it an incentive or disincentive to support the government. The entire population, those who supported the insurgents, those who supported the government, and those who supported neither, were subject to the same controls.[160] They all received the same ration of food regardless of their support for the government and they would all benefit from the lifting of the sanctions once the area was determined to be secure.[161] Therefore, there was no incentive or disincentive to support the government.

There also was not an incentive or disincentive, specifically, to stop supporting the insurgents. While it is true that the controls would be lifted once an area was deemed secure and no longer subject to insurgent influence, this did not prevent portions of the population from wanting to provide support to the insurgents.[162] However, they no longer had the ability to provide any support. Moreover, it is possible that the insurgents could use the same incentive. That is, they could also promise that the food restrictions would be lifted once they achieved control. It is possible that the population and resource controls may have convinced some portions of the population to support the government but it was not the policy's primary purpose.

Some writers have characterized population control measures as collective punishment because they are coercive. The British Army officer Julian Paget regarded them as such and believed that they could be employed in this manner to utilize less force.[163] He drew this conclusion as a result of his examination of the British campaigns in Malaya, Cyprus, and Kenya. This is not an accurate portrayal of how population and resource control measures were employed in Malaya, however.

It is true that the British High Commissioner and Director of Operations from 1952-1954, Lieutenant General Sir Gerald Templer, imposed collective punishments that included longer curfews and reduced rations of rice on some villages during the campaign.[164] However, the overall population and resource control measures regime which Templer and his predecessor, Lieutenant General Sir Harold Briggs, established was not collective punishment. Rather, as discussed above, it was designed to prevent the population from being able to provide the insurgents with any material support and to isolate them from the insurgents.[165] The national identification card system, curfews, movement restrictions, and food controls were implemented across the country and vigorously enforced without regard to specifically punishing given communities.

It seems disingenuous to say that population and resource control measures are not collective punishment but that they could be used in that way. However, if the population is told that they are collectively being punished for actions that most of them are not engaging in, they are likely to be resentful. Moreover, they are unlikely to understand how this is increasing their security or reducing the effectiveness of the insurgents. However, if it is explained that the measures are to prevent specific types of support from being provided to the insurgents and to increase their own physical security, then they can better understand why the measures are being employed. They can also see that because such controls are in place they can no longer be coerced into providing support when they do not want to. They are not in control of their behavior.

Many modern writers do not believe that population control measures can be employed today because they will not be seen as legitimate by the international community. Mackinlay asserts that the direct method by which the British separated the insurgents from the population in previous campaigns is no longer feasible and only indirect methods can be used.[166] Moreover, he recommends that future multinational operations should be conducted using only those means that are considered legitimate by all members of the coalition.[167]

Determining the legitimacy of means would seem to be fairly straightforward. However, what it is legitimate in one situation may not be in another. Trinquier stated, "the people know instinctively what is correct. It is only by substantive measures that we will lead them to judge the validity of our actions."[168] It is dangerous to reference Trinquier, who openly advocated the use of torture, when speaking about legitimacy of means, but in this case he is correct. It is ultimately the affected population who will determine whether actions taken by security forces are legitimate.

It is inconceivable to most Americans that US forces would create walled-in neighborhoods for populations that are only accessible through a single access point and require a detailed search to enter. It would not be legitimate to impose such a regime in their eyes. Yet, this accurately describes the Safe Neighborhood Program in Baghdad, Iraq, during 2007 and 2008. Many residents and local governing councils in Baghdad specifically requested that their neighborhoods be included in the program.[169] In their eyes, the tactic was legitimate and effective.

It should also be noted that while it would be preferable for the host nation government to execute population and resource control measures, this is not the only way for them to be considered legitimate.[170] The Safe Neighborhood Program was conducted in coordination with the Iraqi government and ISF, but it was clear to the population that US forces were involved, particularly with the emplacement of the walls. This did not diminish the program's legitimacy for the population and may have enhanced it.[171]

Limitations of the Current Population and Resource Control Construct

While the population and resource control construct derived from the theorists and encapsulated in current doctrine is useful, it does have some limitations. The first limitation of this construct is that it focuses only on the insurgent, not the population's actions to support the insurgent. The way the definition is framed it leads to the conclusion that there are no active, willing supporters of the insurgency among the population. Thus, if the population can simply be protected and isolated, then support for the insurgency will end. This is not the case, however. There are always some active supporters of the insurgency in the population and if their behavior is not addressed support for the insurgency will continue. Moreover, the insurgents often use intimidation and coercion to force the population to provide it with support. They do not allow the population to be neutral but if the population and resource control construct targets behavior that supports the insurgency, it can prevent such behavior. This gives the population the opportunity to choose neutrality, which is an advantage for the counterinsurgent.

Another limitation is that the construct does not address how population and resource controls can be employed to enable behavior that supports the government. One reason for securing and isolating the population is to ensure that it is not subject to intimidation from the insurgency. Doing so allows those elements of the population who want to support the government to do so. Free of intimidation the population can provide the government intelligence on the insurgents, join local security forces, and participate in local governance. It also, however, enables the population to be neutral. If they are, they are not providing overt support to either side, and this is an advantage for the government.

The construct also does not identify how violations of population and resource controls will be handled. It promulgates some enforcement mechanisms, such as checkpoints and searches, but does not identify what actions should be taken to enforce the controls. The manual mentions rewarding populations for complying but does not address sanctioning violators. This is important because if the counterinsurgents do not enforce the controls with sanctions then their impact will be muted.

The construct also does not stress that population and resource controls must be legitimate. Perhaps this is assumed but it has to be reinforced. If control is to serve as a bridge to ultimately gaining the population's support then the methods employed must be legitimate. Further, legitimacy can only be conferred by the affected population. The government and counterinsurgent forces may consider any measures that might prevent critical support being provided to the insurgency but they must also be legitimate.

Lastly, the stated objective of population and resource controls is vague. The establishment of law and order can mean many different things in many different contexts. If the government and its counterinsurgent forces, or the forces of an intervening power, cannot agree on the meaning behind law and order, confusion will result. Population and resource control measures will be employed for varying reasons by different elements and this will weaken their effectiveness.

Updated Population and Resource Control Construct

The mischaracterizations of population and resource controls in current literature and the limitations identified in the current construct can be addressed if a new construct is promulgated. This construct reinforces critical points about how and why population and resource control measures are implemented and stresses the need to ensure legitimacy. Moreover, this construct allows the counterinsurgent to employ a greater range of measures through a focus on controlling the behavior of the population.

New Definition of Population and Resource Controls

Population and resource controls are employed to restore the state's control over the use of violence and the material resources which enable it. They are legitimate civil and economic restrictions imposed by the government on the behavior of the population that are legally enforced by counterinsurgent security forces to

1. Protect the population from the intimidation and violence employed by the insurgency.

2. Isolate the population from the subversive and armed elements of the insurgency.

3. Control the behavior of the population so as to prevent behavior that supports the insurgency and enable behavior that supports the government and counterinsurgent security forces.

4. Facilitate the destruction of the armed and subversive elements of the insurgency by the counterinsurgent security forces.

This construct may be employed throughout all phases of the "clear-hold-build" strategy that is articulated in current counterinsurgency doctrine. During the clear phase it assists the counterinsurgent in separating the armed elements of the insurgency from the population so that they can be targeted. In the hold phase, the controls deny the insurgency the ability to gain material, intelligence, and other support from the population while facilitating the identification and destruction of the subversive element. In the clear phase it provides a mechanism for the government to maintain its control and prevent the insurgency from returning to the area. Throughout, this construct enables the government to demonstrate its determination to defeat the insurgency and begin the process of persuading the population to provide it their support.

All of the techniques discussed above can be used within this construct. Census operations provide a means of identifying elements of the insurgency, organizing the population, determining the exact population that needs to be protected, and providing identification cards. Curfew and movement restrictions facilitate the isolation and protection of the population and provide a means for the counterinsurgent to determine if the insurgency is attempting to re-enter the controlled areas. Resource controls such as import/export restrictions, rationing, and the establishment of controlled items give the government a mechanism for denying material support to the insurgency by controlling the ability of their supporters to provide it. Resettlement facilitates all of the above by providing the government absolute control over the circumstances in which the population lives.

This list is not exhaustive, however. Other control mechanisms that are not articulated in the literature could be employed. The government could deny the population's ability to communicate with the insurgency by restricting phone, internet, radio, or mail communications. The government could prohibit rallies, political meetings, and other public gatherings to prevent the subversive element from operating under the guise of a legitimate political party. Parties with known affiliations to the insurgency could be banned. Citizens could be restricted from possessing or carrying firearms and other weapons. Other techniques exist and it is only the imagination of the government and counterinsurgent forces that limits the measures to be used. However, they must be employed to accomplish their objective and in accordance with the six critical components of the construct: legitimacy, enforcement provisions, protection of the population, isolation of the population, a focus on behavior, and the destruction of the armed and subversive elements.

Legitimacy

The legitimacy of the government's actions can only be determined by the affected population. It would be anathema to Americans to restrict the ability of a population to move, communicate, or possess weapons, but if the insurgency has reached the level where such stringent controls are necessary they may be legitimate. The majority of the population desires security and freedom from intimidation. If harsh measures can accomplish this they will be viewed positively. The legitimacy of population control measures can only be assessed by a comprehensive understanding of the threat the insurgency poses and the society within which it is being conducted.

Enforcement Provisions

If the government imposes restrictions on the population, but is unable to enforce these provisions through legal sanctions, their efficacy and legitimacy will be negatively impacted. Galula identified that if the counterinsurgent issues orders to the population to deny support to the insurgent that it must be able to enforce those orders or it will have exposed the population to reprisals.[172] Thus exposed, the population cannot view such restrictions as legitimate. Moreover, if the government does not have a legal enforcement mechanism, the willing supporters of the insurgency are able to violate the restrictions without fear of sanctions. This defeats the purpose of establishing the restrictions in the first place.

Legal enforcement also empowers the counterinsurgent security forces. They no longer have to determine who is an actual insurgent; violators of the sanctions have committed a criminal act and can be detained immediately. This eliminates confusion as the counterinsurgent forces no longer have to decide whether and how to enforce the population and resource control measures. They can do so automatically. However, this requirement also means that implementing a population and resource control regime is time consuming and man-power intensive.

Security of the Population

The population can openly support the government only if it feels secure enough to do so. Kitson noted that an unarmed population cannot possibly stand up to violent intimidation from insurgents.[173] Trinquier identified that the only way the counterinsurgent can gain intelligence on the insurgents was if the population felt secure enough to do so.[174] Recent experience in Iraq and Afghanistan indicates that intimidation can cause even a supportive population to provide the insurgents intelligence and material support. It is therefore critical that the population and resource control regime increase the security of the population. Moreover, if it does not increase the population's security it will undermine legitimacy of the control measures.

Isolating the Population from Insurgent Elements

If the population can be thoroughly separated from the insurgency, they will be more secure. Moreover, the government and counterinsurgent forces can target the armed elements of the insurgency more effectively. Isolation makes it more difficult for members of the population who support the insurgency to do so and enables others to engage in behavior that supports the government by providing intelligence, joining local security forces, and participating in local governance.

Focus on Behavior

It is difficult for the government and counterinsurgent forces, especially an intervening power, to change the intention of the population to support the insurgency. This process usually occurs over time and the means utilized to do so may not accomplish the objective. However, specific behaviors that support the insurgency can be identified and addressed through population and resource control measures. This removes the ability of the population to support the insurgency without changing their intention to do so. While defeating the insurgency in the long term requires a change of intentions, the immediate effect of population and resource controls that focus on behavior can severely weaken the insurgency and give the government time and space to change the attitude of the population.

Facilitate the Targeting of the Armed and Subversive Elements

Defeating an insurgency requires the complete destruction of the insurgency's subversive elements.[175] All of the other critical components of the population and resource control construct support this aim. However, if the government and counterinsurgent forces lose sight of this truth, it may encourage them to reduce the use of such controls too early. This is tempting, especially if it is viewed as a reward to the population. However, it may also hamper efforts to root out the remnants of the insurgency and therefore leave the population exposed to future reprisals. The population wants to be secure and the best way to accomplish this objective is to remove all criminal, terrorist, insurgent, and subversive elements from their midst.[176]

Evaluating the New Construct of Population and Resource Control

This new construct will be evaluated by comparing its critical components to those of population and resource control measure regimes used in previous and current counterinsurgency campaigns through the case study method. The first campaign considered will be US counterinsurgency operations in the Philippines from 1899 to 1935. Then a close examination will be made of the efforts of the Government of Vietnam (GVN) and the United States in South Vietnam during two distinct periods: the Diem regime from 1954 to 1963 with a focus on the Strategic Hamlet Program and the role of US ground forces, specifically the 25th Infantry Division, in supporting the pacification campaign from 1966 to 1970. Finally, the US campaign in Iraq from 2003 to present will be considered.

Notes

1. Carl Von Clausewitz, *On War*, ed. and trans. by Michael Howard and Peter Paret (Princeton, NJ: Princeton University Press, 1989), 75.

2. Ibid., 75.

3. Ibid., 75.

4. Ibid., 76.

5. Ibid., 77.

6. Ibid., 77.

7. Michael Howard, *Clausewitz: A Very Short Introduction* (Oxford: Oxford University Press, 2002), 51-52.

8. Clausewitz, *On War*, 80-81.

9. Howard, *Clausewitz: A Very Short Introduction*, 55.

10. Clausewitz, *On War*, 581.

11. Ibid., 86.

12. Ibid., 86-87

13. Ibid., 87.

14. Michael Howard, *War in European History* (Oxford: Oxford University Press, 1976), 76.

15. Clausewitz, *On War*, 88.

16. Howard, *Clausewitz: A Very Short Introduction*, 36.

17. Clausewitz, *On War*, 177.

18. Ibid., 177.

19. Clausewitz, *On War*, 88.

20. Mao Tse-Tung, *On Guerrilla Warfare*, trans. Samuel B. Griffith (New York: Frederick A. Praeger, Inc., 1961), 42.

21. Ibid., 43.

22. Ibid., 43.

23. Although this strategy may not have been exactly in the form that Clausewitz would have anticipated, it is one that he would recognize. Mao is clearly defining the series of engagements that his army will fight in order to win the war. The first four steps are engagements to secure further means of war that will then allow Mao to confront his enemy directly. In so doing, Mao will destroy his enemy's means and will to resist and therefore win the war.

24. Mao Tse-Tung, *On Guerrilla Warfare*, 43.

25. Ibid., 88-89.

26. Ibid., 46.

27. Ibid., 85.

28. Ibid., 57.

29. Vo Nguyen Giap, "Inside the Vietminh," in *The Guerrilla Selections from the Marine Corps Gazette*, ed. T. N. Green (New York: Praeger, 1962), 147.

30. Ibid., 148.

31. Vo Nguyen Giap, *The Military Art of People's War*, ed. Russel Stetler (New York: Monthly Review Press, 1970), 92-95.

32. Ibid., 103-05.

33. Giap, "Inside the Vietminh," 155.

34. Roger Trinquier, *Modern Warfare A French View of Counterinsurgency*, trans. Daniel Lee (New York: Frederick A. Praeger, 1964), 7.

35. Ibid., 6.

36. Peter Paret, *French Revolutionary Warfare from Indochina to Algeria: The Analysis of a Political and Military Doctrine* (New York: Frederick A. Praeger, 1964), 7.

37. Ibid., 22.

38. Ibid., 25.

39. Ibid., 29-30.

40. Trinquier, *Modern Warfare*, 8.

41. Paret, *French Revolutionary Warfare*, 17.

42. Trinquier, *Modern Warfare*, 8.

43. Ibid., 8-9.

44. Ibid., 30. Also see Paret, *French Revolutionary Warfare*, 21.

45. Ibid., 30.

46. Ibid., 33.

47. David Galula, *Counterinsurgency Warfare Theory and Practice* (New York: Frederick A. Praeger, 1964), 4.

48. Ibid., 3.

49. Ibid., 3

50. Ibid., 7

51. Ibid., 8.

52. Ibid., 7-8.

53. Ibid., 75.

54. Ibid., 116-19.

55. Ibid., 123-33.

56. Ibid., 87-88.

57. Ibid., 83.

58. Ibid., 77.

59. Robert Thompson, *Defeating Communist Insurgency: The Lessons of Malaya and Vietnam* (St. Petersburg, FL: Hailer Publishing , 2005), 29-30.

60. Ibid., 47.

61. Ibid., 51.

62. Ibid., 43-44.

63. Ibid., 142-46.

64. Ibid., 146.

65. Ibid., 146.

66. Frank Kitson, *Bunch of Five* (London: Faber and Faber, 1977), 282.

67. Frank Kitson, *Low Intensity Operations* (London: Faber and Faber, 1973), 48.

68. Kitson, *Bunch of Five*, 282.

69. Ibid., 282.

70. Ibid., 283.

71. Kitson, *Low Intensity Operations*, 49.

72. Ibid., 49.

73. Ibid., 50-51.

74. Ibid., 50.

75. Kitson, *Bunch of Five*, 283.

76. Ibid., 289.

77. Ibid., 289.

78. John J. McCuen, *The Art of Counter-Revolutionary War* (Harrisburg, PA: Stackpole Books, 1966), 328.

79. Ibid., 31-37.

80. Ibid., 58.

81. Ibid., 33-34.

82. Ibid., 34.

83. Ibid., 57.

84. Ibid., 64.

85. Ibid., 324.

86. Ibid., 330.

87. John Mackinlay, *The Insurgent Archipelago* (London: C Hurst and Co Publishers Ltd, 2009), 18-19.

88. Ibid., 26.

89. Ibid., 4.

90. Ibid., 4-5.

91. Ibid., 4-5.

92. Ibid., 4-5.

93. Ibid., 5.

94. Ibid., 81-88.

95. John Mackinlay and Alison Al-Baddawy, *Rethinking Counterinsurgency* (Santa Monica, CA: 2008), 51.

96. Mackinlay, *The Insurgent Archipelago*, 164-70.

97. Mark O'Neill, *Confronting the Hydra* (Sydney Australia: Lowy Institute, 2009), 6-7.

98. Ibid., 2.

99. Ibid., 34.

100. Ibid., 35.

101. Ibid., 35.

102. Ibid., 34.

103. Ibid., 34-35.

104. Ibid., 14.

105. Frank G. Hoffman, "Neo-Classical Counterinsurgency?" *Parameters* (Summer 2007): 71.

106. Ibid., 73.

107. David Kilcullen, *The Accidental Guerrilla* (New York: Oxford University Press, 2009), 12-16.

108. The Basques are a good example of this. The Basques do not seek an overthrow of the entire Spanish state, but rather want autonomy for their region.

109. Hoffman, "Neo-Classical Counterinsurgency?," 74-76.

110. Steven Metz, "New Challenges and Old Concepts: Understanding the 21st Century Insurgency," *Parameters* (Winter 2007-2008): 22.

111. Ibid., 23.

112. Ibid., 27.

113. Ibid., 29.

114. Kitson, *Bunch of Five*, 283.

115. Max Weber, "Politics as a Vocation," in *From Max Weber: Essays in Sociology*, trans. and ed. by H.H. Gerth and C. Wright Mills (New York: Oxford University Press, 1946), 78.

116. Ibid., 78.

117. Ibid., 78.

118. Ibid., 80.

119. O'Neill, *Confronting the Hydra*, 35.

120. Peter Chiarelli and Patrick Michaelis, "The Requirements for Full Spectrum Operations," *Military Review* 85, no. 4 (July-August 2005): 4.

121. Ibid., 12.

122. Author's personal experience while serving in Baghdad during 2007-2008.

123. Rod Thornton, "Getting it Wrong: The Crucial Mistakes Made in the Early Stages of the British Army's Deployment to Northern Ireland," *Journal of Strategic Studies* 30, No. 1 (February 2007): 75-76.

124. Richard Iron, "Britain's Longest War," in *Counterinsurgency in Modern Warfare* eds. Daniel Marston and Carter Malkasian (Oxford: Osprey Publishing, 2010), 158.

125. Don Mansfield, "The Irish Republican Army and Northern Ireland," in *Insurgency in the Modern World*, ed. Bard O'Neill (Boulder, CO: Westview Press, 1980), 54.

126. Thornton, "Getting it Wrong," 86.

127. Ibid., 90.

128. Don Mansfield, "The Irish Republican Army and Northern Ireland," 55.

129. Carter Malkasian, "The Role of Perceptions and Political Reform in Counterinsurgency: The Case of Western Iraq, 2004-2005," *Small Wars and Insurgencies* 17, No. 3 (September 2006): 373.

130. Ibid., 381.

131. For more information about the battle for Fallujah, see Bing West, *No True Glory: A Frontline Account of the Battle for Fallujah* (New York: Bantam Books, 2005).

132. Malkasian, "The Role of Perceptions and Political Reform in Counterinsurgency," 383.

133. Carter Malkasian, "Counterinsurgency in Iraq," in *Counterinsurgency in Modern Warfare* eds. Daniel Marston and Carter Malkasian (Oxford: Osprey Publishing, 2010), 306.

134. Ibid., 306.

135. United Kingdom, Ministry of Defence, "Operation TELIC Lessons Learned Compendium," http://www.mod.uk/NR/rdonlyres/F0282A90-99E5-415E-B3BC-97EAD7D7873A/0/operation_telic_lessons_compendium.pdf, (accessed 1 May 2011), 9.

136. There was also some complacency within the British Army that led to a nonchalance in applying experiences from Northern Ireland and Bosnia to Iraq without thinking through them fully. See Daniel Marston, "Adaptation in the Field: The British Army's Difficult Campaign in Iraq," *Security Challenges* 6, no. 1 (Autumn 2010), 73.

137. Senior British Army officer, conversation with author, 30 January 2011.

138. David C. Gompert and John Gordon IV, *War by Other Means* (Santa Monica: RAND Corporation, 2008), 91.

139. Chiarelli and Michaelis, "The Requirements for Full Spectrum Operations."

140. Craig Collier, "Now That We're Leaving Iraq, What Did We Learn?," *Military Review* (September-October 2010): 91.

141. James C. Scott, "Revolution in the Revolution: Peasants and Commissars," *Theory and Society* 7, no. 1/2 (January-March 1979): 98.

142. Mackinlay and Al-Baddawy, *Rethinking Counterinsurgency*, 51.

143. Mansfield, "The Irish Republican Army and Northern Ireland," 52-54.

144. Icek Azjen, "The Theory of Planned Behavior," *Organizational Behavior and Human Decision Processes* 50 (1991): 181-82.

145. Ibid., 182.

146. Ibid., 183-84.

147. Kitson, *Bunch of Five*, 282.

148. Trinquier, *Modern Warfare*, 49.

149. Galula, *Counterinsurgency Warfare*, 120-21.

150. Thompson, *Defeating Communist Insurgency*, 113.

151. Kitson, *Low Intensity Operations*, 50-51.

152. Department of the Army, Field Manual 3-24, *Counterinsurgency* (Washington, DC: Department of the Army, 2006), 5-21.

153. Department of the Army, Field Manual 3-24.2, *Tactics in Counterinsurgency*, (Washington, DC: Department of the Army, 2009), 3-24.

154. Ibid., 3-24-3-25.

155. Ibid., 3-26.

156. Ibid., 3-27.

157. Gompert and Gordon, *War by Other Means*, 91.

158. Ibid., 91.

159. Richard Miers, *Shoot to Kill* (London: Faber and Faber, 1959), 161-62.

160. Ibid., 159.

161. Richard Stubbs, "From Search and Destroy to Hearts and Minds: The Evolution of British Strategy in Malaya, 1948-1960," in *Counterinsurgency in Modern Warfare* eds. Daniel Marston and Carter Malkasian (Oxford: Osprey Publishing, 2010), 111-12.

162. Ibid., 112.

163. Julian Paget, *Counterinsurgency Operations* (New York: Walker and Company, 1967), 169.

164. Stubbs, "From Search and Destroy to Hearts and Minds," 111.

165. Paget, *Counterinsurgency Operations*, 60-61.

166. Mackinlay and Al-Baddawy, *Rethinking Counterinsurgency*, 51.

167. Mackinlay, *The Insurgent Archipelago*, 181.

168. Trinquier, *Modern Warfare*, 50.

169. Author's personal experience as a Company Commander in Baghdad, Iraq, 2007-2008.

170. Wade Markel, "Draining the Swamp: The British Strategy of Population Control," *Parameters* (Spring 2006): 47.

171. Author's personal experience as a Company Commander in Baghdad, Iraq, 2007-2008.

172. Galula, *Counterinsurgency Warfare*, 116.

173. Kitson, *Bunch of Five*, 283.

174. Trinquier, *Modern Warfare*, 35.

175. Kitson, *Low Intensity Operations*, 49.

176. Collier, "Now That We're Leaving Iraq," 88-89.

Chapter 3
The Philippines, 1899-1935

We have only one purpose, and that is to force the insurgents and those in active sympathy with them to want peace.

— Brigadier General J. Franklin Bell, *Address to the Officers in Batangas Province*

The pacification of the Philippines by the United States following the conclusion of the Spanish American war is in many ways the most successful, and yet the least referenced, American counterinsurgency campaign.[1] The unique conditions of the campaign make it an excellent case study for examining the use of population and resource control measures. It is the only counterinsurgency campaign where the US was the colonial power. Pacification was led by military and civil authorities at different times. The US confronted well-organized insurgent movements as well as loosely grouped and led bandit gangs, commonly referred to as *ladrones*.[2] Moreover, US authorities had to repeatedly contest these groups for control of areas of the archipelago.

US authorities responded to these unique conditions by constructing a legal framework to control the behavior of the population through specific restrictions backed up by legal sanctions. These restrictions ranged from the harsh, such as reconcentration of the population into towns, to the more benign, such as requiring municipal officers to report *ladrones*. The measures could be implemented either by the military, during periods of martial law, or civil authorities once a province was declared pacified.

Overview

In August 1896, the *Katipunan*, a secret Filipino organization, began an insurrection against the Spanish colonial regime. Insurgents under the Filipino leader Emilio Aguinaldo, who would later lead the insurgency against the United States, captured a Spanish garrison in Cavite Province and wrested control from the Spanish authorities. The insurrection spread throughout the Tagalog speaking areas of Luzon before Spanish forces were able to put it down using harsh tactics that foreshadowed those used by the US military. The last insurgent surrendered to the Spanish in January 1898 and the insurrection's leaders were exiled in Hong Kong.[3]

Less than four months later, the US Asiatic Squadron under Admiral Dewey sailed into Manila harbor and destroyed the Spanish fleet on 1 May 1898.[4] Accompanying the victorious US fleet were Aguinaldo and the other exiled leaders of the insurrection.[5] The first wave of US Army forces did not arrive in the Philippines until 30 June 1898 and did not capture

Manila until 13 August 1898.[6] This interlude allowed Aguinaldo and his followers to defeat the Spanish garrisons outside of Manila and establish their control over a large portion of the main island of Luzon.[7]

The US Army and the Filipino forces under Aguinaldo maintained an uneasy peace around Manila until February 1899. President William McKinley decided that the US would occupy and temporarily administer the archipelago. He completed a treaty with and purchased the Philippines from Spain.[8] Aguinaldo was unwilling to accept US occupation and administration and decided to force the US out of the Philippines. Aguinaldo's army attacked the US Army in Manila on 4 February 1899, beginning the conventional phase of the war.

From February to November of 1899, the US Army, under the command of Major General Elwell S. Otis[9], waged a conventional campaign that destroyed Aguinaldo's Filipino Army and disrupted his putative national government. The campaign was concentrated in Northern Luzon and US forces did not attempt to control the Tagalog areas of Southern Luzon because of limited forces and a belief that destroying Aguinaldo's army would end the insurgency.[10] US forces entered into agreements with the Sultan of Sulu and other local leaders to assert control over some areas of the archipelago but Southern Luzon was controlled by insurgent elements loyal to Aguinaldo.[11]

In November 1899, with his army decimated and his government on the run, Aguinaldo directed his subordinates to wage guerrilla warfare.[12] The transition to guerrilla warfare initiated a US pacification campaign that continued with varying degrees of intensity until 1935 when the Philippines became a Commonwealth. The US military executed the first phase from November 1899 until June 1902. Although areas that were deemed pacified were transferred to civilian control after the establishment of the Philippine Commission in 1901, pacification efforts remained under the control of the military. The civil government of the Philippines controlled the pacification campaign during its second phase from June 1902 until the start of the Commonwealth in 1935.

The US military's pacification efforts followed in the wake of its advancing forces. After evicting the Filipino Army or guerrilla forces from an area the US military occupied key towns and established local governments to control the area. McKinley wanted the Philippines to be pacified through "benevolent assimilation" and US forces dutifully executed his orders.[13] However, the insurgency dragged on and US commanders began using all their powers under General Orders Number 100 (G.O. 100) of 1863 to gain control.[14] By 1902, organized resistance under recognized Filipino commanders had ended and the civil government assumed control of the campaign.

The civil government of the Philippines continued to face armed threats to its control of the archipelago. Some of these threats were little more than bands of armed criminals but others were run by former Filipino Army Officers and capitalized on the rhetoric of Philippine independence. The Philippine Commission passed a series of acts that provided civil governments powers similar to the military's under G.O. 100.[15] Using these powers, the civil government ended armed threats quickly and with as little violence as possible. The Governor General considered Luzon completely pacified by 1908 and armed resistance after that was rare except in the Muslim Moro areas.[16]

Military Led Pacification, 1899-1902

During the military-led portion of the pacification campaign, US forces employed a variety of tactics and techniques to pacify areas under insurgent control. Official US policy under Otis and his successors was the "policy of attraction."[17] Attraction sought to win the support of Filipinos by demonstrating that US governance of the archipelago would be to their benefit. To this end, the Army built schools, established local governments, and provided medical treatment.[18] However, much of the pacification work consisted of other tactics common to counterinsurgency campaigns.

Offensive patrols sought to destroy or capture insurgent bands. The destruction of food, crops, and homes used by insurgents denied them material support. The reconcentration of the population was a harsh measure used to break insurgent control and separate the population from the insurgents. Many US Army Officers had fought in the Civil War and in the campaigns against Native Americans[19] in the Western United States and so were familiar with the need to control areas engaged in armed rebellion.[20] The military control mechanism was martial law in the form of G.O. 100.

Control Mechanism

The military's experience during the Civil War and fighting Native American tribes yielded an unofficial but well understood doctrine for pacification that sought balance between repression and conciliation.[21] US officers who had fought the tribes learned that controlling populations was critical and it was best to do so without changing local customs and traditions.²² However, in the Philippines, the US inherited not Filipino institutions of law but a Spanish colonial regime. Moreover, Filipino insurgent leaders subverted this system during the conventional campaign while US control was limited to Manila and Northern Luzon.

In the early stages of the campaign, US commanders felt constrained by the policy of attraction and many wanted to be able to use the full range of powers granted them under G.O. 100.²³ While some commanders did so without specific authorization, others waited for the official proclamation of G.O. 100 by Otis' replacement, Major General Arthur MacArthur, in December 1900. This followed a ruling by the US Army Judge Advocate in the archipelago in June 1900 that martial law already applied.²⁴

The confused status of the Philippines caused by the dithering of the McKinley administration, the collapse of many of the Spanish control mechanisms, and the paucity of US forces to simultaneously garrison the country and fight Aguinaldo's army left a vacuum of control into which the insurgents were able to step. To regain control of subverted areas, the military needed to administer martial law. General Order 100 of 1863 is not martial law in and of itself. Rather, "martial law is simply military authority exercised in accordance with the laws and usages of war."²⁵ Since the US did not have any civil administrators in the Philippines in 1900 and the Spanish administrators were no longer effective, the US military was the only body able to administer the country.

General Order 100 defined the powers that the military could use to impose order. General Order 100 had been written for use in occupied areas of the Confederacy during the Civil War. Officers educated at West Point had a common understanding of the laws of war that treated insurgency and guerrilla warfare as illegal.²⁶ Moreover, they believed that it was both legal and legitimate to vigorously repress conquered populations that aided insurgents.²⁷ General Order 100 provided the control mechanism within which the Army could employ population and resource control measures.

<u>General Orders Number 100</u>

The ruling by the Judge Advocate that martial law already existed in the archipelago was in accordance with the opening section of G.O. 100. This section stated that "a place, district, or country occupied by an enemy stands, in consequence of the occupation, under the martial law of the invading or occupying army, whether any proclamation declaring martial law, or any public warning to the inhabitants, has been issued or not."²⁸

Thus, the very act of invading and conquering the Philippines allowed, and in fact, required, the military to impose control through martial law.

General Order 100 also established that martial law did not have to be uniformly applied throughout the occupied territory. Section I, 5 noted that:

> Martial law should be less stringent in places and countries fully occupied and fairly conquered. Much greater severity may be exercised in places or regions where actual hostilities exist or are expected . . . Its most complete sway is allowed–even in the commander's own country– when face to face with the enemy, because of the absolute necessity of the case.[29]

This section empowered the military to adjust the legal measures that it imposed on the population based on the threat to its administration. Thus, commanders had extraordinary power to enforce laws that might not be specifically mentioned in either the civil code of the Philippines or those contained within G.O. 100 itself.

The provision in G.O. 100 regarding military necessity enhanced this flexibility. The orders stated that "military necessity, as understood by modern civilized nations, consists in the necessity of those measures which are indispensable for securing the ends of the war, and which are lawful according to the modern law and usage of war."[30] What is meant by military necessity is open to interpretation, but it undoubtedly was intended to permit commanders to pursue a course of action which they believed would bring the war to an end more quickly, as long as such a course of action were legal.

Moreover, G.O. 100 noted that military necessity, "allows of all destruction of property, and obstruction of the ways and channels of traffic, travel, or communication, and of all withholding of sustenance or means of life from the enemy."[31] This section made clear that military commanders could legally restrict the movement of people and goods, destroy property used to aid the enemy, and impose other restrictions. General Order 100 specifically stated that "war is not carried on by arms alone. It is lawful to starve the hostile belligerent, armed or unarmed, so that it leads to a speedier subjection of the enemy."[32] These sections established a legal basis on which population and resource control measures could be imposed.

The previously discussed sections of G.O. 100 referred to operations during normal hostilities. That is, during times when two uniformed armies confronted one another and the victorious army imposed its control on hostile territory. Use of the powers contained therein by US commanders in the Philippines was therefore expected, particularly during the fighting against Spain and against Aguinaldo's army. However, once Aguinaldo declared the start of guerrilla warfare, other sections of G.O. 100 became applicable that further increased the power of military commanders to impose control.

As noted above, the laws of war at the time took a dim view of insurgency and guerrilla warfare. General Order 100 was no exception. Section III, 52, declared that "if, however, the people of a country, or any portion of the same, already occupied by an army, rise against it, they are violators of the laws of war and are not entitled to their protection."[33] Thus, military commanders could take even harsher measures than allowed under the laws of war to control the population. The US in general did not enforce this rule in its most extreme manifestation but it did enable commanders to conduct operations in a manner which might not otherwise have been legal.

It is Section X of G.O. 100 that specifically dealt with operations during what it called rebellion. It stated that "the term rebellion is applied to an insurrection of large extent, and is usually a war between the legitimate government of a country and portions of provinces of the same who seek to throw off their allegiance to it and set up a government of their own."[34] It could be argued that Filipinos did not consider US rule to be legitimate. However, this was the view of the US, and based on the treaty with Spain and the purchase of the archipelago, was also recognized under international law. The Filipino insurgency against the US was therefore a rebellion under G.O. 100.

Under such circumstances, G.O. 100 stated that:

The military commander of the legitimate government, in a war of rebellion, distinguishes between the loyal citizen in the revolted portion of the country and the disloyal citizen. The disloyal citizens may further be classified into those citizens known to sympathize with the rebellion without positively aiding it, and those who, without taking up arms, give positive aid and comfort to the rebellious enemy without being bodily forced thereto.[35]

This is very important to the concept of population and resource control measures because it speaks to their primary purpose. The difficulty of determining which citizens are loyal and which are open or covert supporters of the insurgency necessitates that the counterinsurgent protect and isolate the population from the insurgent. Moreover, it requires the counterinsurgent to prohibit behavior that may support the insurgency so that offenders can be identified and punished.

General Order 100 directed commanders to "protect the manifestly loyal citizens in revolted territories against the hardships of war."[36] It further instructed them to "throw the burden of the war, as much as lies within his power, on the disloyal citizens, of the revolted portion or province, subjecting them to a stricter police than the non-combatant enemies have to suffer in regular war."[37] Thus, commanders were legally entitled to enforce strict control over the population's behavior and force them to declare their fidelity to the government through their actions.

All of the powers and instructions contained within G.O. 100 provided US commanders a legal basis upon which to impose population and resource control measures. The measures could be harsh as long as they were intended to isolate and protect those members of the population who did not support the insurgency. Those that did support the insurgency could be subjected to harsh restrictions, imprisonment, or even death. Moreover, military commanders could legally enforce the restrictions without recourse to civilian courts.[38] This enabled commanders to dispense punishment against violators quickly and decisively.

In many provinces of the Philippines, the military did not have to resort to the powers detailed in G.O. 100 to gain control. Following occupation, the military established local governments, generally using the same Filipino elites who had assisted the Spanish, and then policed the area as necessary.[39] However, much of Southern Luzon had been unoccupied since the arrival of the US Army in 1898 and Filipino insurgent leaders loyal to Aguinaldo and Filipino independence were in control of these areas. As a result, population and resource control measures had to be imposed to break their control and end the insurgency.

Batangas

Background

Batangas is a province in the southern half of the island of Luzon. It stretches over 1,000 square miles and at the turn of the 20th century had a population of approximately 300,000 people living in 22 towns. The largest town was Lipa with 40,000 people. However, most Filipino towns consisted of little more than a loose aggregation of villages and scattered small holdings.[40] Batangas was not especially poor but its agricultural land was not sufficient to meet the needs of the population and it had to import rice. Most families earned just enough money and produced just enough food to survive.[41] Yet, Batangueños would prove to be ardent supporters of Philippine independence, despite its high personal cost.

Batangueños, both the poor and the prominent members of the community, eagerly supported the insurrection against Spain. Batangas was the last province to succumb to Spanish efforts to end the rebellion. The commander of the Batangueño forces, Miguel Malvar, was the last insurgent leader to surrender and he inspired much loyalty from the population.[42]

Malvar returned to the Philippines with Aguinaldo, rallied his forces, and attacked Spanish garrisons. By June 1898, the province was free of Spanish control. The new government collected taxes, established schools, started newspapers, and petitioned the national government for relief funds.[43] US forces conducted brief expeditions into the neighboring provinces of Tayabas and Cavite during 1899 but not into Batangas itself. Batangas was independent and under Filipino rule.

US Pacification Campaign, January 1900–November 1901

Batangas' independence ended when the US Army captured Santo Tomas on 9 January 1900. Malvar's forces initially fought using conventional tactics and were repeatedly defeated. The conventional fight ended with the capture of Taal on 19 January 1900.[44] Future Filipino journalist, legislator, and aide to President Manuel Quezon, Teodoro Kalaw, observed that after the occupation of Lipa:

> The people began timidly to return to their homes, in the beginning with much apprehension. Seeing, however, that the Americans did them no harm, everyone was soon back in town, living a normal life. The troops of the Republic, and its heroic leaders, kept to the mountains in order to launch that last phase of the resistance movement against the Americans, guerrilla warfare.[45]

Though defeated in conventional battles by the US Army, Malvar's forces had not suffered many casualties and still represented a major threat. Malvar organized his remaining force into three "flying columns" and on January 25 the columns conducted two separate ambushes against the 38th and 45th US Infantry.[46] Moreover, the Filipino control of the population that existed prior to the US arrival had not been fully interrupted. Kalaw noted that his father, the Municipal President of Lipa, and cousin, the Chief of Police, "experienced many bitter moments trying to be faithful to their duties and at the same time loyal to their countrymen."[47] Kalaw stated that on one side his father and cousin were watched by the Americans while on the other they "were pressed by our suffering Revolutionists headed by General Malvar."[48]

US commanders in Batangas focused initially on the destruction of Malvar's guerrillas. Patrols scouted the countryside day and night with little intelligence searching for Filipino fighters.[49] These tactics yielded some success. The report of the Department Commander for Southern Luzon from August 15, 1900, showed that the Second District, which contained Batangas, produced nearly half of the recorded insurgent deaths and over 70 percent of insurgent captures for the entire department during that year.[50] However, this attrition did not seriously hamper Malvar and the insurgency continued. In a letter to his superiors in June of 1901, the commander in Batangas, Brigadier General Samuel Sumner, asked for reinforcements and noted that he thought it advisable to "arrest all the men and bring them to the several posts, force them to surrender arms or give information . . . and let it be known that they will be held till the active *Insurrectos* come in and surrender their arms."[51]

By the summer of 1901, the US Army began to understand that the insurgency in Batangas was different. In his report of 26 August 1901, the Department Commander of Southern Luzon, Brigadier General J.F. Wade, noted that the "great majority of the people [in Batangas, Cavite, and Laguna] are violently opposed to American rule and both hate and fear the Americans."[52] Wade stated that Malvar had "undoubtedly also the material support of a large number of high-class natives and foreigners in Manila and other large towns, who . . . are not satisfied with the course of events and probably not quite convinced as to the honesty of our intentions."[53]

Wade also indentified that an inability to control the population's behavior seriously hindered pacification efforts. He reported that the guerrillas did not stay in the mountains; rather, "the majority of them live at home, even in and about the towns we occupy. When wanted, they are warned through their system of signals and runners, and gather at night at some designated place. The number is limited only by the number required or the number of rifles within reach."[54] After the action was over the insurgent fighter put down his rifle and assumed the guise of an "amigo."[55]

The US Army's tactics did not prevent the population from supporting the insurgency and Malvar intimidated them to deny support to the Americans. He declared all those who worked with American forces to be traitors and their lives and property forfeited.[56] He also established a system of control that compelled the population to provide him manpower and material support.

In an order issued by his headquarters on 28 April 1901, Malvar assumed command of all of Southern Luzon and furthered a system of control already in place.⁵⁷ The order directed the organizing chief of military forces in each area to "take an average of one unmarried soldier for every hundred habitants, apart from the volunteers."⁵⁸ It fixed the war tax at 60 *centimos* per male and 30 *centimos* per female for every six months.⁵⁹ It instructed commanders to ensure that "private individuals sow an abundance of rice, corn, sweet potatoes, egg plants, tomatoes, beans, and other products of prime necessity, for the good of all and in the defense of the nation."⁶⁰

This system of control allowed the insurgency in Batangas to resist efforts by the US to end it only through security measures. Wade asserted that casualties inflicted on Filipino forces were inducing numerous surrenders, which was true in the provinces surrounding Batangas, but not in Batangas itself.⁶¹ American forces burned buildings and crops but this did not inhibit the population's ability to provide support. Eventually, Sumner directed his units to occupy barrios for three days at a time.⁶² This was intended to deny Malvar's guerrillas logistical support but the occupation of barrios was for too short of a time period to change the population's behavior.

The new Philippine Governor General, William Howard Taft, and US Army commander in the Philippines, Major General Adna Chaffee, wanted the insurgency in Batangas to end rapidly so that the province could be transferred to civil control. Sumner was replaced on 30 November 1901 by the US Army's premier counterinsurgent in the Philippines, Brigadier General J. Franklin Bell.⁶³ The success of Malvar and the *Batangueño* guerrillas at controlling the population would now expose them to Bell's most effective tactic, population and resource control measures.

Bell's Pacification of Batangas

Bell had served in the Philippines for several years and had pacified the Ilocos province in Northern Luzon earlier in 1901. Bell demonstrated that he understood the conditions in Batangas and the challenges posed by Malvar's control of the population. In an address to his officers upon assuming command, Bell stated that he believed in the policy of attraction and benevolent assimilation, but "my experience finally convinced me that it alone could not be efficacious in dealing with *Tagalos* (sic)."⁶⁴ He noted that, "Batangas is the very heart of the *Tagalo* (sic) region" and "the insurrection has been more vigorously and numerously sustained here."⁶⁵

Further, he stated that "it is not possible to convince these irreconcilable and unsophisticated people by kindness and benevolence alone that you are right and they are wrong."⁶⁶ Instead, it would be necessary to use force to change their behavior. American forces would have to compel community leaders "to order and counsel him [the common villager] to do that which we want him to do."[67]

Bell told his commanders to protect the population that desired peace and to "deprive the insurgents of supplies and prevent them from getting more."[68] His purpose was to "turn the inhabitants against the insurrection and secure their earnest and loyal assistance in efforts to re-establish peace."[69] Moreover, Bell wanted from the population "respect for the American flag and submission to constituted authority."[70] To accomplish these objectives, Bell implemented population and resource control measures.

Bell issued his orders through a series of telegraphic circulars that began in December 1901. Reconcentration of the population was ordered in Circular No. 2, which directed that:

> In order to put an end to enforced contributions, now levied by insurgents upon the inhabitants of sparsely settled and outlying barrios and districts, by means of intimidation and assassination, commanding officers of all towns now existing . . . will immediately specify and establish plainly marked limits surrounding each town bounding a zone within which it may be practicable, with an average sized garrison, to exercise efficient supervision over and furnish protection to inhabitants (who desire to be peaceful) against the depredations of armed insurgents.[71]

Commanders "will also see that orders are at once given and distributed to all inhabitants . . . that unless they move by December 25th from outlying barrios and districts . . . their property (found outside of said zone at said date) will become liable to confiscation or destruction."[72] Once peaceful conditions were re-established, the population could return to their former homes.[73]

Circular No. 7 established Bell's policy of food denial. He noted up front that G.O. 100 authorized the starving of hostile belligerents and to that end, "every proper effort will be made at all times to deprive those in arms in the mountains of food supplies."[74] Bell believed that it would "not take more than a week to completely clear all outlying districts of food products. Station commanders will begin at once to hunt for and bring in these supplies."[75] These supplies were not merely taken from the insurgents, but were provided to the people under the US Army's protection so that they would not starve nor have an incentive to leave the protected areas. Circular No. 15 directed that "no rice or food products will be permitted to leave the limits of the protected zones."[76]

Bell complemented the reconcentration and food denial policies by establishing movement restrictions. Circular No. 14 prohibited movement on the roads and trails outside of the restricted zones without a pass from the commanding officer that specified the "length of time the said individual has permission to be absent, where permitted to go and for what purpose."[77] If the pass holder failed to return at the designated hour he would be arrested and confined. Additionally, "any able bodied male found by patrols or scouting detachments outside of protected zones without passes will be arrested and confined, or shot if he runs away."[78]

Circular No. 19 established further limits on the population's behavior. Station commanders "convinced that collections are being made for the benefit of the insurgent cause, in public markets . . . are authorized to close the same."[79] Inhabitants "will be required to enter their habitations not later than 8 p.m., and to refrain from again appearing upon the street . . . before the break of day."[80] Those found outside during curfew were to be arrested and fined.

Circular No. 20 addressed the behavior of both the population and the local governing officials. It required the local officials to immediately report insurgents in their jurisdiction. If they failed to do so they would be "tried and punished by Provost Court."[81] Local officials who tried to evade or neglect their duties would also be imprisoned. If the population concealed firearms and did not turn them in after being directed to, their barrio or homes could be burned.[82] Moreover, commanders were instructed to ensure that locals did not possess American uniform parts and "native troops caught selling any portion of their uniform would be severely punished."[83]

Summarizing all of his directives to date, Bell stated that "the purpose of the preceding telegraphic circulars of instruction has been to place the burden of war on the disloyal and to so discipline them that they will become anxious to aid and assist the government in putting an end to the insurrection and in securing the re-establishment of civil government."[84] In assessing whether a town and its population were supporting the insurgents, Bell cautioned his subordinates "not to judge or be mislead by words alone."[85] They had to "rely solely upon acts in order to form a correct judgment of sincerity."[86]

Bell's population and resource control measures went into effect the next day. Over the course of the next four months, Bell issued additional directives to improve the effectiveness of the population and resource control measures. He banned the possession of war *bolos* and *talibons* throughout Batangas, Cavite, and Laguna provinces.[87] He directed his subordinates to collect intelligence to accurately determine the composition of Malvar's force and the number of firearms they had so that when he surrendered it could be ascertained how many of his forces remained in the field.[88] He instructed his commanders to secure firearms by paying the population to turn them in.[89] All surrendered personnel would have their names, insurgent unit information, residence, and other information recorded and tracked.[90]

Bell's population and resource control measures produced rapid success. Kalaw observed that "such stern measures had to produce results. Colonels Katigbak and Kalaw, till then inseparable aides to General Malvar, marched into town with all their men and surrendered."[91] The two officers led a patrol of 500 Filipino volunteers into the mountains in early April 1902 to attempt to capture Malvar. With his wife severely ill, his army either surrendered or starving in the mountains, and his control over the population broken, Malvar surrendered on 16 April 1902. Once his remaining army had also capitulated, Bell ordered an end to the population and resource control measures in his final circular on 16 May 1902.[92]

Malvar explained his decision to Batangueños in a letter written on the day of his surrender. He identified as the first two reasons "the desertion of my most trusted officers" and "the knowledge that the people in all the towns were looking for me, to induce me to surrender."[93] The next reason was the "lack of food in the field, owing to the concentration in the zone, apart from the increased activity of the American troops; because of the adherence of the towns, to the American troops on account of the concentration and the measures taken by General Bell."[94] He concluded by saying that he had sought only "a government of our own, with a flag of our own, under the protection of the American government." Several of Malvar's subordinates and his brother-in-law, an insurgent leader in Tayabas province, indicated that Bell's tactics were the only ones that could have ended the insurgency in Batangas.[95]

Civilian-Led Pacification, 1902-1935

With the pacification of Batangas complete and the near simultaneous end of the brutal campaign on the island of Samar, civilian authority over the entire archipelago of the Philippines was firmly established. From this point forward it was the responsibility of civil officials to lead pacification efforts, though some provinces were governed by serving US Officers. Military forces remained in the archipelago and were utilized in support of civil pacification efforts but did not lead them.

The military's efforts over the previous three years had brought most of the population under the control of the government. However, gangs of bandits and committed insurgents continued to use violence to subvert government control in support of their aims, regardless of what those aims might be. These groups presented threats of varying degrees to US control of the Philippines and the civil government had to respond to them to maintain legitimacy with the population.[96]

US civilian authorities, beginning with Taft, constructed a legal framework to provide them the tools to respond to both armed resistance and political subversion.[97] Some of these tools provided for restrictions on the population's behavior that were in place at all times. Others enabled civil authorities to implement population and resource control measures similar to those used by Bell in Batangas and enforce them using the Philippines Constabulary and, if necessary, US Army forces.

Control Mechanism–Civil Law

McKinley's appointment of Taft as the first Governor General of the Philippines, which may have been largely the result of political maneuvering, was nonetheless fortuitous. Taft was an expert in constitutional law and later served as Chief Justice of the US Supreme Court.[98] As a result, he was well qualified to establish a legal regime in the Philippines that would enable the US to maintain its hard won control of the islands through a system of harsh sanctions against undesirable behavior and emergency powers during times of crisis.

Taft and his successors were aided in this effort by several decisions of the US Supreme Court. These decisions, collectively referred to as the Insular Cases, established that Filipinos were subjects of the US, but not citizens. This gave the US regime in the Philippines power to restrict or revoke certain civil liberties in the Philippines, such as the right to a trial by jury. Thus, the US government in the Philippines could implement and enforce measures to suppress armed revolts and eliminate political subversion that were not available to governments in the homeland.[99]

<u>Legal Restrictions and Powers in Support of Civil Pacification</u>

The civil government of the Philippines established restrictions on behavior and provided civil governments new powers to support pacification. The Philippine Commission passed a series of acts over the years to modify the Spanish Penal Code and Governors General issued Executive Orders when necessary to enforce restrictions. The acts and orders established new definitions for certain crimes, articulated the means of determining proof, and provided civil authorities in the province additional powers to control the population. Furthermore, these acts directed the Constabulary and local officials to enforce the law and gave them the power to do so.

Act No. 518, known as the Bandolerismo Statute, was passed in November of 1902 and defined the crime of brigandage.[100] It established that an armed band consisting of three or more persons formed for the purpose of committing robbery, theft, or abduction was guilty of brigandage.[101] Notably, the law provided extraordinary power to convict people of brigandage with little legal proof. To prove the crime of brigandage it was "not necessary to adduce evidence that any member of the band has in fact committed robbery or theft or abduction, but it is sufficient to justify conviction if, from all the evidence, it can be inferred beyond a reasonable doubt that the accused was a member of a band of robbers organized for such illegal purposes."[102] Moreover, the act provided that any person who abetted such a band by providing it information, material support, or shelter could also be punished.[103] The Bandolerismo Statute was still being enforced as late as 1911 and was included in the 1911 Constabulary manual.[104]

Act No. 781 of June 1903, the so-called Reconcentration Act, was even more powerful. The act was technically a modification to the act which had established the Constabulary but it also provided a new power to the civil government to counter armed resistance. Section 6 established that:

> In provinces which are infested to such an extent with *ladrones* or outlaws that the lives and property of residents in the outlying *barrios* are rendered wholly insecure by continued predatory raids, and such outlying barrios thus furnish to the ladrones or outlaws their sources of food supply, and it is not possible with the available police forces constantly to provide protection to such *barrios*, it shall be within the power of the civil governor, upon resolution of the Philippine commission, to authorize the provincial governor to order that the residents of such outlying *barrios* be temporarily brought within stated proximity to the *polblación* or larger *barrios* of the municipality, there to remain until the necessity for such order ceases to exist.[105]

American civil authorities could now legally reconcentrate Filipinos just as Bell had and for the same reason, to break insurgent or criminal control over the population.

Act No. 781 contained another section that allowed the civil government to assert control over the population. Section 5 established that "it shall be the duty of all municipal officers, as soon as practicable, to give notice to the provincial governor, or inspector of constabulary in the province, of the presence of any bands of *ladrones* or brigands."[106] Municipal officers that did not comply "shall be punished by a fine not exceeding one thousand dollars and imprisonment not exceeding two years."[107] Given the broad definition of brigandage discussed above, Filipino officials in the towns that did not report any gathering of armed men might find themselves in violation of the law. This section was reauthorized later under Act No. 1683. The requirements for municipal officers remained the same but the maximum punishment was changed to a fine of 2000 Philippine pesos and confinement for two years.[108]

The insurrection against Spain and the insurgency against the US both suffered from a lack of sufficient numbers of firearms. This condition continued to hamper insurgents and brigands after 1902. To solidify the government's control over firearms, Taft issued Executive Order No. 9 on 23 March 1903. The order required any resident who wanted to possess a firearm to provide a two hundred dollar bond per weapon and file an application.[109] Municipalities that wished to arm their police forces had to put up a one hundred dollar bond per weapon.[110] Approval for such applications resided with the chief of the Constabulary and the civil governor, respectively. Each firearm application included its kind, make, model, and serial number and the amount, caliber, and make of ammunition for it. Permits were granted for only one year at a time and even registered weapons had to be turned in on demand.[111] Passed later, Act No. 1780 established a maximum punishment of a 500 peso fine and a six month jail term for the unlawful possession of a firearm.[112]

Act No. 1309 provided the final tool to the civil government for controlling the population. It empowered:

The municipal council, with the approval of the provincial governor, when the province or municipality is infested with *ladrones*, to authorize the municipal president to require able-bodied male residents of the municipality, between the ages of 18 and 50 years, to each assist for a period not exceeding five days in any one month in apprehending *ladrones*, robbers, and other lawbreakers and suspicious characters, and to act as patrols for the protection of the municipality not exceeding one day in each week.[113]

This act gave local governments an enormous ability to control and protect their own populations, especially if the local Constabulary unit were called away to other provinces.

It was not just armed threats that the US colonial government sought to control. Laws were passed that banned political parties, made assembly under certain circumstances illegal, and denied Filipinos basic political freedoms. Kalaw joined the euphemistically named "Committee on Filipino Interests" and noted that they had to meet in secret under such a name because working for independence was "considered treason then."[114] The US maintained rigid control over Filipino politics for decades.[115]

The legal restrictions and pacification powers combined to provide the civilian government in the Philippines a tremendous amount of control over the population. The legal restrictions on behavior, such as brigandage, fire arm possession, the joining of political parties, and the reporting requirements for municipal officials, were always in force. Emergency pacification powers included reconcentration and forced manpower support. Together they produced a control mechanism that gave the colonial regime tremendous flexibility in its conduct of pacification. It also made pacification easier because it ensured near continuous control over the population to begin with.

The Philippine Bill and the Insular Cases

The colonial regime was able to impose such restrictions because Filipinos were subjects of the US but not citizens. Congress established their status in the Philippine Organic Act, passed on 1 July 1902. The bill proscribed powers to the Philippine Commission and placed limits on its ability to enforce law and order. However, these limits were not as stringent as they were in the US itself. The Supreme Court affirmed the limitations established by Congress in a series of decisions in the Insular Cases.

Section 4 of the Organic Act, declared that persons residing in the Philippines before the insurrection against the Spanish, and all those born thereafter, were "citizens of the Philippine Islands and as such entitled to the protection of the United States."[116] Crucially, they were not citizens of the United States. They were, however, provided several legal protections in Section 5.

These protections included many of those found in the US Constitution and Bill of Rights. The prohibitions against being tried twice for the same crime, unreasonable search and seizure, and excessive bail remained.[117] Filipinos were also entitled to freedom of speech, religion, the press, and assembly. Notably absent, however, were the right to bear arms, the right to a trial by jury, and the requirement to be indicted by a grand jury. Moreover, while the writ of habeas corpus was affirmed, its suspension was allowed "when in cases of rebellion, insurrection, or invasion the public safety may require it."[118]

The US Supreme Court affirmed Congress' power to decide the status of any acquired territory and to establish laws that differed from those in force within the US for such territory. In 1904 the Court stated in US v. Dorr:

> We conclude that the power to govern territory, implied in the right to acquire it, and given to Congress in the Constitution in article 4, 3, to whatever other limitations it may be subject, the extent of which must be decided as questions arise, does not require that body to enact for ceded territory not made a part of the United States by Congressional action, a system of laws which shall include the right of trial by jury, and that the Constitution does not, without legislation, and of its own force, carry such right to territory so situated.[119]

Therefore, because Congress had not incorporated the Philippines into the territory of the US, Filipinos were only entitled to the rights specifically identified in the Philippine Bill. They could not claim all of the rights of US citizens contained in the Constitution.

The Court affirmed this decision and extended its conclusions seven years later in US v. Dodwell. In Dodwell the Court wrote that:

> As to the objection that no indictment was found by a grand jury, as required by article 5 of the Amendments of the Constitution, there is no such requirement in the Philippine act of July 1, 1902. It is therein provided that 'no law shall be enacted which shall deprive any person of life, liberty, or property without due process of law.' This court has held that due process of law does not require presentment of an indictment found by a grand jury.[120]

While Dodd and Dodwell together do not address all of the rights denied to Filipinos they do illustrate that the Philippine Commission's powers to assert control over the population vastly exceeded the power of the US Government in the homeland. In its pacification campaigns, the civil government would make wide use of its powers.

Civilian-Led Pacification in Southern Luzon

From 1902 to 1935 the US civil government in the Philippines conducted a number of pacification campaigns. It is beyond the scope of this work to address them all. However, a close examination of the campaign in Southern Luzon, especially in the province of Cavite, from 1904 to 1906 will demonstrate how the colonial regime used the legal mechanisms at its disposal to control the population and end armed threats.

While there are other lengthy campaigns that could be examined, especially in the Moro areas where an insurgency continues to this day, only an insurgency that emanated from the Tagalog areas of Luzon posed a threat to US control of the entire archipelago. Luzon included the national capital, Manila, and was the mostly heavily populated island. Tagalogs were the largest single ethnic group and had produced the majority of the insurgent leaders. Moreover, Cavite was the birthplace of both Aguinaldo and the insurrection against Spain. Thus, once it was finally pacified it could be concluded that Filipinos had acquiesced to American rule.

Background

The US military's campaign in Cavite ended quickly relative to that in Batangas when Mariano Trias surrendered in March 1901.[121] Trias was the first major Tagalog leader to capitulate and his doing so led to the collapse of the insurgency in Cavite.[122] This did not, however, end the threat of insurgency in Cavite.

The provincial governor, Major D. C. Shanks, stated in his report of August 15, 1905, that "at the time my last report was submitted, in September, 1904, the province had been free for some time from ladrone movements."[123] However, in the fall of 1904, some of the Constabulary in the province were transferred to the island of Samar and the enlistments of many of the soldiers in the native scouts companies came to an end. This left the province relatively undefended and the situation was taken advantage of by several bands of insurgents operating throughout the Tagolog provinces of Cavite, Batangas, Laguna, and Rizal.[124]

Loosely based at their outset and loyal to specific leaders, the armed bands eventually coalesced into a coherent insurgent organization under the political leadership of Mariano Sakay, who considered himself to be the "president of the Filipino Republic," and the military leadership of Lieutenant General Montalón.[125] Montalón controlled a group of armed men from Cavite and Batangas province and had secured the loyalty of several other armed bands in Southern Luzon.[126]

Fighting began when an armed band attacked the police station and native scout barracks in San Pedro Tanasan, Laguna Province on 12 November 1904.[127] Insurgent successes continued over the next several months, culminating on 15 January 1905, when Montalón's forces disarmed the municipal police in Taal, Batangas province, looted the treasury, and escaped with 20 rifles and 15 shotguns.[128]

Pacification Campaign

Montalón's actions convinced the colonial regime that a massive response was required. Cavite, Batangas, Laguna, and Rizal provinces were grouped into a "provisional constabulary district" under the command of the assistant chief of the Constabulary, Colonel D. J. Baker.[129] However, at no time did Baker or the military assume command of the pacification campaign; all four provinces remained under the control of their civil governors. Constabulary officers were pulled from stations across the archipelago to reinforce the provisional district. Moreover, the Governor General directed the US Army to support the campaign, and the 2d Cavalry and 7th Infantry were sent to Cavite. In his report of 31 July 1905, Baker stated that "the moral effect of these troops, not only in Cavite, where they took station, but also in Batangas, was decisive."[130]

The Governor General suspended the writ of habeas corpus in Cavite and Batangas on 31 January 1905. Baker noted that while no one was arrested without at least a reasonable suspicion of guilt, suspension of the writ did mean that "the arrested law breakers can not (sic) of right obtain bail and again free resume their practices and intimidate the witnesses against them."[131] It also freed up officials who would otherwise have had to prosecute, try, and counsel the offenders to assist the Constabulary in capturing more *ladrones*.

Baker further stated that the suspension of the writ, and the powers of arrest it gave him, "proved an instrument of mercy."[132] Baker and his officers made an effort to turn those who had been captured and "many of those who had confessedly sinned were encouraged to make atonement by giving their influence, by obtaining information through their previous connections, or by abstaining from obstructive tactics."[133] Baker's ability to control the population through the power of arrest thus gave him the ability to change the behavior of former insurgents to support the government.

Baker did not detail the campaign over the next couple of months in his report. However, he stated that it consisted of "weary waits for information, the hard and usually profitless marches, the carefully planned but generally indecisive attacks, the tedious and often fruitless negotiations, and the patient but often disappointing efforts to induce the people to free themselves from the irresponsible bondage of ladronism."[134] Despite the powers of control that the civil government had and the powers of arrest given to the armed forces, traditional methods of campaigning proved insufficient.

Governor General Luke Edward Wright reported on 1 November 1905, that:

> The country was intersected with numberless blind trails known only to the ladrones, which led to their haunts, and it was useless to conduct a campaign in the ordinary way. It was easy for them when pressed to bury their guns and scatter themselves among the people of outlying barrios, many of whom were their relatives or sympathizers and none of whom dare to give information. The *ladrones* were thus in a position to draw supplies at will from the people and to unite or disperse as occasion might require.[135]

Trying to campaign using patrols, marches, and the standard tactics of the Constabulary and the Army under such circumstances would produce only limited success and would not deny the insurgents the support that sustained them. Therefore, because "it was obvious that no real progress could be made so long as this state of affairs existed, and accordingly . . . it was determined to depopulate all of the outlying barrios and draw the people most exposed to ladrone raids and influences in the *poblaciones*."[136]

Reconcentration was ordered for portions of all four provinces but was most heavily utilized in Cavite and Batangas. It was not, however, as pervasive as it had been in Batangas three years earlier. While Bell had reconcentrated almost the entire population of Batangas to gain control, Baker reported that "the extent and degree of each reconcentration was adapted to local conditions and necessities. In no case were the rigors or penalties of a technical or much less of a popularly understood reconcentration enforced."[137] This lesser form of reconcentration was nonetheless still effective and Baker stated that the restrictions were lifted as conditions justified. Reconcentration in Southern Luzon ended by July 1905.

Summing up the campaign, Baker reported that 422 insurgents were killed, captured, or surrendered and the combined force had regained control of 518 firearms.[138] Of the insurgent leaders still at large he stated:

> Of the remnant of the ladrones, Sakay frequents northern Rizal . . . Felizardo disarmed and stripped of companions, lurks between here and Manila. De Vega and his remaining followers skulk in the forest of

Buenavista and Jalan. Montalón, who has been joined by Natividad's remnant of Oruga's band, is hidden now here and now there by the Cólorum society.[139]

While he recognized these men as still dangerous, they no longer posed a serious threat to government control of Luzon.

Less than a year later, the acting Constabulary Chief, Colonel Henry Bandholtz, working through a former Filipino insurgent leader, Dr. Dominador Gomez, secured the surrender of Sakay, De Vega, Montalón, and others, with no conditions except the offer of a fair trial.[140] All were convicted, and Sakay and De Vega were ultimately executed. Governor General James F. Smith reported on 3 November 1908 that "it is eminently gratifying to be able to state that from July 1, 1908, to the date of making this report, a state of complete peace and public tranquility has existed throughout the Archipelago."[141] It is true that Smith downplayed the continuing violence in the Moro areas but his assessment was accurate in that the critical Tagalog speaking areas of Luzon were indeed pacified.

Analysis of Population and Resource Control Measures in the Philippines

Population and resource control measures were undoubtedly effective in the pacification of the Philippines. This was true whether the archipelago was under military or civilian control. Bell's incredibly detailed and interlocking system of population and resource controls ended in less than five months an insurgency in Batangas which had resisted all previous Army efforts to end it for the prior two years. The Governor General, the provincial governors, and the security forces crushed a nascent insurgency in Southern Luzon in slightly more than five months once population and resource control measures were fully implemented. Moreover, they did so with a less pervasive regime than Bell had used. The final death of Tagalog insurgency in the archipelago was a quiet one as Sakay, De Vega, and Montalón surrendered without conditions.

It could be argued that the effectiveness of population and resource control measures in the Philippines is only mildly interesting because such a harsh set of restrictions could not possibly be used today. However, close examination of the population and resource control measures employed yields lessons that can be applied by modern counterinsurgent forces. The population and control measures were all legally enforceable, either under martial law as represented in G.O. 100, or in the acts and orders passed by the US government in the Philippines. They simultaneously protected the population and isolated them from the insurgents. Lastly, they prevented behavior that supported the insurgents and facilitated behavior that supported the government.

Legal Enforcement

The control mechanisms created by G.O. 100 and the laws enacted by the civil government of the Philippine Commission and the Governor General empowered local counterinsurgent commanders to legally enforce population and resource control measures. Legal enforcement gave the counterinsurgent forces a means of incarcerating or otherwise punishing those who violated the restrictions and it allowed them to do so without having to determine if the violator was actually an insurgent. A distinction was no longer necessary since by violating the restrictions the person had committed a crime. This removed one of the main difficulties that confronted the counterinsurgent forces during pacification of the Philippines.

Wade identified how difficult it was in his 1901 report. He stated that "the common solider [of the insurgency] wears the dress of the country; with his gun he is a soldier; by hiding it and walking quietly along the road, sitting down by the nearest house, or going to work in the nearest field, he becomes an 'amigo' full of good will".[142] Bell's population and resource control measures alleviated this problem, however. Anyone who violated the movement restrictions, the curfew, or was found outside of the protected zones could be arrested and charged with a crime, and in some cases, shot. Soldiers no longer needed to distinguish between "amigos" and active insurgents; if someone was violating the restrictions they could be arrested and punished.

Legal enforcement of restrictions during the civil pacification of the campaign offered an additional benefit. Since many of the laws that established the population and resource control measures were in effect all the time, the Constabulary could enforce them and prevent large scale uprisings from ever beginning. The very act of joining an armed band or possessing a firearm without a permit was a crime punishable by incarceration. The insurgency in Southern Luzon that begun in 1904 was primarily the result of the transfer of many Constabulary officers to Samar, leaving the law unenforced and thus weakening the government's control of the province.

Legal enforcement of population and resource control measures produced another advantage for both the military and civilian authorities. Since the burden of proof for a violation was low and the punishments were harsh, the counterinsurgents had enormous leverage over captured insurgents and their supporters to induce them to provide support to the government. If the prisoners offered help they could be pardoned or the sentence reduced, if they did not they would subject themselves and their families to the full hardship of the legal penalties. Bell used the surrendered Malvar subordinates Katigbak and Kalaw to lead a party to capture him. Baker offered amnesty to those he arrested in return for information on the remaining insurgents.

Protection and Isolation of the Population

During the campaign, the Filipino population was not subjected to attacks by insurgents on a regular basis. The insurgents lived among them and had no desire, or need, to attack them. However, the murder of "americanistas," people who assisted US forces or worked for the government, was commonplace.[143] Protecting those who worked with the regime was necessary for it to function, and as Wade identified, protecting them reduced the number of forces that were available to patrol in search of insurgents. Moreover, as noted numerous times, the insurgents were able to blend into the population making it difficult to target them during patrols.

The population and resource control measures imposed, especially reconcentration, alleviated both problems. Everyone who moved into a protected town had to do so without a weapon because of the restrictions on the possession of firearms. This reduced the ability of the insurgency to target americanistas. Governor General Wright stated that reconcentration in 1905 "furnished protection to the law-abiding people against spoliation and outrage."[144] Additionally, because the population was concentrated into a smaller area the military or Constabulary were able to provide protection with a smaller number of soldiers and this freed up forces to conduct patrols to target the insurgents.[145]

Wright highlighted the advantages of isolating the insurgents from the population when he noted that "the immediate effect of this reconcentration was to cut off the ready source of food supply which the outlaws theretofore had and to force them more in the open where they could be reached."[146] The insurgents could no longer hide among the population, because the population was inside of the protected zones. Without this source of cover, the insurgents could only hope to avoid military or Constabulary patrols. If they did not, and did not choose to fight, they could be arrested, as noted above, even if they were unarmed.

Isolating the population from the insurgency greatly facilitated targeting of the insurgents. Obviously, by placing most of the population into protected zones any fighters that remained outside were now easily identifiable. Bandholtz stated that one of the purposes for re-concentrating the population in Albay province in 1903 was "to enable the troops to operate freely without any fear of injuring innocent people." [147] Moreover, by protecting the population and isolating it from the insurgency it was possible to gain additional intelligence. Wright reported that once reconcentration had been imposed "the officers in charge soon began to get reliable information and guides and to track the outlaws to their hiding places."[148] He further noted that the insurgent bands were gradually broken up which enabled the counterinsurgent forces to reduce their patrol size and increase the frequency of patrols.[149] This ensured that Sakay, Montalón, and the others were even more isolated and it accelerated the end of the insurgency.

Focus on Behavior

The previous chapter argued that it is difficult to change the intentions of the population and therefore the counterinsurgent should focus on controlling the behavior of the population. In this aspect, the Philippine counterinsurgents excelled. Recall the comment of Bell to his officers that "it is not possible to convince these irreconcilable and unsophisticated people by kindness and benevolence alone that you are right and they are wrong."[150] He also told them that "you cannot afford to believe what they [Filipinos] say about their relations with the insurrection unless it be backed up by some act which has so committed them to the side of the Americans as to greatly antagonize the insurgents."[151]

Members of the civil government echoed Bell's astute observation. The Constabulary Senior Inspector in Cavite, Captain T. R. Hanson, stated in his 1903 report that despite the appearance of security in the province "the population had apparently decided that they would not be governed. . . . The people in most of the towns are in sympathy with the outlaws and warn them of the approach of constabulary or scouts."[152] In his 1906 report, the governor of Cavite province, Louis J. Van Schaick, stated that "I am convinced that *ladrone* leaders do not produce conditions, but that the conditions and attitude of the public produce ladrones."[153]

These American observers understood that no amount of attraction or benevolence would change the minds of the most committed insurgents. However, by directing population and resource control measures at behaviors that supported the insurgency the US was able to control the population, and thus the insurgent leaders, as a prelude to persuading them to support US administration of the archipelago. Kalaw, in writing about the town of Lipa after Bell had imposed his population and resource control measures, said that "henceforth, neutrality would no longer be recognized. One either had to go out and fight for the Americans or to stay within the town as their prisoner."[154] Note that Kalaw does not say that one's intention to support the insurgency had to change; rather, one's behavior had to change. It was no longer possible to support the insurgency because Bell had made it illegal to engage in any behavior that might do so.

The focus on behavior also produced notable success with regards to the insurgents. Kalaw noted that "the Revolutionists were slowly starved out. With labor forbidden in the fields and communication with their friends impossible, they had no way of obtaining food."[155] Bandholtz observed that because of the population and resource control measures employed in Albay province in 1903 insurgents surrendered "in an emaciated condition, many of them covered with tropical ulcers. Some of them had ulcerated holes in their calves into which a man could thrust his fist."[156] The population could no longer provide them support and this severely inhibited their operations, regardless of whether or not they still had the loyalty of the population.

The population and resource control measure regime also facilitated behavior that supported the government. It has already been noted that both the military and the Constabulary received more information and greater assistance once such measures were in place. Even Malvar identified that the population of Batangas began to search for him to induce his surrender.[157] Moreover, as discussed above, the colonial regime required municipal officers to provide information on ladrones at all times and could also require the population to provide manpower to the police or Constabulary during times of crisis.

Notably, the forced behavior change that the population and resource control measures brought about was often followed up by permanent changes. The Senior Inspector of the Constabulary for Batangas province in 1903 observed that the "better class of people discourage *ladronism*."[158] He also reported that a mass meeting was held in February 1903 to prevent *ladronism*. At this meeting funds were collected so that "a man is employed by the various barrios whose duty it is to give immediate information of existence of ladrones."[159] Long term behavior change was most notable amongst the leaders of the insurgency.

Many insurgent leaders determined that it was fruitless to resist US administration of the archipelago and thus decided that it was best to work for independence through the US rather than against it. Manuel Quezon, the first president of the Philippine Commonwealth, was an officer during the insurgency against the US His commander ordered him to surrender in 1901 to find out if Aguinaldo had been captured. After seeing the captured Aguinaldo and delivering the message to his commander, Quezon was paroled. Two years later, still seething and unwilling to learn English, Quezon met with Governor Paras, a Filipino, of Tayabas province. During the meeting they "talked about the situation of our country. He [Paras] was an honest and a real patriot. He told me that he did not seek the job, but accepted it because it was his sincere opinion that the only way of promoting the freedom as well as the welfare of the Filipino people was by cooperating with the American Government."[160] After the meeting, Quezon recalled that "although I dissented from the opinion of Governor Paras, his words made some impression on me. I wondered, in my own mind, if the freedom which we lost by fighting America could not be won by cooperating with her."[161]

Quezon's intentions, to work for independence, were not changed by this meeting, but his behavior was. Quezon was not the only former insurgent to work with the Americans to govern the archipelago. His opponent in the first presidential election was none other than Aguinaldo. Subsequent to his surrender in Cavite, Trias was eventually made the provincial governor. Countless other insurgent leaders similarly cooperated with the colonial regime.

The behavior of the population was changed too, largely because it was clear that the US would impose control. Wright observed that:

> As it became evident to the inhabitants of the affected provinces that the Government was in deadly earnest and proposed finally to make an end to *ladronism* their attitude underwent a material change, so that when one or two ladrones came into a barrio they were either seized or driven out by the people themselves.[162]

It is not likely that Wright actually knew whether or not the population's attitude towards *ladronism* had changed, but it is clear that their behavior did.

The change in behavior on the part of both the leaders of the insurgency and the people as a result of the population and resource control measures also speaks to their legitimacy. It is hard to say whether or not ordinary Filipinos considered the US tactics legitimate. Kalaw and others have argued that they were not. However, this is belied by the fact that the leaders of the insurgency chose to work with the colonial regime. Moreover, it is likely that ordinary Filipinos considered a government that imposed control to be more legitimate than one that did not, regardless of the methods it used.[163]

The US did face legitimacy crises during its administration of the Philippines. However, these were caused by violations of the law by the Constabulary, such as torture, and corruption within colonial administration, not the restrictions in place or powers employed, including reconcentration, to pacify areas of the archipelago.[164] While working as a journalist for *El Renacimiento*, a nationalistic Philippine newspaper, Kalaw regularly investigated alleged abuses of power by the Constabulary.[165] He did not, however, openly attempt to remove the restrictions that he would later declare so awful. Finally, consider the words of an 18 year-old Kalaw on the day that Governor General Taft visited Lipa following the pacification of Batangas in 1902:

> My town takes this opportunity of greeting you and of giving you the homage of gratitude. Be pleased to accept it. If my town cannot offer this with the brilliance of other more prosperous places you have recently visited, rest assured that it is given with the sincerity of a people who, even in surrender, have not lost an appreciation for its well-wishers.[166]

Notes

1. Anthony James Joes, "Counterinsurgency in the Philippines, 1898-1954," in *Counterinsurgency in Modern Warfare,* eds. Daniel Marston and Carter Malkasian, (Oxford: Osprey Publishing, 2010), 39.

2. Terms such as ladrones, bandoleros, and others are Spanish in origin and reflect the impact of Spain's long colonial rule of the Philippines. The US personnel who participated in the campaign in the Philippines adopted these terms and they will be used throughout this paper where appropriate.

3. Glenn Anthony May, *Battle for Batangas: A Philippine Province at War* (New Haven: Yale University Press, 1991), 48-65.

4. Joes, "Counterinsurgency in the Philippines," 41.

5. Ibid., 41.

6. Brian Linn, *The Philippine War, 1899-1902* (Lawrence, KS: University of Kansas Press, 2000), 23-24.

7. Ibid., 26.

8. Joes, "Counterinsurgency in the Philippines," 41.

9. Linn records that Otis was "one of the most unpopular, maligned, and controversial commanders in the islands." But also asserts that he was "both more interesting and more capable than the caricature 'Granny' Otis created by his detractors." See Linn, *The Philippine War*, 27-29.

10. Linn, *The Philippine War*, 88.

11. Linn, *The Philippine War*.

12. Ibid, 148.

13. Ibid, 30.

14. General Orders 100 will be discussed in greater detail below.

15. Alfred W. McCoy, *Policing America's Empire* (Madison, WI: The University of Wisconsin Press, 2009), 60.

16. U.S. Bureau of Insular Affairs, *Ninth Annual Report of the Philippine Commission, 1908, Part 1* (Washington, DC: U.S. War Department, 1909), 43.

17. Joes, "Counterinsurgency in the Philippines," 46.

18. Ibid., 46.

19. An examination of the US Army's counterinsurgency campaigns against Native American tribes is beyond the scope of this paper. However, many of these campaigns included population and resource control measures. Most obviously, Native American tribes were forced to live on reservations. Moreover, the systematic destruction of the American bison was extremely effective at breaking the will of the Comanches to continue to fight. For more information on the war against the Comanche see S.C. Gwynne, *Empire of the Summer Moon: Quanah*

Parker and the Rise and Fall of the Comanches, the Most Powerful Indian Tribe in American History (New York: Scribner, 2010).

20. Andrew J. Birtle, *US Army Counterinsurgency and Contingency Operations Doctrine, 1860-1941* (Washington, DC: Center of Military History, 1998), 133. Birtle notes that "most officers began their analysis from the premise that force was the sine qua non of Indian pacification. This view stemmed less from vindictiveness than acceptance of the brutal fact that government policy ultimately entailed the destruction of the Indian's traditional way of life, something many Native Americans were unwilling to accept without a fight." Birtle, *U.S. Army Counterinsurgency*, 79.

21. Linn, *The Philippine War*, 9.

22. Birtle, *U.S. Army Counterinsurgency*, 101.

23. Linn, *The Philippine War*, 211.

24. Ibid., 211.

25. Adjutant General's Office, US War Department, *General Orders Number 100* (Washington, DC: 1863), Section I, 4.

26. Birtle, *U.S. Army Counterinsurgency*, 126.

27. Ibid., 126.

28. *G.O. 100*, Section I, 1.

29. Ibid., Section I, 5.

30. Ibid., Section I, 14.

31. Ibid., Section I, 15.

32. Ibid., Section I, 17.

33. Ibid., Section III, 52.

34. Ibid., Section X, 151.

35. Ibid., Section X, 155.

36. Ibid., Section X, 156.

37. Ibid., Section X, 156.

38. Ibid., Section I.

39. Linn, *The Philippine War*, 75-76.

40. May, *Battle for Batangas*, 8.

41. Ibid., 20.

42. Ibid., 50.

43. Ibid., 69-72.

44. Ibid., 125-26.

45. Teodoro M. Kalaw, *Aide-de-camp to Freedom*, trans. Maria Kalaw Katigbak (Manila: Teodoro M. Kalaw Society, Inc., 1965), 20.

46. May, *Battle for Batangas*, 132.

47. Kalaw, *Aide-de-camp to Freedom*, 24.

48. Ibid., 25.

49. May, *Battle for Batangas*.

50. US War Department, *Report of the Lieutenant General Commanding the Army, 1900, Part 3* (Washington, DC: Government Printing Office, 1900), 221.

51. Samuel Sumner quoted in May, *Battle for Batangas*, 228.

52. US War Department, *Report of the Lieutenant General Commanding the Army, 1901, Part 5* (Washington, DC: Government Printing Office, 1901), 389.

53. Ibid., 389.

54. Ibid., 390.

55. Ibid., 390.

56. Ibid., 389.

57. Miguel Malvar, "Provisions and Instructions Issued by the Superior Commander of Southern Luzon for Observation by this Department," 28 April 1901, in John R.M. Taylor, *The Philippine Insurrection Against the United States: a Compilation of Documents* (Fort Leavenworth, KS: Combined Arms Research Library Microfilm), Exhibit 1156.

58. Ibid.

59. Ibid.

60. Ibid.

61. US War Department, *Report of the Lieutenant General Commanding the Army, 1901, Part 5*, 390.

62. May, *Battle for Batangas*, 236-37.

63. General Bell arrived in the Philippines as a junior officer in 1899, but was rapidly promoted to Brigadier General. He participated in every major phase of the US Army's campaign in the Philippines through the pacification of Batangas in 1902. His career was briefly threatened after his return from the Philippines when he was called before Congress to testify about his actions in Batangas. The threat was short-lived, however, and Bell eventually became Chief of Staff of the Army.

64. J. Franklin Bell, address to the officers of Batangas province, December 1, 1901, in Robert D. Ramsey III, *A Masterpiece of Counterguerrilla Warfare: BG J. Franklin Bell in the Philippines, 1901-1902* (Fort Leavenworth: Combat Studies Institute Press, 2007), 34.

65. Ibid., 34.

66. Ibid., 34.

67. Ibid., 35.

68. Ibid., 39.

69. Ibid., 43.

70. Ibid., 41.

71. J. Franklin Bell, Telegraphic Circular No. 2, 8 December 1901, in Robert D. Ramsey III, *A Masterpiece of Counterguerrilla Warfare: BG J. Franklin Bell in the Philippines, 1901-1902* (Fort Leavenworth: Combat Studies Institute Press, 2007), 45.

72. Ibid., 45-46.

73. Ibid., 46.

74. J. Franklin Bell, Telegraphic Circular No. 7, 15 December 1901, in Robert D. Ramsey III, *A Masterpiece of Counterguerrilla Warfare: BG J. Franklin Bell in the Philippines, 1901-1902* (Fort Leavenworth: Combat Studies Institute Press, 2007), 55.

75. Ibid., 56.

76. J. Franklin Bell, Telegraphic Circular No. 15, 23 December 1901, in Robert D. Ramsey III, *A Masterpiece of Counterguerrilla Warfare: BG J. Franklin Bell in the Philippines, 1901-1902* (Fort Leavenworth: Combat Studies Institute Press, 2007), 62.

77. J. Franklin Bell, Telegraphic Circular No. 14, 21 December 1901, in Robert D. Ramsey III, *A Masterpiece of Counterguerrilla Warfare: BG J. Franklin Bell in the Philippines, 1901-1902* (Fort Leavenworth: Combat Studies Institute Press, 2007), 60.

78. Ibid., 61.

79. J. Franklin Bell, Telegraphic Circular No. 19, 24 December 1901, in Robert D. Ramsey III, *A Masterpiece of Counterguerrilla Warfare: BG J. Franklin Bell in the Philippines, 1901-1902* (Fort Leavenworth: Combat Studies Institute Press, 2007), 66.

80. Ibid., 66.

81. J. Franklin Bell, Telegraphic Circular No. 20, 24 December 1901, in Robert D. Ramsey III, *A Masterpiece of Counterguerrilla Warfare: BG J. Franklin Bell in the Philippines, 1901-1902* (Fort Leavenworth: Combat Studies Institute Press, 2007), 67.

82. Ibid., 67-68.

83. Ibid., 68.

84. J. Franklin Bell, Telegraphic Circular No. 22, 24 December 1901, in Robert D. Ramsey III, *A Masterpiece of Counterguerrilla Warfare: Brigadier General J. Franklin Bell in the Philippines, 1901-1902* (Fort Leavenworth: Combat Studies Institute Press, 2007), 70.

85. Ibid., 71.

86. Ibid., 71.

87. J. Franklin Bell, Telegraphic Circular No. 23, 28 December 1901, in Robert D. Ramsey III, *A Masterpiece of Counterguerrilla Warfare: Brigadier General J. Franklin Bell in the Philippines, 1901-1902* (Fort Leavenworth: Combat Studies Institute Press, 2007), 71.

88. J. Franklin Bell, Telegraphic Circular No. 26, 3 January 1902, in Robert D. Ramsey III, *A Masterpiece of Counterguerrilla Warfare: Brigadier General J. Franklin Bell in the Philippines, 1901-1902* (Fort Leavenworth: Combat Studies Institute Press, 2007), 73.

89. J. Franklin Bell, Telegraphic Circular No. 34, 12 February 1902, in Robert D. Ramsey III, *A Masterpiece of Counterguerrilla Warfare: BG J. Franklin Bell in the Philippines, 1901-1902* (Fort Leavenworth: Combat Studies Institute Press, 2007), 81.

90. J. Franklin Bell, Telegraphic Circular No. 36, 15 February 1902, in Robert D. Ramsey III, *A Masterpiece of Counterguerrilla Warfare: Brigadier General J. Franklin Bell in the Philippines, 1901-1902* (Fort Leavenworth: Combat Studies Institute Press, 2007), 82.

91. Kalaw, *Aide-de-camp to Freedom*, 36.

92. J. Franklin Bell, Telegraphic Circular No. 38, 16 May 1902, in Robert D. Ramsey III, *A Masterpiece of Counterguerrilla Warfare: BG J. Franklin Bell in the Philippines, 1901-1902* (Fort Leavenworth: Combat Studies Institute Press, 2007), 83-84.

93. Miguel Malvar, "The Reason for My Change of Attitude," 16 April 1902, in John R.M. Taylor, *The Philippine Insurrection Against the United States: a Compilation of Documents* (Fort Leavenworth, KS: Combined Arms Research Library Microfilm), Exhibit 1172.

94. Ibid.

95. May, *Battle for Batangas*.

96. McCoy, *Policing America's Empire*, 55.

97. Ibid., 60.

98. Taft was elected President of the United States after Teddy Roosevelt. He is the only person in US history to serve as both President and Chief Justice.

99. Ibid., 60.

100. U.S. Bureau of Insular Affairs, *Fourth Annual Report of the Philippine Commission, 1903, Part 1* (Washington, DC: Government Printing Office, 1904), 34.

101. Ibid., 34-35.

102. Ibid., 35.

103. Ibid., 35.

104. Philippine Constabulary, *Manual for the Philippine Constabulary, 1911* (Manila: Bureau of Printing: 1911), 71.

105. *RPC, 1903, Part 1*, 141.

106. Ibid., 141.

107. Ibid., 141.

108. *PC Manual, 1911*, 73.

109. *RPC, 1903, Part 1*, 950-51.

110. Ibid., 951.

111. Ibid., 951.

112. *PC Manual, 1911*, 74.

113. *PC Manual, 1911*, 72.

114. Kalaw, *Aide-de-camp to Freedom*, 45.

115. McCoy, *Policing America's Empire*, 97.

116. *The Philippine Organic Act*, 57th Cong., 2d session. (July 1, 1902), Section 4.

117. Ibid., Section 5.

118. Ibid., Section 5.

119. Dorr v. U S, 195 US 138 (1904).

120. Dowdell v. U S, 221 US 325 (1911).

121. US War Department, *Report of the Lieutenant General Commanding the Army, 1901, Part 5*, 409.

122. Linn, *The Philippine War*, 295.

123. US Bureau of Insular Affairs, *Sixth Annual Report of the Philippine Commission, 1905, Part 1* (Washington, DC: Government Printing Office, 1906), 210.

124. Ibid, 210.

125. US Bureau of Insular Affairs, *Seventh Annual Report of the Philippine Commission, 1906, Part 1* (Washington, DC: Government Printing Office, 1907), 30.

126. US Bureau of Insular Affairs, *Sixth Annual Report of the Philippine Commission, 1905, Part 3* (Washington, DC: Government Printing Office, 1906), 129-30.

127. Ibid., 130.

128. Ibid., 130.

129. *RPC, 1905, Part 1*, 53-54.

130. *RPC, 1905, Part 3*, 132.

131. Ibid., 132.

132. Ibid., 132.

133. Ibid., 132.

134. Ibid., 132.

135. *RPC, 1905, Part 1*, 57.

136. Ibid., 57.

137. *RPC, 1905, Part 3*, 133.

138. Ibid., 133.

139. Ibid., 133.

140. *RPC, 1906, Part 1*, 30.

141. *RPC, 1908, Part 1*, 43.

142. *Report of the Lieutenant General Commanding the Army, 1901, Part 5*, 390.

143. Linn, *The Philippine War*, 222.

144. *RPC, 1905, Part 1*, 57.

145. *RPC, 1903, Part 3*, 139.

146. *RPC, 1905, Part 1*, 57.

147. *RPC, 1903, Part 3*, 139.

148. *RPC, 1905, Part 1*, 57.

149. Ibid., 57.

150. J. Franklin Bell, address to the officers of Batangas province, 34.

151. Ibid., 35.

152. *RPC, 1903, Part 3*, 56.

153. *RPC, 1906, Part 1*, 225.

154. Kalaw, *Aide-de-camp to Freedom*, 36.

155. Ibid., 36.

156. *RPC, 1903, Part 3*, 139.

157. Miguel Malvar, "The Reason for My Change of Attitude."

158. *RPC, 1903, Part 3*, 53.

159. Ibid., 54.

160. Manuel Luis Quezon, *The Good Fight* (New York: D. Appleton-Century Company, Incorporated, 1946), 87-88.

161. Ibid., 88.

162. *RPC, 1905, Part 1*, 58.

163. McCoy, *Policing America's Empire*, 62.

164. Ibid, 141-42.

165. Kalaw, *Aide-de-camp to Freedom*, 45. During the time that Batangas is under the control of the Constabulary in 1904 and 1905, Kalaw reported on a number of abuses committed by individual Constabulary officers. His paper, *El Renacimiento*, became involved in a libel suit as a result. This was the first of several libel suits that the paper would face because of its reporting on the activities of individual members of the Constabulary and the Philippine Commission. Kalaw does not say that the paper specifically advocated for the removal of the laws that the Constabulary was using. Moreover, by the time he assumes the editorship of the paper in 1908 he is a close confidante of future Philippine president Manuel Quezon who has, as noted above, decided that it is best to work for independence through the Americans, rather than against them.

166. Ibid., 38.

Chapter 4
Vietnam, 1954-1963

In destroying the strategic hamlets, we must not only destroy the barbed wire and installations but must also destroy the enemy's grip, regain the population and not allow the enemy to control the population.

—*A Party Account of the Revolutionary Movement in South Vietnam from 1954-1963*

Vietnam is a difficult conflict to characterize. It was neither a pure insurgency nor a state-on-state conventional war. The conflict involved the forces of multiple countries on both sides while equipment and support were supplied by many more. The Republic of Vietnam (RVN) experienced political subversion, targeted assassination, urban terrorism, insurgency, and invasion by conventional main force units and formations. At some points during the conflict all of these occurred simultaneously. Vietnam was a hybrid conflict.[1]

This makes Vietnam an important case study to examine the use of population and resource control measures. Prior to the introduction of US ground forces in 1965, population and resource control measures were implemented by the Government of Vietnam (GVN) and its security forces. However, after the introduction of US ground forces in 1965, it became possible for US units to implement and enforce population and resource control measures. The simultaneous existence of a conventional main force threat and an insurgency during portions of the conflict highlights the difficulty of using such measures when confronting a hybrid threat.

It is possible to divide the war in Vietnam from 1954 to 1975 an innumerable number of ways. In doing so it should be clear what specific aspect of the war is being examined. Then it is possible to divide the war in a way that facilitates this examination. A close study of the entire period of the war is beyond the scope of this paper, which will conduct two specific case studies to examine the use of population and resource control measures. This chapter will examine the programs implemented by the Diem regime from 1954 to 1963. The next chapter will study the use of population and resource control measures by the US 25th Infantry Division in Hau Nghia province from 1966 to 1970.

The period of the Diem regime facilitates an examination of how population and resource controls measures evolved over time under a single government and a single leader of that government. The instability of the GVN government after the coup in 1963 until the ascension of Premier Nguyen Cao Ky and Chief of State Nguyen Van Thieu in 1965 renders any such analysis difficult, if not impossible. However, after the introduction of US ground forces the regime stabilized to the point where it is again possible to examine the use of population and resource control measures. Once US ground forces departed, however, the threat to the GVN from a conventional invasion significantly outweighed the threat posed by the insurgency and renders an analysis of population and resource control measures to counter an insurgency meaningless.

Overview

The Viet Minh defeat of the French Army at Dien Bien Phu in 1954 was closely followed by the signing of the Geneva Accords which divided Vietnam into two independent countries. The northern half of the country, the Democratic Republic of Vietnam (DRV), was controlled by the Vietnamese Communist Party[2] under Chairman Ho Chi Minh and his top military leader, General Vo Nguyen Giap. The area south of the 17th parallel, which included central and southern Vietnam, formed its own government. The Vietnamese emperor, Bao Dai, asked the staunch anti-communist and Vietnamese nationalist, Ngo Dinh Diem, to become premier[3] in June 1954.[4]

From 1954 to 1956 the two halves of Vietnam co-existed as both governments sought to assert control and some portions of the population resettled.[5] However, as it became clear that the GVN was strongly anti-communist and capable of gaining control of the country, and thus thwarting the DRV's intention to unify Vietnam under Communist leadership, the Communist cells that had remained in the RVN after the departure of the French began to conduct what the Party referred to as political struggle.[6] The political struggle was not able to reverse the GVN's intense targeting of the Party apparatus and its increasing control over South Vietnam, however. As a result, in January 1959, the 15th Plenary session of the Party Central Committee in Hanoi[7] resolved to "liberate" the Republic of Vietnam and authorized the use of armed struggle.[8]

In the years following the decision of the Party Central Committee, the Communist cadres in the south expanded the nascent insurgency and openly contested the GVN for control of the country. From 1959 to 1963 the Army of the Republic of Vietnam (ARVN), supported by American advisers, confronted Viet Cong[9] (VC) elements throughout the country. The fight during this time period was waged mainly for control over the population and ebbed and flowed as the GVN, supported by the US, and the VC, supported by the DRV, responded to each other's initiatives with new tactics. Additionally, in 1959 the DRV began construction and use of the Ho Chi Minh Trail, a supply line for war materiel, men, and equipment from the DRV to the RVN.[10] The Ho Chi Minh trail and the accompanying sanctuary areas in Laos and Cambodia significantly complicated the war efforts of the GVN and its allies.

The DRV's war effort was not limited to an increase in armed activity. The VC and its political wing, the National Liberation Front (NLF), formed in 1960, continued their campaign of political subversion and propaganda against the Diem regime. The Party capitalized on, and potentially manipulated and participated in, protests by Buddhists against the Diem regime to discredit him in the eyes of Saigon intellectuals as well as US journalists and government officials.[11] Discontent with Diem was not widespread among US civilian and military officials, however, many of who viewed Diem as an effective leader and did not believe that a credible alternative to him existed.[12] Nevertheless, in November 1963, a group of Vietnamese generals executed a coup against Diem. The coup and the resulting murder of Diem and his brother, Counselor Ngo Dinh Nhu, changed the war dramatically.

The 1963 coup destabilized Saigon and led to a series of coups over the next two years which undermined the GVN's war effort and denied it any continuity. Sensing an opportunity, the DRV introduced main force units from the People's Army of Vietnam (PAVN) into the South in 1964 in an effort to defeat the GVN militarily before the US could intervene with ground forces of its own.[13] The VC main force and PAVN units were not able to end the war quickly, however, and the US deployed ground combat troops to South Vietnam in 1965 to prevent the collapse of the GVN.

The introduction of US ground combat troops significantly changed the dynamics of the war. General William C. Westmoreland, the commander of the US Military Assistance Command, Vietnam, (MACV), decided to employ US forces offensively to destroy VC and PAVN main force units in order to allow ARVN forces to conduct pacification operations among the Vietnamese population in the hamlets and villages.[14] Though this strategy has been derided, it did take account of the situation in existence on the ground, specifically, that the GVN and ARVN could not control the population while they were under threat of attack by VC and PAVN main force units. The U.S war of attrition continued until the 1968 Tet Offensive changed the war once again.

From the time of its intervention in Vietnam until the 1968 Tet Offensive, the US gradually escalated the war. This included a destructive bombing campaign in the north. It was believed that the pressure placed on the north by the combined air and ground campaigns would demonstrate US resolve and force the DRV to negotiate.[15] Also during this period the US increased its support for the GVN's pacification effort and created the Civil Operations and Revolutionary Development Support (CORDS) organization to coordinate all of its efforts to do so.[16]

The 1968 Tet Offensive is popularly viewed in the United States as a major defeat. However, the VC and the NLF suffered grievous losses in the battle and then faced an invigorated GVN.[17] In the aftermath of Tet, VC control over many of their base areas was weakened and this enabled US and ARVN units to execute the Accelerated Pacification Campaign (APC). The APC dedicated a greater amount of resources, both civil and military, to the pacification effort than had been done to that point of the war. Moreover, the new MACV commander, General Creighton Abrams, created what he termed a "one war" strategy at the beginning of 1969 that theoretically balanced the dual mission of US forces between offensive operations against Communist main force units and support to pacification.[18]

Also in 1969 the newly inaugurated administration of President Richard Nixon ordered a change to US strategy to end the war in Vietnam. The new strategy, referred to as Vietnamization, directed a transition of combat responsibilities from the US military to the Republic of Vietnam Armed Forces (RVNAF). This was a major shift from the strategy executed under Westmoreland as it required ARVN to simultaneously confront the insurgents of the VC as well as the VC and PAVN main force units.[19] However, even as the drawdown of US forces and accompanying transition occurred from 1969 to 1971, the opportunity offered by the 1968 Tet Offensive continued to be taken advantage of. The GVN and ARVN expanded their control over the country and seriously damaged the NLF and VC apparatus in South Vietnam through 1970.[20] Unfortunately, by 1971 the last US ground combat unit had departed Vietnam and this altered the war again.

The withdrawal of US ground forces and the 1971 invasion of Laos by ARVN provided the impetus to the DRV and PAVN to adapt their strategy. Rather than supporting an insurgency it now became possible to conduct a conventional campaign to defeat ARVN and collapse the GVN. Their first attempt to do so, the 1972 Easter Offensive, was repulsed by ARVN with the assistance of American air power.[21] However, by 1973 all of the American advisers, air power, and other support had been withdrawn. The GVN and RVNAF were now forced to withstand the coming DRV and PAVN onslaught alone. They could not. The RVN ceased to exist after

PAVN tanks smashed through the gates of the presidential palace in Saigon on 30 April 1975.[22]

GVN Campaign, 1954-1963

At the end of the French Indochina War in 1954, neither of the newly independent nations had total control over the government apparatus or population within its boundaries. This presented a greater threat to the RVN than to the DRV as Ho and Giap had control over PAVN and the loyalty of the Viet Minh organization. Upon his appointment as premier, Diem had no such control over ARVN or the other elements of state power. The Party account of this period states that "Ngo Dinh Diem, the then Prime Minister, still had no control over the army, the government, and the security and police apparatus, not even at the central level."[23] Recognizing this, Diem asked for, and the emperor granted him, total control over all civil and military matters in South Vietnam.[24]

Diem then systematically asserted control over all elements of state power. His first step was to gain control over the ARVN. He dismissed senior commanders, saw off an attempted coup by the French-backed General Nguyen Van Hinh, rejected Bao Dai's appointment of General Nguyen Van Vy as Chief of the General Staff, disarmed the imperial guard, and replaced all of the French military advisers with US personnel.[25] He then set about destroying the armed sects, the Hoa Hao, Cao Dai, and Binh Xuyen, who held sway within the police and political apparatus and represented a threat to his power. By 1956, Diem dominated all elements of state power at the central government level.[26]

The situation at the village and hamlet level[27] was quite different, however. The peasants in Long An province, for example, were not controlled by either the GVN or the VC.[28] Such areas were relatively autonomous. In his account of the evolution of pacification in Duc Lap village, R. Michael Pearce noted that it was free of government control and uncontested by either side from 1954 to 1957.[29] To secure the RVN, Diem needed to extend his control to the lower levels of government and ultimately to the population itself.

Initial Efforts at Control

Beginning in 1956, Diem initiated a series of measures to gain control over the population. Some were relatively successful while others were failures. The programs were generally executed in isolation from one another. That is, there was no overarching control mechanism that they explicitly connected to and therefore they were not integrated into a comprehensive campaign. Despite this shortcoming, Diem's early efforts diminished the VC and disrupted their attempts to dominate the population.

<u>Population and Resource Control Measures, 1956-1958</u>

In 1956, Diem began implementing population and resource control measures through a campaign to identify Communists within the RVN and have them arrested. This campaign is commonly referred to as the "Denounce the Communists" Campaign.[30] The Party apparatus in place in South Vietnam upon the departure of the French did not completely decamp to the DRV and this posed a threat to the GVN. The outlawing of the Communist Party, and ultimately any public gathering of opponents to the regime, provided Diem's government with a tool to dismember the latent Party organization.

Rather than simply pronounce Communism as illegal, Diem also counter-organized and counter-propagandized the population and members of his government to deepen his control. Party accounts[31] of the period noted that the Diem regime "set up counter revolutionary organizations such as the Can Lao Nhan Vi Party, the National Revolutionary Movement, the People's Council for Denunciation of Communism, the Republican Youth and Republican Women Movements."[32] The Party also recorded that the regime organized rallies and demonstrations against Communism and required government workers to attend anti-Communist education classes.[33] These tactics echo those employed by Communist regimes, including the one in North Vietnam. This is likely because Diem and many other GVN leaders had been a part of the Viet Minh in its earliest days, understood its strategy and tactics, and recognized that controlling the population was the critical first step in gaining their unconditional support.

To further connect his government to the population at the village and hamlet level, Diem required the hamlet chiefs to organize the population into family groups. The Long An province chief from 1957 to 1961, Mai Ngoc Duoc, recounted that:

The task of the hamlet chief was to keep track of any occurrences in his hamlet and to report them to the village council. To do this the people were organized into family groups, each headed by a family group chief, who reported to the hamlet chief. . . . Aside from the job of controlling the people in the hamlet, he received instructions from above, for example, to make reports on how many poor there were in his hamlet and so forth. His main job was just to keep his eyes and ears open and make reports back to the village council.[34]

The Party account asserts that this system allowed the Diem regime to control "all the people's activities" to include forcing them to join the government organizations and perform guard duty.[35] As pervasive as this system was, it was still not a holistic control mechanism that integrated all elements of population and resource control. In 1959, however, the Diem regime made its first attempt at creating such a mechanism through Law 10/59 and the agroville program.

Law 10/59 and the Agroville Program

In May 1959, Diem promulgated Law 10/59[36] which gave the government power to arrest anyone accused of acting in opposition to it and punish them without trial, even with death.[37] While this law was extremely harsh, it was enacted in response to the threat that the Communist subversive element posed to the GVN. Diem realized that the Communists could assume the guise of another, ostensibly non-Communist, opposition movement and continue to subvert his government. It should also be noted that this action was implemented through law. This demonstrated that the Diem regime understood the importance of making its actions lawful and the actions of the Communists unlawful.

Law 10/59 was a major blow to the VC. Party documents refer to the law in a vitriolic manner, calling it fascist and part of an organized terror campaign by the US and Diem.[38] Additionally, the Party recounted that the law forced the people "to leave the Party and the revolution, surrender and to carry out the enemy's reactionary policies–failing which they would be outlawed and subjected to punishment under the 10/59 law."[39] Diem then attempted to create a holistic control mechanism.

In July 1959, Diem instructed his government ministers to create fortified, concentrated villages.[40] The government instruction to the province chiefs stated that this was necessary because:

> The population, especially in the South, is living in such a spread out manner that the government cannot protect them and they are obliged to furnish supplies to the Viet Cong. Therefore, it is necessary to concentrate this population, especially the families who have children still in the North or who are followers of the Viet Cong here.[41]

By resettling the population, especially those with known VC connections, the government could both isolate them from the VC and maintain surveillance on those under suspicion. Party accounts indicate that in addition to the resettlement of the population the regime enforced movement controls, curfews, and restrictions on public gatherings.[42] By restricting such a large extent of the population's behavior it became possible for the government to break the VC's hold over them.

The program was also part of a broader control mechanism that consisted of four central components: regrouping the population into agrovilles and connecting them with a strategic route system, development of competent cadres for village councils and administrative posts, improvement of village self-finance resources, and the formation of a vigorous youth movement.[43] Such a mechanism, if fully realized, could have provided Diem the means to completely wipe out the subversive element, a requirement noted by Kitson as being necessary for victory in counterinsurgency.[44]

The VC recognized the danger that the agrovilles posed to them. The Party account identified that the government had set up the agrovilles "with the primary purpose of concentrating the population in remote base areas to keep them under tight control and to attack and destroy our organizations."[45] The agrovilles became a focus of VC attacks and they attempted to incite the population to resist the government's efforts at establishing them.[46] However, the Party account notes that the GVN continued to build and fortify the hamlets, thus challenging their control over the population.[47]

Unfortunately, the Agroville program suffered from a number of shortfalls. The program was overly ambitious for the GVN. Each agroville was to have a school, market, irrigation canals, and an artificial fish pond.[48] The agrovilles were to contain around 400 families making them rather large and difficult to defend.[49] The program was costly and Diem did not ask the US for financial support because he feared interference.[50]

The GVN also had difficulty demonstrating the benefits of the program to the affected population. The agrovilles disrupted the traditional modes of work and family life. The peasant farmer "was now obliged to walk from the agroville to his own rice fields and gardens. He could not give them the constant attention they required to be protected from intemperate weather, torrential rains, the ravages of rodents, and theft."[51] Families had to leave behind water buffaloes and other valuable animals as well as their ancestral shrines.[52] All of this may have been tolerable if the agrovilles had delivered on their promise of a better life and greater security but they did not.

Despite the shortcomings of the Agrovilles and the lack of a truly comprehensive control mechanism, Diem was defeating his Communist enemies by 1959. The official PAVN history of the war notes that in 1955 "many provinces in South Vietnam still had several thousand cadre and

Party members and every village had a village Party chapter. By 1958-1959 many villages had no Party chapter, and many Party chapters numbered only two or three members."[53] The damage to the Party apparatus was substantial. In some of the lowland districts of Central Vietnam it had been destroyed.[54]

The destruction was not complete, however. The Party acknowledged the effectiveness of the Diem regime's actions but it believed that they had ultimately provided an opportunity which could be exploited.[55] The Party account noted that "the enemy failed in his evil scheme to eliminate our Party, the revolutionary armed forces and our movement. Even though the enemy caused severe losses to our Party and revolutionary armed forces, both still survived and our movement remains active."[56]

Communist Response

Diem effectively consolidated his control over the government apparatus and had begun to gain control of the population in South Vietnam between 1954 and 1959. The Party account credited him saying:

> The US-Diem administration was relatively stable. It was able to control the rural areas through its oppressive system, and at the same time, it also increased its oppression in the cities. The enemy's administrative system, which reached down to the house-block level, enabled him to control the people fairly tightly, thus restraining and impairing our Party's structures and causing us much difficulty. With his espionage network and his security organization, the enemy forced the majority of the peasantry in many areas, including the former resistance base areas, to cooperate with him in his oppression of the peasants themselves.[57]

The Party also noted that Diem "could draft a great number of youths; he could build up and promptly equip his army from the popular to the regular forces; he could get laborers to build more and more strategic roads, military bases, fortifications, airfields, etc."[58]

Despite the inflammatory language, there is in these statements a note of respect for Diem and his ability to control the population and deny such control to the Party. The Party and the VC reacted strongly to the challenge. As noted above, the Central Committee in Hanoi authorized armed struggle in January 1959. The Agrovilles were an early target of the armed struggle. The VC "burned and sacked agroville sites when possible. They ordered those under their persuasion not to cooperate with the government in implementation of the program. They shrewdly selected for special punishment those officials who were active in Agroville work and also unpopular among the villagers."[59]

The special punishment referenced usually meant assassination, though kidnapping and intimidation also occurred. The VC targeted the very best and very worst government officials. Assassinating the best officials ensured that the GVN's control mechanism in the countryside broke down and sowed fear among other government officials and those in the population who might support the government. Eliminating the most cruel or corrupt officials ingratiated the VC with the population.[60]

The VC campaign produced significant success by the end of 1959. A March 1960 letter from the Nam Bo[61] Regional Committee noted that the campaign had "made important progress in the last two months of 1959 and the first two months of 1960 in a number of regions. In many places in the rural areas, the masses have been able to utilize the enemy's (word illegible) and have won the first victory for democratic freedom and economic rights."[62] This produced a notable change on the ground as "a number of regions where there was previously no movement, or where the movement was weak, there are now many campaigns, a few relatively strong."[63] Some of these campaigns were able to call on as many as two thousand people.[64]

The Nam Bo Regional Committee believed that "the reason for this initial success is that we have correctly carried out Central's resolutions . . . It is also due to the spirit of enthusiasm, the determination for the task, and the unflagging efforts of all our comrades."[65] The Party believed that their ability to link the armed struggle with their political struggle would set the stage for their ultimate victory.[66] It was the violence that was the critical element of the campaign, however.

The Regional Committee stated that:

The most significant point is that in the past period we have boldly made use of armed activity in combination with the political struggle. Thanks to our work in eliminating traitors, striking at those who will not learn, and thanks to our offering appropriate resistance to terrorism, the masses in many places have been able to step up the struggle with the enemy.[67]

The violence changed the dynamic of interaction between the VC, the GVN, and the population. The Regional Committee identified that "the enemy are alarmed and in a state of panic, especially those in the bases. In many villages the enemy administrative machinery has broken down."[68] Previously, government officials had been able to move about the countryside with relative ease but were no longer able to do so.

The fear produced by VC violence meant that some officials "fled to sleep inside their military outposts and did not dare to arrogantly conduct searches as they had before. Hundreds resigned or were too afraid to carry out their duties."[69] Thus, government officials could not gather the information and enforce the laws that were critical to controlling the population. Moreover, in areas where the government was not in control, the VC and the Party now were.

The Regional Committee directed its members to capitalize on the changed dynamic by reinforcing the Party's own apparatus in the villages and hamlets. It directed them "to push ahead urgently with the task of consolidating and developing the Party, Groups, and the network of active key personnel."[70] It also ordered them to focus more of their effort on building up bases and organizing the masses to resist the GVN when it returned.[71] In other words, the Party's strategy was to counter the government's control of the population by breaking it and then using the Party's mechanisms to establish its control over the population.

The Party executed its strategy with brutal efficiency. The PAVN history of the war notes that "tens of thousands of puppets, spies, tyrants, and enemy armed forces at the grassroots level had been eliminated. Many of the enemy's new agricultural areas, concentration areas, and collective living areas had been destroyed."[72] The Party infrastructure had succeeded in expanding its numbers with over 500 villages forming guerrilla squads, nearly 200 forming guerrilla platoons, and a total of 7,000 armed local guerrillas in the Nam Bo region alone.[73] To support these full time forces the Party collected "contributions from the people in the area where the unit was stationed and for which our revolutionary governmental apparatus at the village and hamlet level was responsible."[74]

The VC were now in control of large swathes of territory and could maintain control through a governmental structure supported by armed force. They consolidated their domination and connected villages to one another in order to deny large chunks of the country to the GVN. Retaking these areas would require Diem's government to execute major military operations to defeat the VC guerrillas, dispatch the Party infrastructure, and then secure the population from reprisals, a significant undertaking. This was not the only threat that Diem faced, however.

The resolution of the 15th Plenum of the Party Central Committee in Hanoi authorizing armed struggle spurred the General Military Party Committee to discuss "such pressing matters as building bases and developing revolutionary armed forces in the South, expanding North Vietnam's role in the revolution in the South, and preparing our armed forces to crush any aggressive scheme the enemy might try to carry out."[75]

Moreover, "preparations for sending the army [PAVN] to South Vietnam to join the battle were begun."[76]

Rather than facing only a rejuvenated, locally supported insurgency, which presented a significant threat on its own, the GVN would have to confront PAVN and an insurgency explicitly supported by the DRV. To this end, PAVN began construction and operation of the Ho Chi Minh Trail. By the end of the year, it had successfully delivered small arms, knives, explosives, and other military equipment to VC units and transported over 500 PAVN cadre who "immediately began to form battalions, companies, platoons, and sapper teams" in the Central Highlands and Mekong Delta.[77]

By October 1960, two overland routes ran from North Vietnam through Laos and Cambodia into South Vietnam, terminating in the Central Highlands and the Mekong Delta. The Ho Chi Minh Trail could be used primarily to transport arms, ammunition, and military equipment because the VC units received food and life support from the population. Thus, the limited capacity of a route operated initially by human porters could be conserved for the most critical military supplies. Controlling the population was now even more critical to the GVN because doing so would require the Ho Chi Minh Trail to deliver food and manpower rather than just military supplies.

The Communist campaign in 1959-1960 threatened the very survival of the Diem regime. This was acknowledged by the US Embassy in Saigon. In a cable to the Secretary of State in September 1960 Ambassador Durbrow related that the:

> Diem regime [is] confronted by two separate but related dangers. Danger from demonstrations or coup attempt in Saigon could occur earlier . . . Even more serious danger is gradual Viet Cong extension of control over countryside which, if current Communist progress continues, would mean loss [of] free Vietnam to Communists. These two dangers are related because Communist successes in rural areas embolden them to extend their activities to Saigon.[78]

Not only did Ambassador Durbrow recognize that the survival of the RVN was threatened, he also identified that the GVN would need to take a series of interrelated actions to confront it. His cable stated that

> For Saigon, danger essentially political and psychological measures required. For countryside, danger security measures as well as political, psychological and economic measures needed. However both sets measures should be carried out simultaneously and to some extent individual steps will be aimed at both dangers.[79]

Such were the challenges that Diem confronted in late 1960 and early 1961. Whereas previously his population and resource control measures could be implemented separately from security operations, he would now have to execute them simultaneously. Failure to do so would expose GVN officials and the population to reprisals by VC guerrilla units. This problem set required a new program that created a holistic control mechanism. Diem responded by implementing the much derided and misunderstood Strategic Hamlet Program.

Control Mechanism–Strategic Hamlet Program

The Strategic Hamlet Program has been condemned as an abysmal failure or worse by many historians.[80] Eric Bergerud derided it as "an irrelevant response to the insurgency and consequently doomed from the outset."[81] However, much of the documentation that these assessments are based on was produced by US observers early in the program's execution.[82] Many US government documents, captured NLF and VC documents, and official Party accounts of the war are now available that allow the Strategic Hamlet Program to be re-examined more thoroughly.

Moreover, the Strategic Hamlet Program is often examined in the light of a hearts and minds campaign to win the support of the population.[83] As discussed in the second chapter, the concept of hearts and minds and what it means to win the support of the population is often misunderstood. The Strategic Hamlet Program was not intended to be part of a larger popularity contest between the GVN and the VC. Rather, it was intended to serve as a holistic control mechanism through which Diem could control the behavior of the population and connect them more fully to the government. He intended to use this control to wipe out the remaining VC and Party elements and end the war.

Purpose

The Strategic Hamlet Program was not solely about concentrating the population behind a barrier to protect and separate them from the VC insurgents. Rather, it was a comprehensive counterinsurgency strategy initiated by Diem's government to regain control over the portion of the countryside that had been lost during the previous two years. The purpose of the program was:

> To achieve the widest possible popular response to the government's counterinsurgency effort by providing the peasants with an increasing degree of physical security from Communist intimidation and by

enacting social, economic, and political reforms meaningful to the peasants in the context of their own traditions and expectations.[84]

This political purpose was to be achieved by accomplishing two subordinate security objectives:

> First, to sever Communist communication and control lines to the rural populace and thus deny the Communists the local resources (manpower, food, intelligence, and weapons) necessary to their operations; and second, to promote a nationwide self-defense effort at the rice-roots level by providing the peasant with weapons and other defense facilities.[85]

Once these immediate objectives were accomplished, ARVN and the GVN's other counterinsurgent forces could use their control over the population and domination of the terrain to target and destroy VC units. Moreover, they could use the intelligence collected during the formation of the strategic hamlet to identify and eliminate the Front's subversive element within the village. However, to maintain their control the GVN needed to take the process one step further and create a determination within the population to resist Communist subversion.

This was reflected in documents indicating that the Strategic Hamlet Program's other purpose as "stated by President Diem, was to create a 'state of mind;' the commitment of the peasants to the support of their government and resistance to the Viet Cong."[86] It was this commitment to support the government that transformed a group of people who had been concentrated and organized into a strategic hamlet.[87] The actual components of the program, primarily coercive in nature, were intended to create the conditions that would allow the population to support the government openly without fear of intimidation and reprisal by the VC.

The Front also understood the purpose of the program very clearly. An anti-Strategic Hamlet Program pamphlet published by the Front in 1962 listed four objectives: "a - to control, 'to protect', to 'get a hold of the people,' especially the rural people; b - to collect necessary information in order to destroy the organizations of the so-called 'Vietcongs' among the population; c - to isolate the armed forces of the revolution; d - to establish and maintain the 'white' zones."[88] They also recognized that the program was a "*general synthesis* of all the military, political, economic, social, schemes, together with other policies."[89]

The purpose behind the implementation of the Strategic Hamlet Program as laid out in the GVN, US, and Communist documents cited clearly indicates that Diem and his government, particularly his brother Nhu who was in charge of the program, understood the need to conduct a comprehensive counterinsurgency campaign to defeat the threat from the VC. However, if the program was to achieve its fundamental purposes and create the general synthesis cited by the Front, all of the components of the program had to support the purpose and mutually reinforce one another.

Components

The Strategic Hamlet Program's components included security operations, population and resource control measures, counter-organization of the population, information operations, formation of self defense forces, and the creation of a fortified area to protect and isolate the population from the insurgents. It was the interaction of all of these components, however, that truly gave the program the strength to present a serious threat to the VC.

The first step in establishing a strategic hamlet was an ARVN offensive operation to force VC units out of the area where the hamlet was to be established. This operation was not conducted to search for the enemy but was conducted to deliberately drive the enemy from the area.[90] By driving the enemy out of the area, the GVN could ensure that it had the necessary operational space to implement the other components of the program.

Once this operation was complete a Strategic Hamlet Operational Team would arrive and begin organizing the hamlet and implementing control measures.[91] If possible, the hamlet would be organized so that families would not have to be relocated. The GVN implementing document specifically stated that "*it is absolutely forbidden to force the people to leave their houses and lands behind and go to establish new hamlet villages. The people can stay in their respective hamlets and villages and set up their own strategic hamlets and villages as already mentioned above.*"[92] In their report on the initial implementation of the program, John Donnell and Gerald Hickey noted that "in most strategic hamlets only a small percentage of the population is regrouped."[93] They also reported that "most families that move inside the perimeter do so voluntarily."[94]

Families were regrouped, however. This was especially true in the Mekong Delta where the settlement pattern was more dispersed than it was in the Central Highlands. If the population in the Mekong Delta area was not regrouped, it created defensive works that were in some cases four to five kilometers around, far too much for the hamlet's small self-defense team to protect.[95] As a result, some families were moved within the perimeter of the strategic hamlet. This was absolutely necessary if the program was to accomplish the security objectives that had been established for it. Moreover, if the government could demonstrate its ability to protect the population then the population could support the government by participating in its own defense, serving in the government, and providing information to the security forces.

Once the population had been regrouped, the civil defense team within the Strategic Hamlet Operational Team would create the hamlet's defenses. The team would utilize the population to build the fences, gates, defensive positions, and obstacles.[96] The defensive works were "not intended to help the village *offer resistance* to our enemy's violent attack but it is merely aimed at protecting the village from infiltration by the enemy. Provided with this fence, each hamlet has only a few known entrances and exits, all under constant control."[97] That is to say, the fence and defensive works were not the decisive element of the strategic hamlet program, which was the "internal organization of the village."[98]

The internal organization was carried out to eliminate the Communist infrastructure within each hamlet. The security team within the Strategic Hamlet Operational Team partnered with the village and hamlet officials to take a new census.[99] The results of the census were maintained by the village officials, the head of the household, and the local ARVN battalion commander. Additionally, the security team would nail a census board to each home that identified all of the authorized inhabitants.[100]

After the completion of the hamlet's defensive works and the census, the government imposed population and resource control measures to further isolate the insurgents. The government enforced curfews, movement restrictions, and "shoot on site" zones.[101] It established control over the "quantity of paddy, rice, land, and cattle of each family in each hamlet."[102] The government also delivered plastic identity cards to each resident. All of these actions set the conditions for the organization of the population.

The population of the strategic hamlet was organized by age and sex into groups and each group was assigned specific responsibilities for the continued defense of the hamlet.[103] The GVN recognized that "after the organizational phase, we have to trust the work to the groups concerned and guide them as to what needs to be done."[104] It was this final step that produced the commitment of the population to resist the Communists. That was the program's essential purpose. Furthermore, it expanded the physical isolation of the population into a "*psychological* separation of the people from the VC."[105]

The organization of the population was the final component of the Strategic Hamlet Program. After it had been accomplished satisfactorily the government teams could move to another hamlet and begin the process again. The GVN believed that if the program was executed properly that the hamlet could resist infiltration and small VC attacks.[106] It did not expect them to withstand large attacks. Rather, it wanted the defense forces to delay the VC attack while the population cached supplies and the adults left the hamlet.[107] This would leave the VC in control of a village that had been stripped of supplies and contained only old people and children.

The alarm raised by the self defense forces would draw an ARVN unit.[108] This forced the VC to leave the hamlet rapidly and therefore they could not regain control of it. If they attempted to leave behind subversive personnel, the population control measures in place could identify them. The Strategic Hamlet Program's components created a holistic control mechanism that provided the Diem regime with a means of effectively targeting the Communist insurgency. However, in order to be fully effective the program had to be properly executed and resourced, a major challenge for the GVN.

Execution and Results

Creating strategic hamlets required the effective execution of all components of the program by GVN officials at the hamlet, village, district, and province level. This was a major challenge as "the details of the program were worked out by a small group of Vietnamese officials (many of them former Viet Minh, including young Major Tran Ngoc Chau), assigned to the Presidential planning staff."[109] Thus, the execution of the program had to be explained in depth to the lower level officials who would run it. Moreover, "there were no known precedents for many aspects of the Strategic Hamlet Program and new procedures of all sorts had to be established on an *ad hoc* basis."[110]

These conditions meant that the execution of the Strategic Hamlet Program would rely heavily on the abilities of individual officials at the province level and below.[111] The Diem regime recognized this and was attempting to develop effective leaders who were staunch anti-Communists, but in many areas the program suffered because of a lack of such leaders.[112] Moreover, the regime pressured leaders to produce results quickly. This yielded a large number of strategic hamlets being reported as complete that had not yet executed all of the components of the program.

United States officials identified this problem as early as the summer of 1962. A report from the Central Intelligence Agency (CIA) to the Secretary of Defense stated that:

> As of 30 June [1962], there were approximately 2,000 strategic hamlets completed. This represents increase of 1300 since January 1962. . . Qualitatively, there is a considerable variation, some being virtual fortresses and others having only token size fences or other defensive devices which could be easily breached by Viet Cong.[113]

Such a rapid expansion threatened the program's viability. Strategic hamlets that were only partially completed were not in a position to defeat small scale assaults and did not have the infrastructure in place to destroy the Communists cadres. Therefore, the population would not be sufficiently protected from intimidation and coercion by the VC. If the security benefits of the program were not realized then anyone who helped to establish the strategic hamlet would be subject to retaliation. This undermined the program's legitimacy with the population.

However, the CIA report also noted that "local observers rightly state that until country considerably more saturated with strategic hamlets, many of those already in being will be exposed to Viet Cong destruction."[114] Thus, there was also pressure to expand the number of hamlets rapidly in order to reinforce existing hamlets through the establishment of new ones but, if the government did not sufficiently concentrate its efforts in a specific area, it risked creating exposed hamlets that were vulnerable to VC attack. Rapid expansion also caused significant difficulties for ARVN. As noted above, the first step to establish a strategic hamlet was the execution of a military operation to drive VC units out of the area. The ARVN was not large enough at the time to conduct so many major, simultaneous operations. This created a weakness that was identified by the Front.[115] The Front noted that by expanding the number of strategic hamlets "the enemy falls into a grave contradiction, to spread out the troops for occupation and to concentrate the troops for attack. This is a vicious circle for them: when they concentrate their troops on one strategic hamlet, the people have revolted in another strategic hamlet, forcing them to move elsewhere."[116]

The program's requirement to emplace population and resource controls, conduct a census, provide identification cards, and organize the population also created a heavy burden. If these portions of the program were not properly delivered, the hamlet establishment phase often became a period of unpleasant, meaningless, forced labor for the villagers. Although all of the physical steps might have been carried out, the hamlet was really nothing more than the population grouping now surrounded by a worthless mud wall, with a group of men who had been trained in military tactics and provided weapons, but had no desire to use them, a hamlet charter which was torn up by the Viet Cong agents who returned to the hamlet once the government cadre had left, and with 'elected officials' who either fled the hamlet or agreed to cooperate with the Viet Cong.[117]

It was absolutely critical that the program be executed fully for it to be successful.

Where good leaders executed the Strategic Hamlet Program properly and delivered on the promises of increased security made to the population, it performed as intended. A summer 1963 assessment by the State Department stated that:

> On balance, however, the strategic hamlet has been a success. Much of the concern and hesitation originally shown by the peasants has disappeared, partly because of the Vietnam Government's improved public information program but also because of the security and other benefits the peasants have received once they moved into the hamlets... there are increasing reports of peasants volunteering intelligence on the Communists and of welcoming the strategic hamlet program because it has freed them from Communist intimidation and 'taxation.'[118]

In Kien Hoa province in the Mekong Delta, the strategic hamlets established by Lieutenant Colonel Tran Ngoc Chau, resisted VC attacks even as those in the surrounding provinces, such as Long An, collapsed during the fall of 1963.[119]

This demonstrates the difficulty of evaluating the Strategic Hamlet Program. Country-wide assessments, such as the State Department's above, provided only an aggregate picture of the progress and accomplishments of the program. Because the program was intensely local and relied almost exclusively on the abilities of the province chief to be executed effectively, its progress can really only be evaluated at the province level and below. Even in areas where the program was not executed particularly well, such as Long An, it did help the government stabilize the situation in 1962 and 1963.[120]

As execution of the program improved, the Strategic Hamlet Program grew more effective. In a 1962 report, the State Department concluded that "effective GVN control of the countryside has been extended slightly. In some areas where security has improved peasant attitudes toward the government appear also to have improved. As a result, the Viet Cong has had to modify its tactics and perhaps set back its timetable."[121] Despite this improvement, the memorandum also noted that the VC still controlled around 20 percent of the villages and had influence over nearly another 50 percent of the population.[122]

By the summer of 1963, the program was picking up momentum rapidly. The State Department report this time stated that the:

> Strategic hamlet program has already reduced the total area and population under Communist control or influence and has weakened Communist strength and logistics capabilities. Communist guerrillas are reportedly experiencing morale problems and shortages of food and supplies in many areas, and have resorted increasingly to outright theft and harassment of the peasant in order to gain supplies and recruits.[123]

The report concluded that "the strategic hamlet program in Vietnam is moving from infancy to solid growth in a relatively short time and against determined Communist opposition."[124]

Were evidence of the increasing success of the Strategic Hamlet Program limited to US and GVN documents there would be every reason to be skeptical of the program's efficacy. However, captured enemy documents and the official PAVN history of the war indicate how dangerous the Communists believed the program was. Moreover, the intense efforts they exerted to counter it make clear that they saw it as a significant threat.

Communist Response

As with Diem's earlier use of population and resource controls, the Strategic Hamlet Program initially caught the Communists off guard. Their success at regaining control of the countryside in 1960 and 1961 using a combination of armed and political struggle seems to have produced a certain amount of complacency that allowed the program to develop. In a sort of after action report published in October or November 1962, the Front noted that "some comrades even thought that the enemy would construct strategic hamlets for our benefit, therefore they neither opposed nor made reports to higher authorities."[125]

This failure to oppose the establishment of strategic hamlets had severe consequences. The report identified that "when the enemy had completed the construction, our movement, naturally weak, declined very rapidly."[126] This occurred because the government's counter-organization within the strategic hamlet was able to target both VC armed forces and political cadres. The report stated that "each time penetrating the area, we are all rounded up and pursued by the enemy. Our cadres and village self defense members are attacked and driven away, and consequently they can only adhere to hamlets at the outskirt."[127]

The experience of this Front organization was not uncommon and it led to an assessment of the Strategic Hamlet Program that was markedly different than that offered by some American observers at the time and since.[128] A document written in late 1962 or early 1963[129] that was classified "Top Secret" declared that "*to destroy 'strategic hamlets' is a life or death struggle between the enemy and our troops.*"[130] This assessment was echoed in another Front document which stated that

> For the enemy, if the 'national policy of the strategic hamlets' fails, without the addition of any new factors, then the entire program of the enemy's policies of aggression will fail because the enemy's entire program has been reduced into 'the national policy of the strategic hamlets.' On the contrary, if the enemy can carry out his national policy of the strategic hamlets, then he will win.[131]

The Party and the Front viewed the Strategic Hamlet Program as an existential threat to the insurgency and the entire war effort. The official PAVN history recounts that in 1962:

> Our full-time armed units encountered many difficulties when they tried to operate in the rural lowlands. In the mountains and contested areas, our units were forced to move constantly to evade enemy sweeps and commando operations, lowering their combat efficiency. Our soldiers endured many hardships because food production was unreliable and our warehouses, crops, and food stocks were being attacked and destroyed. Rightist and negativistic tendencies began to appear among our soldiers.[132]

As a result of the deteriorating situation, the North Vietnamese Politburo met in December 1962 to discuss the situation. It was determined that "to overcome the situation it would be necessary to mobilize the entire Party and the entire population to build up our armed forces and to develop a widespread pattern of guerrilla warfare."[133] Additionally, "the Politburo decided to quickly send combat forces to South Vietnam and to expand our mobile main force troops and our specialty branch units."[134]

As the North was increasing its support for the war effort, the Front and VC apparatus in the South were developing and disseminating their techniques for countering the strategic hamlets. They understood the Strategic Hamlet Program much better than US observers did, possibly because its architects were former members of the Viet Minh. The tactics and techniques to counter and subvert the strategic hamlets were highly developed and reflected a deep understanding of the program's strengths and weaknesses.

A document intended for Front and VC members stated that "the principal force to destroy strategic hamlets is the people's forces in strategic hamlets, armed forces coming from outside will only be used in support of this struggle."[135] It also instructed that "the people should be organized secretly, or publicly or semi-publicly and change the enemy's popular organizations to ours."[136] These instructions reflect the need to counter the government's organization of the people and its ability to deploy ARVN to destroy concentrations of VC units.

Moreover, the Front recognized that it did not need to destroy strategic hamlets as soon as they were built if it could utilize their organizations for its own purposes. The pamphlet directed that "we must allow only the framework of these strategic hamlets to be under enemy control but the core (infrastructure) must belong to the revolutionary people. The progress of the struggle should smolder and only at a propitious time should efforts be made to destroy strategic hamlets."[137] Once the time was right, the VC could execute a synchronized plan to dismantle the strategic hamlets.

One Front element reported how this could be accomplished based on their experiences in "H" village.[138] Using the local Party organization and cadres, the VC subverted the strategic hamlet's organizations and prepared them for a single effort to destroy the hamlet's defensive works.[139] Upon initiating the plan:

> Self defense members will closely watch the enemy stations, stop their reinforcement elements, 200 people outside will be directed to come and help those inside to revolt. Cadres will use loudspeakers to call the people to rise up to destroy strategic hamlets thus to liberate themselves and suppress the US and Diem scheme.[140]

After the hamlet's defensive works had been destroyed, the Front's cadres "proceed on warning and educating some collaborators and spies so to make the people understand the enemy future scheme."[141] Thus intimidated, the Front expected the population to resist government efforts to rebuild the hamlet's defensive works. However, even if the fences were rebuilt, "the party committee has been able to adhere to the area, and self-defense members to carry on their activities."[142] This result was more dangerous to the Strategic Hamlet Program than the mere loss of the fence.

As the various pamphlets and instructions were disseminated and support flowed in from the North during 1963, VC attacks against strategic hamlets increased. The Long An Province representative's report from June-July 1963 reported that "Viet Cong activity has picked up considerably–concentrating on attacking strategic hamlets, tearing down walls and fences, kidnaping (sic) young men, assassinating hamlet officials and in general, destroying the morale and will to resist of the rural population."[143]

Not only did the number of attacks increase but their effectiveness increased as well. The PAVN history of the war notes that in Cochin China "in 1962, we had destroyed 100 'strategic hamlets' but were only able to retain control of 15 of them."[144] However, "in 1963 the enemy was no longer able to rebuild the 'strategic hamlets' that we destroyed. The liberated area in Cochin China grew back to the size it had reached during the time of insurrection in 1960."[145]

This likely resulted from two factors. First, as discussed above, was the over-extension of the Strategic Hamlet Program beyond the GVN's ability to properly execute it. The ARVN forces were too few in number to react to attacks on a large scale and the defense forces and organization of the hamlets were too weak to resist major attacks on their own. Second, PAVN determined in 1962 that in order to counter the GVN's strategy it needed to develop the capability to defeat ARVN's mobile troops when they were supported by helicopters and armored personnel carriers.[146] This "demanded that our army rapidly strengthen our mobile main force elements on the battlefield . . . and that we elevate the combat capabilities of our armed forces in South Vietnam to a new, higher level."[147] The GVN was no longer only confronting insurgent forces, it now had to counter well trained, equipped, and organized main force units.

The Strategic Hamlet Program was not designed to protect the population from an assault by such main force units. It was intended only to defeat small bands of lightly armed guerrillas. Main force units could only be countered by ARVN. Unfortunately, there was not enough ARVN available in 1963 to defeat the main force units as they were created. Simultaneously, the position of the Diem regime was weakening.

End of the Strategic Hamlet Program

Despite his early success against the Communist insurgency and in forging the beginnings of a nation, by 1962-1963 Diem had fallen out of favor with some senior members of ARVN, the US government, US journalists, and members of the Saigon intelligentsia. As early as November 1962, there was already discussion in US policy circles about the possibility of another coup against Diem and its effects. The State Department reported that the coup most likely to succeed would be one with non-Communist leadership and support, involving middle and top echelon military and civilian officials. For a time at least, the serious disruption of government leadership resulting from a coup would probably halt and possibly reverse the momentum of the government's counterinsurgency effort.[148]

Events would reveal this assessment to be completely accurate.

Diem had meticulously asserted control over all elements of power within the GVN over a period of several years. During that time, he defeated several coup attempts, improved the organization of the RVNAF and the government, and executed a campaign that at times was defeating the Communist insurgency. It is unlikely that any new government, no matter how well or quickly organized, could possibly assert the control that had taken Diem nearly a decade to build up.[149]

Moreover, the Strategic Hamlet Program, now the centerpiece of the government's counterinsurgency strategy, was reliant on leaders within the GVN from top to bottom that were loyal to Diem. The program was under the overall direction of Diem's brother, Nhu. The province, district, and military officials who executed the program had been groomed and appointed by Diem over several years. Any coup that ousted Diem would also have to repudiate the Strategic Hamlet Program.

The coup against Diem occurred on 1 November 1963 and plunged the government into chaos. The Party was quick to react and "taking advantage of the convulsions and contradictions within the puppet army and the puppet regime, all our battlefields increased their operations."[150] Strategic hamlets were destroyed throughout the country: over one thousand in Cochin China, more than 400 in the Central Highlands, and in Pleiku Province alone 289 villages returned to their previous status.[151]

The increased military operations of the VC and PAVN coincided with near total paralysis in the GVN, especially at province level and below. A memorandum to President Johnson from National Security Council staff member Michael V. Forrestal on 11 December 1963, stated that "a certain amount of inertia has occurred in provincial administration since the coup. A large number of the province chiefs have been changed and some of the newly appointed ones have been changed again."[152] Thus, the coup leaders could not effectively respond to VC and PAVN attacks against the strategic hamlets.

Moreover, the coup leaders did not want the Strategic Hamlet Program to continue given its close association with Diem and Nhu.[153]

The US position was no better. Forrestal told Johnson that:

> In light of the above, you might wish to tell McNamara that you hope he will be able to focus the attention of the Vietnamese generals on their first priority problem, the immediate restoration of administrative initiative in the provinces . . . Secretary McNamara might also tell them that in his opinion it is of utmost importance to establish a new program for the villages and immediately issue the necessary implementing directives. He might also offer our help in getting up such a program, something which should be rather easy for us to do, since it would draw heavily from the old Strategic Hamlet Program.

As the Party and Front were responding aggressively to the opportunity presented to them to destroy a program that they considered an existential threat, the GVN and its ally, the US, were allowing the very same program to die rather than reinforcing it. Simultaneously, they were searching for a new program that would be largely the same as the one they were killing. Reinforcing and continuing the Strategic Hamlet Program would not have guaranteed success over the long term. However, the coup and the accompanying dissolution of the program facilitated the Communist offensive and resulted in a loss of control in the countryside that the GVN would not begin to recover from until after the 1968 Tet Offensive.[154]

Analysis of the use of Population and Resource Control Measures under Diem

It would be easy to write off the Diem regime's use of population and resource control measures from 1954 to 1963 in Vietnam as a failure because of the ultimate outcome of the war and the fate of the regime itself. However, such an analysis would be shallow and does not take into account the complexity of the conflict and the threat that the regime confronted. All of the measures employed by the Diem regime had shortcomings, particularly in their execution. However, when properly executed they presented a significant threat to the Communists who acted aggressively to counter them.

The Strategic Hamlet Program was a major undertaking for a nascent government that was facing a well organized and supported insurgency. This was recognized in the US Operations Mission report on the program in 1963 which noted that "it is a costly program and a daring one, a program which, if successful, should certainly end the insurgency and if unsuccessful will certainly end the counter-insurgency."[155] The report acknowledged that the Strategic Hamlet Program was an appropriate strategy, but "like any good strategy, the greatest risk it entails is the risk that it may not be resolutely pushed to final victory."[156]

The Strategic Hamlet Program was certainly pushed hard by the regime, overextending GVN and ARVN resources beyond their capability to support it. This certainly contributed to its collapse. However, this was a problem of execution, not design. Furthermore, the collapse of the Strategic Hamlet Program cannot be considered in isolation from the coup that deposed the Diem regime and the resulting chaos in governance that it produced. Had the regime, and the province and district level officials that supported it, remained in power it could have adjusted the execution of the Strategic Hamlet Program over time to address the shortcomings in execution.

The other factor that must be considered in the analysis of the Diem regime's use of population and resource control measures is the change in strategy of the Party and its military forces in reaction to them. Diem's early efforts forced the VC to begin conducting armed struggle, which changed the dynamic of the war. The success of ARVN and the Strategic Hamlet Program's efforts to counter the insurgency in 1962 drove the Party and PAVN to develop and employ main force units in the South which denied the regime the ability to conduct a pure counterinsurgency campaign. At most, the regime's population and resource control efforts, including the Strategic Hamlet Program, can be graded an incomplete, while acknowledging both their successes and failures.

Protection and Isolation of the Population

It is clear that Diem understood the need to protect and isolate the population from the VC insurgents and cadre that operated within the countryside. Failure to do so, ceded control to the VC and allowed them to intimidate and coerce the population into providing support. Moreover, the attitude of the average rural Vietnamese peasant was that they would follow whichever side was strongest in their area. An old man from Duc Hanh, a hamlet in Duc Lap village stated that "outside [the hamlet] the people follow the Liberation Front, inside they follow the government. They follow whoever is strong."[157]

However, the settlement pattern within South Vietnam made protecting and isolating the population difficult, especially in the Mekong Delta. Hamlets consisted of a number of houses scattered across a wide area with dense jungle and inaccessible terrain nearby that could easily conceal insurgent elements. The only way to ensure that the population was protected and isolated was to concentrate them into denser, more defensible groupings.

Diem's first attempt to do this, the agroville program, was largely a failure. The agrovilles were too large for the small self defense units to protect. Insurgents could easily infiltrate the defenses to intimidate the population. If the agroville was attacked in strength, it would be easily overrun. Moreover, the agroville program was not part of a larger counterinsurgency strategy. It was, despite the simultaneous promulgation of Law 10/59, largely an isolated effort.

The Strategic Hamlet Program, on the other hand, was a more holistic strategy to protect and isolate the population. Before a strategic hamlet was created, ARVN would conduct a large operation to drive armed insurgent elements out of the area. The hamlets themselves were more compact and easier for a small element to defend. The program also included a census, the issue of identification cards, and the counter-organization of the population to deny Party cadre the ability to infiltrate and subvert the hamlets.

When all elements of the program were executed properly, this strategy succeeded in protecting and isolating the population from the insurgency. This allowed the government to gain control over the population and deny the VC food, shelter, manpower, and intelligence. This caused them a number of difficulties and forced them to change their strategy to counter it.

Many detractors of the Strategic Hamlet Program, including Race, Bergerud, Pearce, Donnell, and Hickey have focused on the massive disruption to the lives of the population that the program caused and on the forced labor required to build the strategic hamlets.[158] The program, like the agrovilles before it, did require the rural population, especially those in the Mekong Delta, to move away from their farmlands and the ancestral shrines where they practiced their religion. It obviously would have been better not to force the population to move in this way but the GVN faced a major dilemma. The VC had a pervasive infrastructure throughout the rural areas to control the population. The GVN did not have the military, police, or government capability required to destroy this infrastructure and simultaneously protect and isolate the population while they were spread out over a wide area. Therefore, the only means the government had to break VC control and destroy the subversive infrastructure was to isolate the population in new settlements, establish governing structures in these settlements, and use them to target the VC infrastructure.

The VC also placed onerous requirements on the population. One villager who formerly lived in the Viet Cong zone recalled, "I had to pay them a tax of over a thousand piasters for my house. They don't call it tax but call it a contribution."[159] They also required the population to join work parties and assist Communist military forces. The PAVN history notes that rice "was transported by civilian porters and by local means of transportation (boats, vehicles) belonging to the civilian population."[160] It is unlikely that all of this support was voluntary. The VC infrastructure could intimidate and coerce the population at will if they were not isolated and protected from it. Therefore, if the GVN could deliver security and protect the population in the strategic hamlets, it could at least ensure that the population would be neutral.

The Strategic Hamlet Program's isolation and protection of the population was working in some areas of the country in 1962 and 1963. However, when the Party and Front changed tactics and began using main force units to support the operation of the guerrillas, the program could no longer effectively do so. The main force units could easily overwhelm the hamlet's defenses, which were not intended to defeat large-scale attacks, and ARVN was spread too thin to be able to react to all of the threats. The presence of main force units complicated execution of the program and in 1963 did so to an extent that in the chaos following the November coup it rapidly collapsed.

Focus on Behavior

Because the regime's population and resource control measures did not effectively protect and isolate the population throughout the countryside, this made it more difficult for it to affect the behavior of the population. Those among the population who wanted to support the insurgency could at times do so, while those who wished to remain neutral or support the government could not. In this, the regime faced the challenge not encountered by Bell and the other leaders in the Philippines, of how widespread the insurgency was. It affected nearly every area of the country rather than the isolated pockets that the Americans targeted in the Philippines.

Diem did attempt to prevent behavior that supported the Party or the VC. Law 10/59 was promulgated in order to make joining the Communist movement, or any other subversive element, illegal. The census of people and their agriculture assets, identification cards, curfews, and movement controls that were executed as part of the Strategic Hamlet Program were intended to prevent the population from providing food, shelter, and other support to the insurgency.

The control measures also required the population to engage in behavior that supported the government. By counter-organizing the population and requiring them to participate in their own defense, the GVN tried to more effectively connect the peasants in the countryside to the government. In securing and isolating the population, the government made it possible for some to openly support the government, provide intelligence, or join the security forces.

This combination did negatively affect the Front and the VC. The VC units in 1962 started to run low on food and had to shelter in the jungle instead of in the hamlets. The VC units moving from one area to another were exposed to targeting by ARVN as well as the local security forces that could shoot on site. The VC had difficulty recruiting additional manpower and suffered defections which drove PAVN and the DRV to send more manpower south along the Ho Chi Minh trail. In addition, the government was able to recruit manpower of its own to defend the hamlets and participate in the administration of the local area.

Unfortunately, when the protection and isolation provided by the program failed, so did the government's ability to control the behavior of the population. If the VC succeeded in penetrating or infiltrating the hamlet, the most active supporters of the government were targeted for assassination. Being a particularly competent hamlet or village administrator was akin to a death sentence if the VC returned.[161] Upon their return, the VC could reassert their control over the population and once again require contributions to the cause.

This state of affairs created a situation exactly opposite of what the controls intended. Those among the population who wanted to support the insurgency could do so without fear of arrest. It denied the neutral population the ability to remain neutral. They could be intimidated and coerced to support the insurgency. Finally, those who desired to support the government could not because they would be targeted by the VC. Thus, because of the lack of security, the ability of the population and resource control measures to control the behavior of the population broke down.

Facilitate the Targeting and Destruction of the Armed and Subversive Element

Diem clearly understood the threat posed to his government by armed and subversive elements. As early as 1955, he dismantled the armed sects that had influence within some portions of the GVN. After dispatching this threat, he immediately began concentrating on the Communist armed and subversive elements, which presented an existential threat to his regime.

Every aspect of the regime's population and resource control measures were designed to facilitate this targeting. From 1956 to 1959, while the VC was content to engage only in political struggle, Diem used the Denounce the Communists campaign and Law 10/59 to arrest members of the Party and their sympathizers. The agroville program's concentration of the population included counter-organizations that could identify subversive elements within them for detention. These efforts were effective but did not completely destroy the Party's apparatus.

When the Communists transitioned to armed struggle in 1959 they forced Diem to target the armed and subversive elements simultaneously. The Strategic Hamlet Program, when properly executed, did both. ARVN operations drove armed VC elements away from villages where strategic hamlets were to be created. The hamlets were then fortified, armed, and population and resource controls imposed. Curfews, movement restrictions, and the regrouping of the population into the strategic hamlet allowed ARVN and the other local security forces to target VC elements operating outside. Inside the hamlet, the census, identification cards, and organization of the population into groups gave the GVN a mechanism for identifying and arresting the subversive element.

When properly executed, this interlocking system was highly effective. The Communists lost control of significant amounts of territory throughout 1962 and the beginning of 1963. However, the system began to fail as the Strategic Hamlet Program was rapidly and less effectively expanded. Hamlets where the population was not counter-organized or that did not have a complete census could be easily infiltrated and subverted. Self defense forces that were not confident that ARVN would support them if attacked, did not dare identify VC units moving through the area.

Furthermore, the development and deployment of main force units made it more difficult for the regime to target local VC guerrilla bands. Only ARVN had the capability to confront main force units and therefore it had to be dedicated to the task. This left the local security forces in the hamlets, villages, and districts to confront the VC guerrilla bands. However, they often were not strong enough, without the backing of ARVN, to do so and many collapsed in the face of determined attack.

Ironically, it was the very effectiveness of the regime's targeting that produced this situation. Recall that it was PAVN's assessment that to counter the Diem regime's strategy, it would have to be able to defeat ARVN's successful sweep operations that led to the development and employment of highly capable main force units. Otherwise, the lightly armed VC guerrillas, isolated and easily targetable as a result of the Strategic Hamlet Program, would have been destroyed over time by repeated ARVN attacks.

The effectiveness of the Diem regime's population and resource control measures altered the dynamics of the war twice. The combination of Law 10/59, agrovilles, the Denounce the Communist campaigns, and other measures forced the Party to abandon its commitment to political struggle only and launch an insurgency. When the regime adjusted to this strategy by introducing the Strategic Hamlet Program, the Party expanded the war into a hybrid conflict involving an insurgency and conventional battles between main force units. This threat was more than the succession of GVN regimes in 1964 and 1965 could handle and ultimately led to the commitment of US forces to ground combat in 1965.

Notes

1. The terms hybrid conflict, hybrid war, and hybrid threat have been used recently by US military planners and academics to describe situations in which a conventional military is confronted by an enemy that is employing "a full range of different modes of warfare including conventional capabilities, irregular tactics and formations, terrorist acts including indiscriminate violence and coercion, and criminal disorder." See Frank Hoffman, *Conflict in the 21st Century: The Rise of Hybrid Wars* (Arlington, VA: The Potomac Institute for Policy Studies, 2007), 8. Although such conflicts are presented in much of this writing as new or novel, with the 2006 Israeli-Lebanese war being the most prominent example, hybrid conflicts have in fact existed throughout history. The Peninsula Campaign during the Napoleonic Wars was a hybrid conflict. Even World War II contained elements of a hybrid conflict as both sides used partisans or raised irregular forces to support the conventional war.

2. In their own documents, the Vietnamese Communists refer to the Vietnamese Communist Party as "the Party." Rather than use an acronym such as VCP, this paper will follow the same convention.

3. Ngo Dinh Diem's official position and title is referred to differently in a variety of documents and accounts of the war. U.S government documents often refer to him as "President," Communist documents label him "prime minister." Some of this confusion reflects the changing nature of the GVN over his rule. In the text, Diem will be referred to as "premier" as a generic and accurate representation of his position and power. However, quoted text of original documents will retain the title as written.

4. Mark Moyar, *Triumph Forsaken* (New York: Cambridge University Press, 2006), 33.

5. Ibid, 55-56.

6. Vietnamese Communist Party, "A Party Account of the Situation in the Nam Bo Region of South Vietnam from 1954-1960," Douglas Pike Collection: Unit 6, Texas Tech University Vietnam Archive [hereafter cited as TTU], 4.

7. The official accounts of the war by the Vietnamese Communist Party put to rest the debate about whether the insurgency in South Vietnam was a purely local insurgency. Some elements of the war may have been directed by local Party leaders and commanders in South Vietnam, but the strategic and operational directives emanated from Hanoi.

8. The Military History Institute of Vietnam, *Victory in Vietnam: The Official History of the People's Army of Vietnam, 1954 – 1975*, trans. Merle L. Pribbenow (Lawrence, KS: University Press of Kansas, 2002), 50.

9. Though some historians have eschewed use of the term Viet Cong because it is a pejorative for Vietnamese Communist, it was the most commonly used term in the contemporary documents and therefore its meaning is well established and

understood. Moreover, the term has lost its pejorative connotation since the end of the war and is understood by serving officers to be accepted shorthand for Vietnamese Communist.

10. Military History Institute of Vietnam, *Victory in Vietnam*, 50-52.

11. Moyar, *Triumph Forsaken*, 214-218.

12. Ibid., 226.

13. Military History Institute of Vietnam, *Victory in Vietnam*, 125-126.

14. William C. Westmoreland, "A Military War of Attrition," in *The Lessons of Vietnam*, eds. W. Scott Thompson and Donaldson Frizzel (New York: Crane, Russak and Company, 1977), 57-71.

15. Ibid., 60-61.

16. Pacification and CORDS will be described in more detail in the next chapter.

17. Eric M. Bergerud, *The Dynamics of Defeat* (Boulder, CO: Westview Press, Inc., 1991), 236-237.

18. Ibid., 241.

19. James Willbanks, *Abandoning Vietnam* (Lawrence, Kansas: University of Kansas Press, 2004), 20.

20. Bergerud, *The Dynamics of Defeat*, 308. The spring of 1970 also witnessed the invasion of Cambodia by US and ARVN forces that forced Communist main forces to retreat further into their sanctuaries and away from the population. The invasion and its implications will be discussed further in the next chapter.

21. Willbanks, *Abandoning Vietnam*, 152-153.

22. Military History Institute of Vietnam, *Victory in Vietnam*, 420.

23. VCP, "Party Account from 1954-1960," 4.

24. Moyar, *Triumph Forsaken*, 33.

25. VCP, "Party Account from 1954-1960," 4-6.

26. Ibid., 6.

27. The political structure of Vietnam built upwards from the hamlet. The hamlet was a loose grouping of houses containing between 500-1000 people. Several hamlets were then grouped into villages. Villages were contained within districts, akin to US counties, and districts in provinces, akin to US states.

28. Jeffrey Race, *War Comes to Long An* (Berkeley: University of California Press, 1972), 41.

29. R. Michael Pearce, *Evolution of a Vietnamese Village-Part II* (Santa Monica, CA: RAND Corporation, 1966), 7.

30. Moyar, *Triumph Forsaken*, 65. Also see VCP, *"Party Account from 1954-1960,"* 8-9.

31. The Communist Party accounts from this period are valuable because they present a picture of how the enemy viewed Diem's actions. While they contain some outrageous accusations against the regime, the narrative remains consistent across multiple documents and is in general agreement with accounts from US and other sources from the same period.

32. VCP, "Party Account from 1954-1960," 8.

33. Ibid., 8-9.

34. Mai Ngoc Duoc, interview by Jeffrey Race, quoted in Race, *War Comes to Long An*, 52.

35. VCP, "Party Account from 1954-1960," 32.

36. Unfortunately, very little has been written about Law 10/59 and an original text of the law has not been discovered by the author.

37. Military History Institute of Vietnam, *Victory in Vietnam*, 49. Also see Race, *War Comes to Long An*, 19n.

38. VCP, "Party Account from 1954-1960," 10.

39. Ibid., 11.

40. The Agroville program and its implementation in 1959 is a strong indicator of Diem's thorough understanding of the need to gain control over the population and the tools for doing so. Diem initiates the program without Western advice and three years before the arrival of Sir Robert Thompson in Vietnam.

41. GVN official correspondence quoted in Joseph T. Zasloff, "Rural Resettlement in South Viet Nam: The Agroville Program," *Pacific Affairs 35*, no. 4 (Winter 1962-1963): 328.

42. VCP, "Party Account from 1954-1960," 8-16.

43. Zasloff, "Rural Resettlement," 331-332.

44. Kitson, *Low Intensity Operations*, 49.

45. VCP, "Party Account from 1954-1960," 11.

46. Zasloff, "Rural Resettlement," 337.

47. VCP, "Party Account from 1954-1960," 11.

48. Moyar, *Triumph Forsaken*, 82.

49. Ibid., 82.

50. Ibid., 82.

51. Zasloff, "Rural Resettlement" 336.

52. Ibid., 336.

53. Military History Institute of Vietnam, *Victory in Vietnam*, 44.

54. Ibid., 44.

55. VCP, "Party Account from 1954-1960," 54.

56. Ibid., 54.

57. Ibid., 53.

58. Ibid., 53.

59. Zasloff, "Rural Resettlement" 337.

60. Race, *War Comes to Long An*, 83. Also see Moyar, *Triumph Forsaken*, 79.

61. Nam Bo is the traditional Vietnamese term for the southern portion of the country. Nam Bo includes the Mekong Delta and the areas around Saigon.

62. Nam Bo Regional Committee, "Letter from the Regional Committee to All Members of Cells," 28 March 1960, Douglas Pike Collection: Unit 5, TTU, 1.

63. Ibid., 1.

64. Ibid., 1.

65. Ibid., 1.

66. Military History Institute of Vietnam, *Victory in Vietnam*, 50.

67. Nam Bo Regional Committee, "Letter from the Regional Committee," 1.

68. Ibid., 2.

69. Military History Institute of Vietnam, *Victory in Vietnam*, 55.

70. Nam Bo Regional Committee, "Letter from the Regional Committee," 7.

71. Ibid., 7-8.

72. Military History Institute of Vietnam, *Victory in Vietnam*, 66.

73. Ibid., 66.

74. Ibid., 67. This account is corroborated by the history of the war in Long An province recorded by Race. In it, he notes a massive increase in Party violence and Party membership after the 1959 decision to expand the war to armed struggle. See Race, *War Comes to Long An*, 113-120.

75. Military History Institute of Vietnam, *Victory in Vietnam*, 51.

76. Ibid., 51.

77. Ibid., 53. Also see Moyar, *Triumph Forsaken*, 84-85.

78. Elbridge Durbrow, "Cablegram from Elbridge Durbrow, United States Ambassador in Saigon, to Secretary of State Christian A. Herter, Sept. 16, 1960," in *The Pentagon Papers* as published by *The New York Times* (New York: Bantam Books, Inc., 1971), 115.

79. Ibid., 115.

80. See Race, *War Comes to Long An*, 192 and Bergerud, *The Dynamics of Defeat*, 37.

81. Bergerud, *The Dynamics of Defeat*, 37.

82. Bergerud's assessment of the program relies heavily on Race and the work done by Donnell and Hickey for the RAND Corporation in early 1962. Race's work is in depth, but focuses only on Long An Province. Donnell and Hickey examined a small number of villages in provinces around Saigon for a limited period of time at the beginning of the program. Another problem in using Donnell and Hickey's work as heavily as Bergerud does is that the authors explicitly note that they considered only the effects of the non-security aspects of the program on the life of peasants in the hamlets. This leaves out a critical portion of the program and negatively skews the analysis.

83. The term hearts and minds as used in analyzing the conflict in Vietnam has generally been construed as an effort to "win the allegiance of the South Vietnamese population." This presents the campaign as a contest between the two sides to provide inducements to the population to support them rather than an outright battle for control. See Bergerud, *Dynamics of Defeat*, 141.

84. US Department of State, Bureau of Intelligence and Research, Research Memorandum RFE-58, *Strategic Hamlets*, 1 July 1963. Texas Tech University Vietnam Archive, 1.

85. Ibid., 2.

86. John B. O'Donnell, "The Strategic Hamlet Program in Kien Hoa Province, South Vietnam: A Case Study of Counter-Insurgency," (paper presented at the conference on Southeast Asian Tribes, Minorities and Central Governments, Princeton, New Jersey, 11 May 1965,) TTU, 11.

87. Office of Rural Affairs, US Operations Mission Saigon, "Notes on Strategic Hamlets," 15 Aug 1963, Douglas Pike Collection: Unit 2, TTU, 3.

88. National Liberation Front, "Anti-Strategic Hamlet Program," VC Document 93,Douglas Pike Collection: Unit 1, TTU, 9.

89. Ibid., 11.

90. Government of Vietnam, "Discussion Paper - From Strategic Hamlets to Self Defense Village," TTU, 30.

91. Ibid., 36.

92. Ibid, 46.

93. John C. Donnell and Gerald C. Hickey, *The Vietnamese "Strategic Hamlets": A Preliminary Report* (Santa Monica, CA: RAND Corporation, 1962), 7.

94. Ibid., 15.

95. O'Donnell, "The Strategic Hamlet Program in Kien Hoa Province," 24.

96. GVN, "From Strategic Hamlets to Self Defense Village," 37.

97. Ibid., 37.

98. Ibid., 37.

99. Ibid., 38.

100. Moyar, *Triumph Forsaken*, 157.

101. NLF, "Anti-Strategic Hamlet Program," 10.

102. GVN, "From Strategic Hamlets to Self Defense Village," 38.

103. Ibid., 38-39.

104. Ibid., 39.

105. US Operations Mission Saigon, "Notes on Strategic Hamlets," 4.

106. GVN, "From Strategic Hamlets to Self Defense Village," 42.

107. Ibid., 42.

108. Throughout the campaign, the GVN established several versions of self-defense forces to provide security in the hamlets and villages. The two most well known are the Regional Forces (RF) and Popular Forces (PF). They are generally referred to as "Ruffs and Puffs" and abbreviated as RF/PF. Both forces were lightly armed and dedicated to serve in the area where they were raised. RFs were a company that supported a province, while PFs were a platoon that supported a village. There were also dedicated security forces in the hamlets which were composed of approximately one squad.

109. O'Donnell, "The Strategic Hamlet Program in Kien Hoa Province," 10.

110. Ibid., 20.

111. US DOS, *Strategic Hamlets*, July 1, 1963, 4.

112. O'Donnell, "The Strategic Hamlet Program in Kien Hoa Province," 25.

113. Central Intelligence Agency, Memorandum for the Secretary of Defense, 13 July 1962, Texas Tech University Vietnam Archive, 4.

114. Ibid., 5.

115. NLF, "Anti-Strategic Hamlet Program," 29.

116. Ibid., 29.

117. O'Donnell, "The Strategic Hamlet Program in Kien Hoa Province," 25.

118. US DOS, *Strategic Hamlets*, 5.

119. O'Donnell, "The Strategic Hamlet Program in Kien Hoa Province," 32.

120. Race, *War Comes to Long An*, 133. Race is a strong critic of the program particularly because of its ultimate failure in Long An. However, his narrative demonstrates that the program did stabilize the situation in the province and only began to severely deteriorate after the replacement of the province chief in mid-1963 and an increase of VC and PAVN main force activity. The VC and PAVN destroyed the last strategic hamlets in Long An only in early 1964, after the fall of the Diem regime and when the program was no longer supported by the GVN.

121. Roger Hilsman, "The Situation and Short-Term Prospects in South Vietnam," in *The Pentagon Papers* as published by *The New York Times* (New York: Bantam Books, Inc., 1971), 155. Hilsman was the director of the State Department Bureau of Intelligence and Research. The memorandum was written based off of information available as of November 1962 and was sent to Secretary of State Dean Rusk on 3 December 1962.

122. Ibid., 155.

123. U.S. DOS, *Strategic Hamlets*, 6.

124. Ibid., 7.

125. "Experiences of Struggle with and Elimination of Strategic Hamlets of H Villagers," October-November 1962, TTU, 2.

126. Ibid., 2.

127. Ibid., 3.

128. As noted above, Race and Bergerud are extremely critical of the program. Moyar also details the antipathy towards the program from John Paul Vann and the reporters he influenced, notably Neil Sheehan and David Halberstam.

129. The document is not dated and was not captured until 1968. However, it includes references to the number of strategic hamlets as of October 1962 which indicates that it was written and published sometime after that.

130. National Liberation Front, "Measures Against Village Merging and People Concentration," TTU, 13.

131. National Liberation Front, "Anti-Strategic Hamlet Program," 22.

132. Military History Institute of Vietnam, *Victory in Vietnam*, 112.

133. Ibid., 114.

134. Ibid., 114.

135. NLF, "Measures Against Village Merging and People Concentration," 15.

136. Ibid., 17.

137. Ibid., 18.

138. NLF, "Measures Against Village Merging and People Concentration." It is not clear from the document where in South Vietnam H village is. However, since this document was replicated and sent to cadres in other areas of the country it can be assumed that the tactics described were generalizable to a significant portion of the country.

139. Ibid., 3.

140. Ibid., 4.

141. Ibid., 4.

142. Ibid., 5.

143. Long An Provincial Representative's Report, June-July 1963, in O'Donnell, "The Strategic Hamlet Program in Kien Hoa Province," 29.

144. Military History Institute of Vietnam, *Victory in Vietnam*, 121.

145. Ibid., 121.

146. Ibid., 113.

147. Ibid., 113.

148. Hilsman, "The Situation and Short-Term Prospects in South Vietnam," 157.

149. This is not meant to assert that Diem was the only possible leader who could successfully prosecute the war against the Communists. Rather, it is intended to illustrate that a coup that required a significant amount of change in the leadership and organization of the GVN and its counterinsurgency strategy would necessarily be chaotic.

150. Military History Institute of Vietnam, *Victory in Vietnam*, 121.

151. Ibid., 121-122.

152. Michael V. Forrestal, Memorandum for the President, 11 December 1963, Douglas Pike Collection: Unit 1, TTU, 1-2.

153. Ibid., 2.

154. The GVN's pacification programs after the fall of Diem will be discussed further in the next chapter.

155. USOM, "Notes on Strategic Hamlets", 5.

156. Ibid., 16.

157. Quoted in R. Michael Pearce, *Evolution of a Vietnamese Village-Part I* (Santa Monica, CA: RAND Corporation, 1965), 55.

158. It should also be noted that the Communists did not intend to leave the population in their dispersed hamlets when the war was over. The PAVN history states that in the North in 1961 "eleven million working peasants were organized into agricultural production cooperatives." See Military History Institute of Vietnam, *Victory in Vietnam*, 91

159. Pearce, *Evolution of a Vietnamese Village - Part II*, 29.

160. Military History Institute of Vietnam, *Victory in Vietnam*, 85.

161. O'Donnell, "The Strategic Hamlet Program in Kien Hoa Province," 52. Also see Race, *War Comes to Long An*, 83.

Chapter 5
Vietnam, 1966-1970

It essentially amounted to going out and beating the jungle every day and every night looking for the enemy. There were all kinds of fancy names given to the 'tactics': search and destroy, cordon and search, sweep and search, anvil and hammer, etc. and etc but it all amounted at the tactical unit level to going out, looking for the enemy, and trying to kill him."

—Carl Quickmire, Troop Commander, Quoted in *Red Thunder, Tropic Lightning*

The involvement of American ground combat forces in Vietnam is a complicated and difficult operation to analyze and make sense of. As the quote above indicates, the reality for tactical units was often very different than that presented by commanders above them. American ground combat forces were primarily tasked to seek out and destroy the armed forces of the DRV and the Front but the tools and methods for doing so were quite limited. US units attempted to develop tactics and techniques that would produce success in this mission, but because of the nature of the war and the tenacity of their enemy, such success was difficult, if not impossible, to realize.

They also faced the challenge of confronting the insurgent infrastructure in the hamlets and villages of rural Vietnam. The pacification effort that was intended to defeat this infrastructure was supposed to be the mission of the Vietnamese forces that US units operated with. However, US units often found themselves providing support to pacification but the need to confront the PAVN and VC main forces, both to protect the pacification effort itself and to prevent the conventional invasion that the US rightly feared, often forced US units to choose between one or the other. The two efforts were inextricably linked and combat power dedicated to one was not available to the other.

Overview of US Ground Combat Operations in Vietnam

The succession of different regimes that ran the GVN following the 1 November 1963 coup that deposed President Ngo Dinh Diem proved incapable of prosecuting the war against the VC insurgency or repelling the invasion of South Vietnam by elements of PAVN.[1] They could not agree on a comprehensive counterinsurgency strategy to succeed the Strategic Hamlet Program which had ended coincidently with the coup against Diem. At the same time, ARVN was not strong enough, despite the presence of American advisers and the support of American airpower, to defeat the VC and PAVN main force units that had begun operating throughout the country.[2]

In response to this situation and concerned over the possibility of an imminent collapse of South Vietnam, President Johnson decided to gradually escalate the war in 1964, first through air strikes against North Vietnam and then by introducing US ground forces in a limited role. It was believed that these steps would send the DRV a clear message regarding US resolve and that the resulting damage would convince it to end its support for the insurgency.[3] They did not, however, and the ground war in South Vietnam grew more intense as the DRV and the Front attempted to capitalize on the situation and win a quick victory.[4]

In April 1965, President Johnson authorized the enclave strategy in which US forces would defend five coastal enclaves and assist ARVN forces within 50 miles of them. This move also failed to significantly change the dynamic of the war and so in July 1965 Johnson committed US forces to ground combat. The US commander, General William C. Westmoreland, envisioned using US forces in three phases.[5]

In the first phase, US forces would stabilize the situation and secure logistical bases. In the second phase, they would seize the initiative by operating against VC and PAVN main force bases and sanctuaries. During the final phase, the remaining enemy units would be defeated and forced across the border into Laos and Cambodia. Westmoreland believed that US ground forces were better equipped to confront the VC and PAVN main forces and that ARVN would be better utilized providing security to the Vietnamese population and confronting VC local and guerrilla units.[6]

Westmoreland was also concerned that if US units were dispersed into small elements to fight VC local and guerrilla forces, that they could be exposed to a major attack by main force units. A major US defeat might prematurely end the war.[7] Thus, as US units flowed into South Vietnam in 1965 and 1966, they were deployed under division and brigade-sized headquarters and were dedicated to the mission of confronting and defeating the PAVN and VC main force units. The United States Marine Corps (USMC) was given responsibility for the I Corps Tactical Zone (CTZ), just south of the 17th parallel, while US Army and other Free World Military Armed Forces (FWMAF), such as those of South Korea and Australia, were given responsibility for operations in the II and III CTZs, and eventually in IV CTZ as well.[8]

During 1966 and 1967, US ground forces conducted offensive operations to find, fix, and destroy enemy main force units throughout the country. Many units, such as the 173d Airborne Brigade and the brigades of the 101st Airborne Division, were not assigned a specific area of operations; rather, they were deployed throughout the country in response to intelligence about the location of enemy main force units. Some offensive operations, such as Junction City[9], were multi-divisional in strength.[10]

However, in addition to large scale offensive operations, many US Army units engaged in smaller operations, like Operation MAILI[11], that focused on securing the local population and assisting the GVN's pacification effort. The USMC executed the Combined Action Platoon program which had USMC squads fight and live along side Vietnamese territorial forces within a village.[12] However, most of these operations were short in duration and did not receive the same amount of resources as major offensive operations.[13]

The deployment of US ground forces stabilized the GVN and allowed the pacification[14] effort to take shape. US units inflicted significant losses on PAVN and VC forces in terms of personnel, materiel, and supplies. Offensive operations had not been sufficient, however, to destroy the main force units. In response, the Party decided to alter their strategy and seek a "decisive victory" through the execution of a "general offensive-general uprising."[15] The offensive began during the Vietnamese holiday of Tet in 1968.

The Party strategy for the Tet Offensive envisioned luring US forces away from populated areas so that VC main force and guerrilla units could defeat ARVN units and seize control of the major urban areas including Hue, Da Nang, and Saigon.[16] While the strategy was initially successful, it also presented a tremendous opportunity to US forces. VC and PAVN main force units had to engage the more heavily armed US units. Once the initial shock of the attacks were over, US units rapidly regrouped and decimated the VC and PAVN main forces. The attack was defeated around Saigon by mid-February and though hard fighting continued through March, PAVN and VC units were soundly defeated.[17]

The Tet Offensive was not a one off event, however. PAVN and VC units launched a second offensive targeted at Saigon in May of 1968. The attack failed to penetrate the US screen that had been established around Saigon and resulted in even greater losses for the PAVN and VC units that took part. Throughout the summer of 1968, US units conducted operations to find and destroy the now retreating enemy main force units. The PAVN and VC main force units assiduously avoided contact but were largely forced out of the populated areas of the country. This enabled the GVN to launch their Special Pacification Plan, referred to by the Americans as the APC.[18]

In 1969, the new commander of US forces, General Creighton Abrams, inaugurated his "one war" strategy that was intended to unify the efforts of US units in support of pacification and the battle against PAVN and VC main and local force elements.[19] The new administration of President Richard Nixon further altered the fight for US forces by introducing the strategy of Vietnamization. This strategy envisioned a gradual withdrawal of US forces and a transition of all security responsibilities to Vietnamese forces. The strategy would require US units to operate more closely with ARVN and prepare them to confront PAVN and the VC simultaneously.[20]

The Party and Front launched another offensive following the Tet holiday in 1969. This time they hoped to strike American units hard enough in order to force the US to withdraw its forces from South Vietnam as part of the conditions of a cease fire.[21] The offensive failed and did not result in the general uprising that the Party and Front had hoped for. Moreover, it again allowed US units the opportunity to deploy their superior firepower against VC and PAVN main force units and severely degrade their strength.

After the 1969 Tet Offensive, US units continued to execute the one war and Vietnamization strategies. They ostensibly focused on small unit, combined operations, but continued to be used to fight major battles against PAVN, such as the infamous battle at Hamburger Hill.[22] However, the decimation that PAVN and VC forces had experienced over the last two years provided a major increase in security in the countryside of Vietnam and the pacification effort began to accelerate.[23]

US units provided increasing amounts of support to the pacification effort, but one major operation remained, the May 1970 invasion of Cambodia. US units supported ARVN and conducted combat operations along the border with and into Cambodia to destroy PAVN and VC supply points and base camps.[24] The invasion of Cambodia represented the final step in Westmoreland's three phase plan for the use of US forces and provides an example of how US operations did not change significantly despite the one war and Vietnamization strategies implemented by US leaders and policy makers. It also illustrates that the strategy developed by Westmoreland and endorsed in the PROVN study to destroy main force units first to create space for pacification was still operative.[25]

Following the invasion of Cambodia, US units returned to their role of supporting pacification and improving the combat effectiveness of ARVN. As they did so, US units continued their withdrawal from Vietnam. US operations became smaller as ARVN division commanders were handed responsibility for prosecuting the war against the Communist main forces.[26] In the end of involvement of US ground combat forces in the war, the 101st Airborne Division left Vietnam in the spring of 1972, .[27]

Control Mechanism - Pacification

Following the end of the Strategic Hamlet Program coincident with the coup against Diem on 1 November 1963, the GVN was without a holistic control mechanism through which it could define a comprehensive counterinsurgency strategy and employ population and resource control measures as a part of that strategy.[28] However, such a mechanism did evolve in the form of pacification.[29] The official definition from the 1968 MACV *Pacification Handbook* stated that:

> Pacification, as it applies in the Republic of Vietnam, is the military, political, economic, and social process of establishing or re-establishing local government [that's] responsive to and involving the participation of the people. It includes the provision of sustained, credible territorial security, the destruction of the enemy's under-ground government, the assertion or reassertion of political control and involvement of the people in government, and the initiation of economic and social activity capable of self-sustenance and expansion.[30]

This definition demonstrates just how comprehensive, and complex, the system of pacification was. Pacification consisted of a number of component programs, encompassed a wide range of military and civilian activities, and sought to achieve a variety of aims.[31] Notably included in those aims are local security and the destruction of the enemy subversive infrastructure. The handbook noted that:

> The key to pacification is the provision of sustained territorial security. Territorial security is security from VC local forces and guerrilla units and VC/NVA [North Vietnamese Army] main force units, if any are in or threatening the area. It also includes the protection of the people within a hamlet from the VC infrastructure and bullies.[32]

Thus, the first step in pacification was to provide meaningful security to the population from all possible threats, including VC and PAVN main force units. This is important to note as some writers, such as Andrew Krepinevich, contend that pacification presented an alternative strategy to Westmoreland's attrition strategy.[33] However, the definition makes clear that attrition, and the search and destroy tactics associated with it, formed one part of the overall pacification strategy. The other elements of pacification could not begin until the population was sufficiently protected from the VC and PAVN main force units.

The other problem with presenting pacification as an alternative strategy to attrition is that pacification as defined above and as understood by historians and writers looking back on the conflict was not a fully formed concept in 1964 or 1965 as the US contemplated intervening with ground combat forces. Pacification with its concepts, objectives, and component programs, evolved over time beginning with the Diem regime's efforts to gain control of the country discussed in the previous chapter. Its evolution did not occur in a vacuum but in the midst of the dynamic conflict that surrounded and was a part of it.

Evolution of Pacification after Diem

Despite the persistent criticism of Diem by those who opposed his policies and who ultimately overthrew his government, the new leaders of the GVN realized that they needed to assert control over the population, particularly in the rural areas. They also recognized that the Strategic Hamlet Program, despite is noted shortcomings, provided a starting point to do so. Vietnamese Brigadier General Tran Dinh Tho had long experience in pacification and recalled in a monograph written after the war that:

> In the face of the deteriorating situation, the GVN was in a dilemma. On the one hand, there was no way to reinstate the Strategic Hamlet program since it had been linked with the old regime and officially abolished. On the other hand, the GVN could not give the enemy free reign over the countryside. As a solution, the government instituted a new pacification program, the 'New Life Hamlet' program. As a matter of fact, there was nothing that could distinguish this program from its predecessor, only a change in name.[34]

This assertion is supported by the experience of R. Michael Pearce in Duc Lap Village, Hau Nghia province. Pearce noted that the requirements for what he called a "New Rural Life Hamlet" were: a census completed and the VC infrastructure destroyed, a hamlet self defense force formed, defensive works constructed, a communications system in place to call for reinforcements, organization of the population into groups, and a new hamlet government selected.[35] The establishment of the New Rural Life Hamlet was itself one step in a larger pacification process which included a military operation to clear the area of VC and PAVN main force units and the insertion of teams to improve local governance and development.[36] The New Rural Life Hamlet requirements and the pacification process that it was a part of were nearly identical to the components of the Strategic Hamlet Program.

In an attempt to avoid the problem of overreach that had plagued the Strategic Hamlet Program, the GVN executed the pacification programs in the context of an "oil-spot" strategy in 1964, the first of which was called Chien Thang (Will to Victory).[37] As this program failed, the GVN was encouraged by MACV and the US embassy to pursue a less ambitious plan, referred to as Hop Tac (Victory).[38] Hop Tac pursued pacification in only three provinces around Saigon.[39] Despite the attempt to reduce the scope and improve the focus of the GVN's pacification efforts, the degrading military situation and the succession of different governments prevented the New Rural Life Hamlet program and its associated pacification strategies from ever achieving any momentum.

When Premier Nguyen Cao Ky and Chief of State Nguyen Van Thieu assumed power in June 1965 they understood the need to address the GVN's lack of control in the rural areas and this led to the creation of a new pacification strategy.[40] Tho noted that:

> The RVN government was fully aware of the Communist dependence on the rural area, and the national strategy of 'Pacification and Development' was designed to separate the Communists from it. The strategy also sought to establish the GVN presence in less secure, contested areas with a view of controlling the nation's manpower and resources and denying them to the enemy.[41]

The strategy was not well developed in 1965 when the US intervention began, however. The concept of pacification continued to evolve within the GVN and in 1966 it became the Revolutionary Development (RD) program. With this change came a unification of the pacification effort within the GVN. A standing committee, with the Prime Minister as chair and representatives from civilian ministries and the military, was formed to direct the RD effort.[42] MG Nguyen Duc Thang became secretary general of the committee and in early 1966 he created the RD cadre program.[43] The RD cadre was a team of young men and women who were trained to execute the GVN's pacification in the hamlets after the military had secured the area. They were expected to secure themselves as they did so and this would prove to be a major challenge to the pacification program.

RD also brought the Chieu Hoi program formally under the umbrella of pacification. Chieu Hoi, or Open Arms, was the GVN's amnesty program and was intended to allow the non-Communist elements within the VC to surrender and return to the GVN. The Vietnamese had never placed much emphasis on the program and the effort had previously been run outside of pacification. At the insistence of the US, it was brought within RD. This did not, however, change the attitude of the GVN to the program and it continued to receive little in the way of resources or effort.[44] The GVN spent just 31 percent of the funds obligated to the program in 1966.[45] Though this increased in later years, the Vietnamese remained distrustful of any ralliers that came in and thus did not view them as an asset that could be leveraged in the fight against the VC in the rural areas.[46]

In 1967, the pacification program changed names again and became the New Model Pacification program.[47] The New Model Pacification program included an ambitious set of 11 objectives to be accomplished by the RD cadre. The objectives included carryovers from earlier programs, such as the completion of a census and the organization of hamlet self-defense forces, and new objectives like the elimination of illiteracy, improvement of health and sanitary conditions, development of agriculture and craft industries, and the implementation of land reform.[48] A hamlet that was designated an *ap doi moi* (Real New Life Hamlet) during that year's pacification plan was to accomplish all 11 objectives. An *ap binh dinh* (Pacification Hamlet) would only achieve the first two objectives, which were primarily focused on security.[49]

The New Model Pacification Program was thus far more ambitious than the Strategic Hamlet Program had been. It required a major reform to the administrative structures in the rural areas of the country and a massive change in the everyday life of peasants in the hamlets. It was also far less coercive than earlier efforts had been. Tho stated proudly that "the spirit of democracy was strong and pervasive, precluding the use of harsh measures."[50] Despite this he noted that, "yet the people seemed indifferent to the GVN courtship. If successful, the pacification effort would replace this indifference with a solid commitment on the part of the people, a commitment that would support the defense of the nation and achieve a just peace."[51]

Despite the heavy commitment of resources to it by the GVN and the unification of US support for it under CORDS, the New Model Pacification program failed to achieve its objectives in 1967.[52] This was primarily due to the inability of US ground forces, ARVN, and the local security forces to provide sustained security in the hamlets. This exposed the RD cadre to attacks, undermining their ability to conduct the development activities that they were responsible for.

When the Party launched the Tet Offensive in early 1968 it disrupted and rolled back pacification efforts as US and ARVN units had to be redeployed around the country. Many areas that had previously been under government control or contested were now abandoned to the PAVN and VC forces.[53] The aftermath of the Tet Offensive, however, created an opportunity for the GVN and its allies to jumpstart pacification. The loss to the Front of so many experienced cadre in the towns and the decimation of VC and PAVN main force units allowed the GVN and the US to execute the APC in late fall 1968 and early 1969. The APC did not represent a major change to the structure of pacification but was instead a major commitment of resources to pacification.[54]

After the end of the APC and the defeat of the Party's 1969 Tet Offensive, the GVN vigorously pursued pacification. In doing so, the GVN made one major modification. Development and pacification efforts in 1969 were directed towards villages because "the village was the basic administratively organized unit which controlled resources and had a budget of its own."[55] The change was also meant to halt the displacement of the population from unsecure hamlets to secure hamlets, as this was "deemed unnecessary and disadvantageous."[56] This was a dramatic shift as all previous incarnations of pacification had focused on the hamlet. Moreover, it was a strange change to make as the population actually lived in the hamlets. If the population was not secure in their hamlet then pacification would necessarily fail.

The change was partly at the urging of US officials in CORDS who believed that improved development and government at the village level could produce greater gains in the pacification effort.[57] Unfortunately, the village development efforts were limited by the fact that the authorities and resources given to the village were in addition to those already ongoing, which meant that the province chief retained the majority of power in the governmental structure.[58] Moreover, the security situation, while improving, was still not certain enough for the population within the villages to risk supporting the government and candidates for village elections were difficult to find.[59]

Nevertheless, the massive increase in security brought about by the defeat of VC and PAVN main force units and the loss of significant numbers of VC cadre in the rural areas allowed the GVN pacification program to make rapid gains throughout 1969 and 1970.[60] By 1971, the "situation was so good that the GVN deemed it a most appropriate time to pass on to the nation-building phase, particularly development and social reform. Pacification was considered an anachronistic term since its most important objective [ending the war and achieving peace] had been achieved."[61]

Though the GVN had made progress in its battle against the VC, the war was by no means over. Robert Komer had cautioned in 1970 that:

> The VC, though greatly weakened, is still a force to be reckoned with. Indeed, despite the growing evidence as to pacification's short-term impact on rural insurgency, such other factors as new NVA offensives, political changes in Saigon, or the terms of a negotiated settlement may so affect the final outcome in Vietnam that no real test of pacification's ultimate impact may ever be feasible.[62]

His analysis proved to be prescient.

Although ARVN defeated PAVN's 1972 Easter Offensive with the assistance of US airpower, it caused major disruption in the nation building program and the loss of government control in some hamlets. This had been one of the major goals of the offensive. The PAVN history of the war states that during the offensive "we would simultaneously mount wide-ranging military attacks coordinated with mass popular uprisings aimed at destroying the enemy's 'pacification' program in the rural lowlands. These actions would totally change the character of the war in South Vietnam."[63]

They did. The offensive gave PAVN and VC control over significant amounts of territory, some of which they would never relinquish. In the hours before final implementation of the January 1973 cease fire, PAVN units attacked hundreds of villages to further expand their control.[64] Although the PAVN units had been badly hurt during the offensive, ARVN no longer had the support of US advisers or air power and was nearly as damaged as their opponents.[65]

As a result, pacification was dead in 1973. ARVN and the local security forces could no longer provide the security that was the sine qua non of the process and the GVN could not draw on the resources of the United States to implement such an ambitious program.[66] The GVN continued the fiction of pacification all the way through 1975 but it could no longer mount the coordinated and comprehensive effort required to gain the control over the population that it had lost. Whether or not doing so would have prevented or merely delayed PAVN's invasion which ended South Vietnam's independence is not clear.

US Support to Pacification

The US was slow to support the GVN's pacification efforts. The majority of US assistance in the years prior to 1963 was directed towards the improvement of the RVNAF. As noted in the previous chapter, Diem had avoided asking the US for support for both the *agrovilles* and the Strategic Hamlet Programs because he feared that his allies would interfere with his execution of the programs. When the US did contribute to the Strategic Hamlet program the outlay was a paltry $10 million to support an extremely ambitious and costly program.[67]

American support for pacification remained sparce throughout 1964 and 1965. Much of the assistance was directed to the various self defense forces through the military's assistance program. The embassy and MACV assisted the GVN in making the plans for both Chien Thang and Hop Tac. Moreover, MACV assumed the lead for American support of pacification during Hop Tac and directed its advisers in the countryside to prepare reports on the progress of pacification.[68] The lack of US support contributed to the failure of both plans, but it was not the major cause of failure.

The constantly changing regimes at the head of the GVN made it difficult for any pacification program to be properly supported. The chaos that regime changes caused contributed to a lack of coordination between the various components of the pacification program. Without a solid government or a comprehensive pacification program to provide support to, there was little point in dedicating resources to pacification. Moreover, because the military situation was deteriorating so rapidly, it made more sense to focus resources that were going in on reinforcing ARVN.

As the GVN stabilized under Thieu and Ky in 1965, it became possible for the US to support the pacification programs more vigorously. The US was already providing support to some of the components of pacification through the United States Agency for International Development (USAID) and the CIA but the bulk of resources were going to the military. Robert Komer portrays this as a situation where pacification was given second priority to the military's attrition strategy.[69] However, it should be recalled that the GVN's pacification strategy was dependent upon the rural areas being secure from all threats before the process of pacification could begin. This included the threat from VC and PAVN main force units, against whom Westmoreland's attrition strategy was directed.

As the US military's fight against VC and PAVN main forces continued in 1966, questions began to be raised by President Johnson and Ambassador

Lodge about how much effort should be directed to support pacification.[70] A study produced by members of the Army staff entitled "Program for the Pacification and Long-Term Development of South Vietnam," or PROVN, was published in March of 1966. Krepinevich and Komer maintain that PROVN advocated a central role for pacification and that the study's main conclusions were ignored by Westmoreland and MACV.[71] While it is true that PROVN emphasized pacification much more strongly than other strategies had to that point, it nevertheless concluded that in order for pacification to be successful, the necessary first step was to destroy VC and PAVN main force units.[72]

Westmoreland was therefore confronted with a dilemma. Destroying the VC and PAVN main force units was required to provide the necessary space for pacification to succeed but doing so left little in the way of resources to provide to the pacification effort. The Combined Campaign Plan 1967, AB 142, attempted to set specific roles and responsibilities for the military units involved and "established definite RD missions for ARVN and US/FWMAF forces. ARVN's primary responsibility was to provide the military support to RD, while the primary responsibility of US/FWMAF was to seek out and destroy VC/NVA main force units, base areas, and LOCs."[73] Even with this division of labor it was noted that:

> The great number of military forces employed in support of pacification never seemed to keep up with the requirements occasioned by the necessity to deploy a permanent occupation force to every hamlet. The situation was such that when protection forces were deployed from a certain area considered 'secure', that area might relapse into insecurity and the local population would lose confidence in the GVN.[74]

The challenge of supporting pacification was made more difficult by the fact that such support was not unified under a single US agency. The GVN had conceptually unified its pacification efforts but US support was provided through the agency which had responsibility for a specific program. Thus, USAID provided support to development efforts and the Chieu Hoi program, the CIA provided money and advisors to the RD cadre, and the US military supported pacification through its advisory effort inside of ARVN. The resulting disunity of effort concerned the President and some of his top advisors who felt that MACV was not sufficiently supporting pacification and that it would be better to unify pacification under a single agency, preferably the military.[75]

This led to the creation of the short-lived Office of Civil Operations in late 1966. The new office was intended to unify the pacification effort but it never achieved this goal because it did not gain control over personnel, logistics, or funding from the responsible agencies.[76] Nor was the office integrated under the military command structure. As a result, President Johnson decided to unify the pacification effort under the command of Westmoreland who established a new organization called CORDS.[77]

CORDS resolved many of the issues that had plagued US support of pacification to that point. CORDS was a part of the military command structure and its leader, initially Robert Komer, was made a full deputy, referred to as DepCORDS, to Westmoreland. The DepCORDS at each level was responsible for developing pacification plans that unified the civil and military effort and for supervising the execution of those plans.[78] Additionally, US units were directed in the 1968 Combined Campaign Plan "to coordinate their military plans with provincial RD plans."[79] These arrangements gave the DepCORDS access to more resources and greater authority to employ them to support pacification.

Moreover, CORDS gained control over nearly all of the US programs associated with pacification to include: Chieu Hoi, RD cadre, civic action and civil affairs operations of the US military, and all of the associated reports and evaluations.[80] The consolidation of reports[81] provided a useful check on the execution of pacification programs. A senior civilian responsible for compiling pacification reports for II CTZ recalled that Ambassador Colby would often take the reports out to the field and verify their accuracy causing some discomfort to US advisers, particularly military officers.[82]

The lack of security at the local level continued to hamper pacification efforts, however. In an attempt to improve the situation, Westmoreland gave CORDS responsibility for all territorial security forces in May of 1967.[83] This gave CORDS access to further resources from the US military and the military personnel who advised Vietnamese territorial security forces. Despite this change, security in the countryside remained poor because the threat posed by VC and PAVN main force units was still high. Even unified pacification efforts could make little progress in this situation.

However, the Tet Offensive, and the decimation of VC and PAVN main force units that accompanied it, gave the unified pacification efforts the chance to gain ground. The APC in late 1968 and early 1969 showcased this as US units and the CORDS organization deployed the bulk of their resources into the three month pacification effort.[84] This occurred despite the fact that doubts had begun to arise about pacification due to the performance of the Vietnamese RD cadre during the Tet Offensive.[85] Many had been forced to leave the villages where they operated and shelter at the district headquarters.[86] The APC theoretically represented the initial commitment by the new MACV commander, General Abrams, to execute a "one war" strategy in which population security, and thus pacification, would assume primacy over the destruction of enemy units.[87]

United States and GVN operations in support of pacification increased from 1969-1971 but large-scale conventional military operations, such as the invasion of Cambodia in 1970, continued to take place. United States units executed more small unit (company and below) and combined operations with Vietnamese forces but much of the focus remained on destroying VC units.[88] The actions of US units appeared to be different from the message being sent by the US chain of command.

Vietnamization and the withdrawal of US ground forces significantly altered US support for pacification. Limits imposed on the total strength of US military forces in the country resulted in US advisers being withdrawn from areas that were deemed secure and significantly reduced their numbers elsewhere.[89] The civilian agencies involved in pacification also wanted to regain control of their personnel and programs and recommended that CORDS be stripped of most of its responsibilities.[90] This proposal was not acted on but did not need to be as the terms of the 1973 Paris Peace Accords essentially prohibited CORDS existence.

The Peace Accords permitted a minimal US presence located in the Defense Attaché Office in Saigon but it could not provide advice or assistance to military operations.[91] No longer able to function, CORDS ceased operations in February of 1973.[92] The US Congress also began to reduce the amount of aid provided to the GVN, so the resources required to execute an expensive pacification program and upgrade the capabilities of ARVN were no longer available.[93] US support to pacification dwindled alongside the US support to ARVN and the GVN itself, finally expiring when the 1975 PAVN invasion ended the RVN.

US Ground Forces Role in Pacification

The GVN's pacification effort, and the broad US support of that effort, evolved significantly during the course of the war. The role of US ground forces in pacification also evolved, but not nearly as much as the pacification effort itself, the change to a one war strategy under Abrams in 1969 notwithstanding. Westmoreland believed that the most appropriate use of US ground forces in 1965 and 1966 was to locate and destroy the VC and PAVN main force units that threatened the very survival of the

RVN.⁹⁴ This remained the primary mission of US ground forces throughout the war.

The 1967 Combined Campaign Plan stated that "the primary responsibility of US/FWMAF was to seek out and destroy VC/NVA main force units, base areas, and LOCs."⁹⁵ Despite the changed dynamic of the war following the Tet Offensive and the increased emphasis on pacification operations, US ground forces were still directed to focus on enemy main force units as late as 1971. The *Territorial Security in Vietnam* handbook published by Military Assistance Command, CORDS in January 1971 noted, "the best method of protecting the people is to deny the enemy access to populated areas. . . . Preventing main forces from reaching the population is the task of ARVN, US, and FWMAF units."⁹⁶

While this emphasis on the enemy main force units has drawn criticism, it was in fact critical if pacification was to achieve any success. As discussed above, the pacification strategy required sustained security in the countryside before the other activities could proceed. Observing US ground force operations in the Mekong Delta in 1966-1967, a pair of American researchers reported that there was an "inextricable connection between the 'search and destroy' and the 'pacification' tasks. If one failed, the other would also be doomed to failure."⁹⁷

While the importance of US ground force operations against VC and PAVN main force units was clear, it was not sufficient to win the war. The researchers in the Mekong Delta observed that for the Front "the relationship between armed force and territorial control is complex. Initially, armed force is used to break the control of the opposition. . . . The armed units, in turn, protect the political apparatus, and enable it to consolidate and further expand its control."⁹⁸ This complex relationship was true for the GVN and its allies as well. US operations against main force units could achieve only so much, pacification had to follow in their wake and US manuals recognized as much. The 1968 MAC-V *Pacification Handbook* stated that "operations to annihilate the enemy while clearly essential to pacification are, by themselves, inadequate."⁹⁹

This recognition meant that US forces would not be limited to conducting search and destroy operations. The 1966 *Handbook for US Forces in Vietnam* instructed that "US and Free World Forces of approximately brigade size may often be deployed into a province, or even a district, for sustained operations over two, three, or four week periods designed to destroy local and guerrilla forces and the political and military infrastructure of the VC."¹⁰⁰ At their conclusion, these operations were supposed to have accomplished a number of objectives, including: the destruction of village and hamlet VC elements, increased opportunities for civic action, and improved GVN control of the area.[101]

The operations described above were part of a two-phase strategy to provide the security required for pacification. In the first phase, US ground forces and ARVN would clear the area of VC and PAVN main force units and VC guerrilla forces.[102] They would then conduct patrols, establish outposts, and destroy any remaining VC local forces.[103] Then, the Vietnamese territorial security forces assumed responsibility for securing the area.[104] After they did so, US and ARVN forces would move to another area to begin the process again.

Unfortunately, as soon as US and ARVN forces left the area, VC units often began operating in them again. The problem was identified in the Mekong Delta where it was noted that the implication of the US strategy for the Viet Cong was obvious in that "their military units, even Main Force units, should not directly challenge the US troops, but should strike in relatively undefended areas, and force the opposing troops to spread themselves thin."[105] This strategy meant that US ground forces would spend the majority of their time simply trying to locate and engage PAVN and VC forces throughout the war.

While the 1968 Tet Offensive and the new strategy of Vietnamization dramatically altered the course of pacification and US support of it, it did not significantly change the role of US ground forces. US units did conduct an increasing number of joint operations and spent more time executing small unit operations but the emphasis remained on keeping the main force units away from the populated areas. In fact, as pacification progressed and the Vietnamization process accelerated it could be argued that US ground forces became even less involved in pacification.

This shift resulted from the need to transition responsibility for confronting VC and PAVN from US ground forces to ARVN. By 1970 the GVN was making a concerted effort to "to alleviate division commander's territorial responsibilities and to permit them to concentrate more on mobile tactical operations since divisions were to gradually take over combat responsibilities from the departing US forces."[106] Therefore, even when US ground forces were conducting combined operations with Vietnamese forces they were most often doing so in order to prepare ARVN for combat operations against main force units. This left pacification in the hands of GVN cadre teams, territorial security forces, and US advisers.

Moreover, US ground forces were gradually being withdrawn from across Vietnam beginning in 1969. This meant that each remaining US unit was responsible for a much larger area of operations, further reducing its ability to dedicate forces to provide security for pacification. When major operations were conducted, such as the 1970 invasion of Cambodia, US units participated at a high rate and left few, if any, forces behind to support pacification.[107]

US ground force support to pacification throughout the war was, therefore, always relatively limited. However, the task that it performed was critical. A Vietnamese observer of pacification noted that "while US forces did not always participate in pacification operations, their powerful combat support assets and intervention capabilities directly contributed to the clearing of several pacification areas. Their most significant effectiveness was the destruction of enemy bases and lines of communication."[108]

This was echoed by Robert Komer, the first head of CORDS, who observed that "it is hard to assess the *relative* extent to which undoubted changes in the countryside can be properly attributed to the *pacification* program as opposed to other factors. How much is attributable to the shield provided by the allied effort in the 'big unit' war, which largely drove the VC/NVA main forces from most populated areas?"[109] That being said, it is also difficult to assess how pacification affected the fight against VC and PAVN main force units. The American researchers in the Mekong Delta reported that "if Local Force battalions and companies can be kept out of an area, the entry of heavy Main Force battalions becomes more risky for the Viet Cong, and small unit pacification operations can be conducted with greater freedom, which can curtail the movement of critical cadres."[110]

In other words, if pacification activities were occurring, disrupting the operation of VC political cadres, this would deny VC local forces and guerrillas the ability to operate in an area. This in turn limited the ability of main force units to enter the area. The main force war and pacification cannot be separated. Therefore, US ground force units, though not always executing pacification tasks per se, were supporting pacification through their actions against VC and PAVN main forces.

Population and Resource Control Measures in Support of Pacification

Given the limited role of US ground forces in support of pacification, it could be concluded that population and resource control measures would not have been useful. However, in addition to their primary role of fighting the enemy's main forces, US ground forces also participated in clear and secure operations in support of pacification. For these operations to be successful, US ground forces had to target and destroy not only the main force units in the area, but the VC local and guerrilla units as well.

Moreover, because of the relationship between the effectiveness of VC local and guerrilla forces and the ease with which VC and PAVN main force units could then operate in any specific area it was necessary to disrupt VC local forces and infrastructure to protect the population from main force threats. The statement of a former VC cadre from the Duc Hoa district in Hau Nghia province about local supply operations supports this contention. He reported that:

> Cash taxes were forwarded to higher headquarters but rice taxation was kept by the finance section of the village committee and stored in 'safe' peoples' houses. When combat units passed through the village they simply requisitioned rice from the finance section. People were also expected to keep one jar of rice for the village guerrillas and one bushel of paddy in reserve to sell to mobile units when necessary. Thus our military units had many advantages. They didn't have to carry rice and could carry more ammo. They also didn't have to warn a village in advance of their arrival and thus safeguarded the security of operations.[111]

The ability of all levels of VC forces, as well as the PAVN main forces, to disappear into the dense jungle of South Vietnam also made gathering intelligence on the location of the enemy of paramount importance. This could not be accomplished without the support of the population, who knew if PAVN or VC units were passing through the area and requisitioning supplies. Therefore, population and resource control measures could be a useful tool to target and disrupt the local, guerrilla, and main force units.

In practice most of the standard population and resource control measures such as issue of identification cards, census operations, curfews, movement controls, were employed by Vietnamese government or military personnel.[112] These actions generally occurred after an area had been cleared and US ground forces had departed but US units did sometimes support ARVN units as they implemented population and resource control measures. Moreover, US ground forces employed a variety of tactics and techniques which could be considered population and resource control measures.[113]

Cordon and Search

Cordon and search operations were a corollary of the more widely known search and destroy operations. In a cordon and search operation, a US unit, usually in conjunction with ARVN and territorial security forces, would surround a given area, perhaps a hamlet, a known safe haven, or even an entire village, and systematically search the area for VC personnel, supplies, or physical infrastructure. Suspicious personnel were interrogated, supplies confiscated or destroyed, and physical infrastructure disabled.[114]

This tactic was described as a "search and seizure" operation in the 1963 Army FM 31-16, *Counterguerrilla Operations*.[115] The manual stated that it could be used to "apprehend guerrilla force members, and uncover and seize illegal arms, communication means, medicines, and other items of a critical nature. A search and seizure operation may be conducted at any time and may be used as a preventive measure against the possible accumulation of critical items by the population."[116] Viewed as a means to prevent the population from storing supplies for the enemy and therefore as a method to target their behavior and isolate them from the insurgents it is clear that cordon and search operations were a population and resource control measure.

US units also conducted cordon and searches with Vietnamese forces to execute Hamlet Festival, Go Team, or County Fair operations.[117] In these operations, US and ARVN units cordoned a selected hamlet and then Vietnamese forces would search the hamlet and identify residents for screening by intelligence personnel. The remaining residents were then gathered together and propagandized. The primary intent of the propaganda was to assure the people of the GVN's concern for their well being.[118]

The operations differed in that the Hamlet Festival would be conducted in area where the security presence was intended to be permanent, while the GO TEAM and COUNTY FAIR operations were executed in areas where security presence would be temporary. Therefore, upon completion of all of the other activities in a Hamlet Festival the residents would be issued identification cards and family books.[119] This action initiated the implementation of other population and resource control measures but these were not employed by US forces.

In addition to providing the initial cordon element, US ground forces might also provide humanitarian supplies and medical treatment. The intent of such operations was to separate the population psychologically from the VC and garner support for the GVN. Though US units did not perform many of the tasks associated with these operations, they were an essential part of the population and resource control measures employed.

Terrain Denial and Terrain Transformation

The terrain in South Vietnam often provided cover and concealment for enemy forces to rest, re-fit, and store supplies. This was especially true in areas of dense jungle such as the Ho Bo and Boi Loi Woods near Saigon or the swamps of the Plain of Reeds along the Cambodian border west of Saigon. United States units employed techniques to deny VC and PAVN units the ability to use these areas freely. If this did not work, US forces attempted to completely alter the terrain to make it unusable as a sanctuary area.

Terrain denial usually employed Harassment and Interdiction (HI) fires. HI consisted of unobserved artillery fires onto known and suspected enemy base and supply areas.[120] The intent was to prevent these areas from being used, not only by the enemy but also by the population.[121] While it was difficult to assess the effectiveness of HI fires, they were undoubtedly a population control measure as they forced the complete evacuation of an area by civilian personnel, a recognized technique in the counterguerrilla field manual.[122]

Terrain transformation was terrain denial taken to its extreme logical conclusion. Terrain transformation operations "involved the use of heavy bulldozers to level bunkers, trees, and destroy underground shelters during a period of several months."[123] United States units also used napalm or other incendiary materials to burn the foliage or airborne defoliants such as Agent Orange in these areas to deny the enemy the ability to operate under the concealment provided by the jungle canopy.[124] Such operations therefore completely altered the prevailing terrain conditions and forced the complete evacuation of the areas where they were employed.

Movement Control

Standard movement control measures, such as controlling the passage of civilians in and out of secured hamlets, were used mostly by Vietnamese forces. United States forces did employ some such measures in areas outside of those controlled by GVN forces. One example was "Checkmate" operations in which US units would establish road blocks and conduct random searches of vehicles to prevent the transportation of VC supplies and personnel.[125] The intent of such operations was to deny the VC freedom of movement in and around the area of operations. It also targeted the behavior of those members of the population who either supported the VC or were forced to support the VC and prevent them from transporting supplies and materiel.

United States units also enforced movement control by executing patrol operations in areas where clearing operations had been recently performed. Saturation patrolling, in which a large number of small patrols was sent out into a specified area, in combination with the establishment of outposts or ambushes, was used to deny enemy forces the ability to infiltrate into or exfiltrate out of the cleared area.[126] The primary purpose of such operations was to provide security to the population and the pacification effort. However, they could also deny Communist supporters the ability to provide assistance to nearby VC or PAVN units and provided US units a means to target them. Therefore, such operations were another means of implementing population and resource control.

Civic Actions

United States units also employed various civic actions as a means of population and resource control. The most common civic actions performed by US units were the Medical Civic Action Programs or MEDCAPS.[127] During MEDCAPS, US units would provide medical care to the population either as a standalone operation or as part of a combined cordon and search operation. They were intended to connect the US unit to the population, provide the opportunity to collect intelligence, and continue the process of separating the population psychologically from the Front and the VC.

Similar to MEDCAPS were US civic action programs in which US units provided basic humanitarian supplies such as food and clothing to the population or assisted villagers to dig wells or build sanitation facilities.[128] These operations are referenced in the counterguerrilla manual and US units are instructed to be prepared to conduct them, though not specifically as a means of population and resource control.[129] However, like MEDCAPs, such actions were undertaken to psychologically separate the population from the VC and gave them the opportunity to support the counterinsurgent forces through the provision of intelligence. Viewed in this manner, they can be considered population and resource control measures.

25th Infantry Division Campaign in Vietnam

The operations of the 25th Infantry Division (25ID), known as the "Tropic Lightning," are an interesting case study through which to examine the use of population and resource control measures by US ground combat units in Vietnam.[130] The division deployed to Vietnam fairly early in the war, 1966, and remained in Vietnam through much of 1970. The division thus experienced all the major events associated with the US ground combat intervention in Vietnam, which provides a rich body of experiences to examine. It also permits an assessment of how changes in leadership and policy above the division level affected the operations of tactical units.

Moreover, unlike many other units deployed to Vietnam, the division operated primarily in the same geographic area. This provides an opportunity to determine how, if at all, the division altered its operations over time in response to changes in that area. That this area encompassed the strategically important region north and west of Saigon to the Cambodian border and a number of critical Communist base and supply areas such as the Ho Bo Woods, the Plain of Reeds, and the Iron Triangle makes the division's experiences all the more important to study.

1966–1968 Tet Offensive

The Tropic Lightning deployed to Vietnam in phases during the first four months of 1966.[131] As soon as it arrived, the division began conducting combat operations in the provinces surrounding its base camp, located at Cu Chi in Hau Nghia province. Hau Nghia[132] was a major focal point for the US and GVN war effort because of its closeness to Saigon and the critical role it played in supporting Communist forces. Its favorable terrain and position on the border with Cambodia had made it "a passageway for insurgent men and material bound for other parts of Vietnam."[133] Moreover, because of the population's favorable disposition towards the VC "whole insurgent units of battalion size can be moved through the area intact."[134]

When the division arrived in Hau Nghia in 1966, the Front and the VC were in control of the area and their armed forces were superior to the ARVN and territorial forces in the province. The Front had established a political apparatus that was supported by the majority of the population and VC attacks and intimidation had either silenced or forced into government outposts the few GVN officials and security forces that were operating in the province.[135] The Cu Chi district in Hau Nghia had also been a part of Operation SUNRISE, one of the Diem regime's early executions of the Strategic Hamlet Program.[136] The program was not well executed in the area and this had further strengthened the insurgency.

The division therefore confronted multiple challenges in Hau Nghia and the surrounding provinces. The first was to clear the area of any PAVN and VC main force units that could threaten the population and Saigon. Then it would have to destroy the VC local and guerrilla units that provided the force that allowed the VC political apparatus to control the population. Once these had been destroyed, the division had to provide security to allow the GVN pacification process to take hold and end the enemy's control of the population. Simultaneously, the division had to deny VC and PAVN forces the ability to use the Ho Bo, Boi Loi Woods, and Filhol Plantation areas as a supply point, and the entire region as a transportation corridor for the movement of men and materiel.

Pre-deployment Training

The division was based in Hawaii and as a result had always figured prominently in contingency plans for intervention in Vietnam.[137] It took advantage of the terrain in Hawaii to prepare for operations in the tropical jungles of Vietnam:

> It constructed 12 SE Asia type 'villages' located throughout the training area. These villages were used by units during counterinsurgency training exercises from company through brigade level. Village search techniques, civic action and community relations activities received equal consideration with combat operations in the planning of major unit exercises.[138]

The division also established a Special Warfare and Orientation Center that included jungle, guerrilla warfare, and small unit counterinsurgency training facilities.[139] When the division was alerted to deploy it put each brigade through "an accelerated training program with emphasis on tactics and techniques particular to the type of enemy to be encountered in Vietnam."[140] Robert Conner, a junior enlisted man who trained with the division in 1966, observed that "the jungle warfare training in Hawaii helped tremendously."[141] As the division remained in Vietnam it was filled by replacements who did not receive the same pre-deployment training and Conner noted that "they didn't have enough time to train and become soldiers."[142]

While the division's pre-deployment training concentrated on combat operations, it also included time spent conducting civic actions and operations near to the population. To this end, the division executed an accelerated Vietnamese language training course which produced 48 personnel who were qualified in speaking and reading.[143] The division also initiated Operation HELPING HAND, which collected over 350 tons of "clothing, health and sanitation items, basic work items, children's items, and miscellaneous items such as milk and canned goods" from the residents of Hawaii for the division to distribute during civic action programs.[144]

As a result of its training the division was well positioned to confront the challenges presented to it in Vietnam. The division commander, Major General Fred Weyand, had tried to balance its preparation between combat operations against PAVN and VC main forces and the small unit counterinsurgency and counterguerrilla operations that would necessarily take place within the villages. Unfortunately, the division's training would only be a benefit in the village war if the tactical situation and directives from its higher headquarters allowed it to fight in this manner. Furthermore, this training would benefit only the initial contingent of Tropic Lightning soldiers who deployed to Vietnam. The many replacements that filled the division's ranks over the years would receive only the standard training provided by the Army.

Early Operations

The division's mission upon arrival in Vietnam consisted of a number of parts. The first three give an indication of the priorities assigned to the division by its higher headquarters, II Field Force, Vietnam (IIFFORCEV). The division's mission was to:

(a) Conduct search and destroy operations against VC/NVA forces and base camps in TAOR [tactical area of responsibility].

(b) Conduct search and destroy operations against VC/NVA forces and base camps outside of assigned TAOR in accordance with operation schedules now in effect and to be put into effect by IIFFORCEV.

(c) Conduct clearing operations and reserve reaction operations in support of III Corps GVN Revolutionary Development Program with emphasis on the national priority areas in Hau Nghia Province.[145]

The division was therefore directed to focus primarily on combat operations against VC and PAVN main force units. Though pacification support was listed, the division was to support it through clearing operations and "coordination of civic action and psychological operations."[146] This was despite the fact that Weyand and other leaders in the division understood the importance of the political struggle in Hau Nghia and the surrounding areas.[147]

The division's initial operations would conform exactly to the above priorities. Its first major operation[148] was Operation CIRCLE PINES from 30 March to 4 April 1966. The operation "was a search and destroy operation in conjunction with III ARVN Corps to locate and destroy VC forces and base camps in the FILHOL plantation."[149] Four battalions conducted a detailed search of the area, making the operation more like a cordon and search than a search and destroy, and captured a significant amount of supplies and munitions, including over 57 tons of rice.[150]

The division executed four more battalion or larger search and destroy operations over the course of the next month, none of which produced as much in the way of captured supplies as Circle Pines had. This pattern would seem to support the conclusion that from 1966 to 1967 US ground force operations were almost entirely based on Westmoreland's strategy of attrition.[151] However, the last operation reported during the division's first quarterly Operational Report–Lessons Learned (ORLL) challenges this conclusion, if only modestly.

Near the end of April, the 1st Battalion, 27th Infantry began execution of Operation MAILI. The battalion established a temporary base of operation near Duc Lap village and conducted search and destroy operations with Vietnamese units to clear hamlets within the village.[152] The operation in the village was supported by one company from another battalion that established blocking positions along the Oriental River to interdict VC supply lines into the area.[153] The division also executed several MEDCAPS and distributed aid items as part of Operation HELPING HAND. The division stated that Maili was "a determined effort to pacify an area using an American infantry battalion in conjunction with Vietnamese forces over a two to three week period."[154]

The operation lasted just two weeks but the division reported that "initial results have been gratifying in that many of the local populace is returning to the villages."[155] Unlike in reports on other operations, the division did not highlight the number of enemy casualties that had been recorded. Moreover, in the section of the ORLL dedicated to analysis by the commander, Weyand noted that "although the operations [like Maili] are not spectacular by the standard of VC body count, this combined effort is highly successful. In one such operation, a hamlet of 10 families became one of thirty families. Such actions as this, disrupts and eventually destroys the VC infrastructure."[156]

The technique of combining search operations, movement controls, civic actions, and temporary occupation of an area appeared to be effective in the short term. However, despite the commander's analysis, no effort was made by the division to target the Front's infrastructure. Therefore, without consistent US or ARVN presence PAVN and VC main and local force units could easily return to the area. The change in control suggested by the population shift was only temporary and, as with so many other units in Vietnam, the division would have to return time and again to the area.

The Tropic Lightning primarily executed battalion and larger search and destroy operations through 1966 and into 1967. The quarterly report spanning the period from February to April 1967 recorded the division's execution of four major operations, all search and destroy missions.[157] These operations produced varying degrees of success. When the operations were conducted in known VC supply base areas, such as Operation MANHATTAN in the Ho Bo and Boi Loi Woods area, searches resulted in the capture or destruction of large amounts of supplies. In the case of Manhattan, the division reported that over 15 tons of rice, hundreds of rounds of mortar ammunition, and more than 100,000 rounds of small arms ammunition were captured in just the first seven days.[158] Operations that were not in such areas produced few tangible results.

Overall, 25ID's search and destroy operations produced little contact with VC and PAVN main force units, which was their essential purpose. In March 1967 it commented that contact with enemy forces "was with small enemy elements from three to six men, left behind to harass US Forces."[159] The division recognized this problem and in the lessons learned section of the report recommended that units make a distinction between hasty and deliberate search operations.

The report observed that "generally, the Hasty Search Op is planned to move through an AO [area of operations] quickly to catch VC off guard. The Deliberate Search is planned with the idea of destroying VC food, supplies, equipment and fortifications."[160] Therefore, "the initial phase of an op should consist of Hasty Search of the entire AO preferably by the use of highly mobile units, such as Mech or Heliborne forces. Subsequent phases should employ phase lines which require units to do a thorough job prior to moving on."[161] Dividing an operation in this way gave the division a better chance of making contact with large enemy elements while still preserving its ability to destroy essential supplies. It continued to adapt its operations in this manner and began to employ more population and resource control measures as time went on.

In the report on operations for the months of May, June, and July 1967, the division noticeably increased its use of population and resource control measures. As part of the continuation of Operation MANHATTAN it employed the engineer battalion's "Rome Plows"[162] to clear vegetation in the area and deprive "the VC of the sanctuary they had long established throughout the area, especially in the Ho Bo and Boi Loi Woods."[163] The operation ultimately resulted in the capture or destruction of 250 tons of rice, 5.5 tons of other food stuffs, and a significant amount of weapons and munitions.[164]

The division recorded its first execution of a hamlet festival as part of a cordon and search and pacification operation called Akumu. During the festival, a Civil Affairs team "explained the purpose of the US presence in the village to over 19,000 persons. MEDCAPs . . . were held throughout the operation."[165] Similar to Maili, Operation AKUMU was limited in duration, lasting less than three weeks. Nonetheless, the division reported that it "challenged the VC in a formerly secure stronghold, and greatly diminished VC influence 'at the back door' of Camp Cu Chi. In addition VC supply and movement routes through the Filhol Plantation to the Ho Bo Woods were severely disrupted."[166]

It is difficult to determine how accurate that assessment is. It is almost certainly true that supply and movement were disrupted but the results of later operations in the area suggest that such disruption was minimal. Moreover, it is unlikely that the division appreciably reduced VC influence in such a short period of time, especially as it departed the area after the operation was complete. Akumu was, however, part of a much larger and more significant pacification effort, Operation BARKING SANDS.

BARKING SANDS began in May 1967 and continued through December 1967.[167] The operation was "conducted by the 1st Brigade, 25th Infantry Division for the pacification of Cu Chi and Trang Bang Districts in Hau Nghia Province and in PHU HOA District of Binh Duong Province."[168] The operation emphasized the execution of small unit operations to include saturation patrols, "Checkmates," and company cordon and searches.[169] The division believed that the initial phase of the operation had limited the ability of the VC to operate freely and "therefore VC control of the AO has been reduced."[170] A subordinate operation to clear the Ho Bo Woods, Operation KUNIA, was begun in September 1967.

KUNIA expanded on the initial use of Rome Plows to clear vegetation that had occurred during MANHATTAN. The objective of KUNIA was "to eliminate the Ho Bo Woods as a safe haven for the VC through extensive clearing operations and destruction of VC base camps and forces."[171] By the end of the reporting period in October, the division recorded that 9,645 acres of the Ho Bo Woods had been cleared of vegetation.[172] Where MANHATTAN could be considered a terrain denial operation, KUNIA went the next step and was a terrain transformation operation. After clearing the Ho Bo Woods, the division continued KUNIA in the Filhol Plantation during the final months of 1967.[173]

In addition to the terrain transformation operations conducted by the Rome Plows, the division was also executing terrain denial using HI artillery fires. In the quarterly period ending in October 1967, over 124,000 rounds of artillery were fired in support of HI missions.[174] Just over 26,000 rounds were expended during the period ending in January 1968.[175] It is not clear what caused the reduction in HI fires. However, it is possible that the terrain transformation of KUNIA reduced the need for HI fires on known supply areas such as the Ho Bo Woods and Filhol Plantation.

Terrain transformation operations generally coincided with search operations that captured large amounts of supplies. Therefore, they did produce an effect on the enemy's ability to stockpile materiel in that area for a time. However, the division had to return to these areas repeatedly in the coming years either to re-clear the vegetation or to search for supplies so it is unlikely that the effect was long lasting.

The unobserved artillery fires used for terrain denial are even less easy to assess. Firing at known and suspected VC positions may have disrupted operations for a time but given the extensive tunnel and bunker networks found during division clearing operations, it is unlikely that the disruption was severe. The division did report that HI fires during the day on suspected mortar firing positions reduced mortar attacks against US bases.[176] They did not halt them, however.

In support of its pacification and search and destroy operations 25ID continued to execute civic action programs. Hundreds of MEDCAPS were conducted during each reporting period and the initial 350 tons of supplies dedicated to Operation HELPING HAND were exhausted in late 1967.[177] Assessments of such operations were always positive. The division reported that "the entire Helping Hand concept was extremely worthwhile and has gone a long way toward winning the 'other war' in Vietnam."[178] Because health care in rural Vietnam was so poor, MEDCAPS were "especially beneficial to the local population living in US areas of operation."[179]

It is not obvious how HELPING HAND was assisting the division to win the support of the population, other than to note that giving away materials and supplies was very popular.[180] Nor is it clear what affect MEDCAPS, which soldiers liked and believed relieved significant amounts of suffering, were having on the process of pacification.[181] Notably, the VC did not attack MEDCAPS. The division reported that "although a definite pattern was established there have been no VC incidents at any of the scheduled MEDCAPS."[182] The lack of attacks could indicate that the Front did not believe that MEDCAPS and other civic actions threatened their control of the population as the Strategic Hamlet Program had.

The Tropic Lightning's operations continued to produce little contact with the VC and PAVN main force units. From August to October 1967 it made no contact with PAVN units and observed that "VC activity consisted primarily of efforts to delay allied clearing operations."[183] The same delaying tactics were reported during the end of 1967 and beginning of 1968.[184] Given the huge amounts of rice that were captured, over 133 tons during BARKING SANDS alone, it is not surprising that the VC attempted to delay cordon and search and terrain transformation operations for as long as possible so that supplies could be evacuated.[185] However, it also appears that they were following the pattern observed in the Mekong Delta of avoiding contact with superior US units and firepower and thereby forcing the Tropic Lightning to spread itself thin.

Moreover, despite the division's reported success in all of its operations, they had yet to allow the GVN to establish control over any part of its area of operations. It reported that as of the end of October 1967 "the RD programs in the designated hamlets are behind the projected time schedule."[186] Yet it believed that the VC's guerrilla forces were finding it more difficult to gain support from the population.[187] The enemy's next action would put that claim to the test.

Tet 1968–1969

The Party, supported by the Front and PAVN and VC units, launched its general offensive and general uprising at the end of January 1968. The offensive completely disrupted all pacification efforts and operations in support of pacification as US and ARVN units were deployed across the country to defeat the attack. RD Cadre had to be withdrawn from their hamlets to the relative safety of the district headquarters.[188] IIFFORCEV recorded in its after action report (AAR) for the Tet Offensive that the "VC penetrated about 50 percent of the hamlets pacified during the 1967 campaign."[189]

It is arguable that any of these areas were actually pacified to begin with. In the AAR, IIFFORCEV assessed that:

> The enemy moved sizeable groups of personnel and significant materiel support into Saigon and other critical areas before the offensive began. Friendly forces were not warned of these actions by the local population which was either indifferent to the enemy's presence, supported him passively, or was afraid of enemy reprisal in the event his presence was disclosed.[190]

This was despite IIFFORCEV's analysis that VC terrorism in the months before the offensive had increased because "the VC political infrastructure was losing its influence over key sectors of the population."[191]

Such a belief was common. A number of captured VC documents in the months before Tet were assessed by US intelligence as showing a definite loss of VC control over the population.[192] Recall also that 25ID believed that the VC guerrilla forces were no longer able to garner significant support from the population in late 1967. Yet it is likely the case that the Communists were able to move the bulk of the supplies to support the attack on Saigon directly through the division's area of operations.[193] However, these contradictions also produced better analysis as units examined conditions in their areas before the Tet Offensive through the lens of what had occurred during it.

The 25ID observed in its report for the period ending on January 31, 1968 that "the large number of attacks by fire [at the end of the reporting period] are believed to have been conducted to cover the movement of VC forces to the Saigon area and to cause as many casualties and as much damage as possible."[194] If such improved analysis continued it might be possible for the division to adjust its operations to better support pacification. Before it could do so, however, the Tet Offensive had to be defeated.

Operations During Tet

When the Tet Offensive began, the division was executing its 1967-1968 Dry Season Campaign. The major component of which was Operation SARATOGA, begun in December 1967.[195] SARATOGA was intended "to pacify 25th Infantry Division's TAOI [Tactical Area of Operational Interest] in the provinces; to secure that portion of the allied base area in the Division TAOI; to prevent VC rice taxation, harvesting, or transportation within the Division TAOI; and to destroy VC/NVA forces within the Division TAOI."[196] The operation was very similar in execution to BARKING SANDS. This is not surprising given how successful the division believed BARKING SANDS had been.

Once the Tet Offensive began, however, the division suspended Saratoga. Instead it mounted counteroffensive operations from 1 February to 10 March 1968 to defeat VC and PAVN attacks around Saigon.[197] The battle in Saigon was largely defeated by the middle of February, but the division continued to fight hard in the area surrounding it into March.[198] As enemy units began to retreat from Saigon, 25ID transitioned and began executing major search and destroy operations with ARVN forces from 11 March to 22 April in attempt to engage the fleeing enemy.[199] On 7 April, it initiated a new operation, TOAN THANG (Complete Victory).

The mission of the Tropic Lighting in TOAN THANG was to "complete destruction of enemy battalions and company sized units, prevent infiltration of major forces from the western zone"[200] and "conduct combined offensive operation in conjunction with 25th and 5th ARVN Infantry Divisions throughout TAOI to destroy enemy forces with priority to elements of 7th NVA and 9th VC Divisions."[201] The only operations in support of pacification that would be conducted under TOAN THANG were MEDCAPS and civic actions. All other operations were suspended to focus resources on the destruction of the PAVN and VC main force units.

TOAN THANG generated a much greater amount of contact with large enemy elements than any of the division's operations had to that point. 3rd Battalion, 22d Infantry defeated an attack against its night perimeter on 12 April by a battalion sized enemy force, killing over 150 enemy personnel and capturing more than 40 AK-47s and 10 crew-served weapons.[202] However, this may have been more the result of PAVN and VC main force units using Hau Nghia and the surrounding areas as a staging point for a second offensive against Saigon and their insistence on attacking superior US units than because of the effective execution of operations by the Tropic Lightning.[203]

The division's units were repositioned around Saigon in the last week of April to defeat the Communist offensive against Saigon that was expected to begin on 1 May.[204] The offensive was quickly defeated and VC and PAVN main force units began retreating through the 25ID's area of operations, by 15 May the division's units "were now employed to pursue the fleeing enemy."[205] On that day 3d Squadron, 4th Cavalry intercepted a VC local force battalion and decimated its remaining numbers, killing 82 and capturing three.[206]

Such contacts continued throughout the month. Whereas previous operations had most often encountered only a handful of enemy personnel at a time, the division's units were now making contact with platoons, companies, and even battalions.[207] Each encounter resulted in the killing of dozens of enemy personnel. By the end of May, the division recorded a total of more than 2,200 confirmed enemy dead.[208] It had taken an all out enemy offensive to provide the division the opportunity to confront and defeat large enemy forces, what it had been sent to Vietnam to do over two years earlier.

Operation TOAN THANG, Phase II

The damage inflicted by the Tropic Lightning and ARVN on the Communist forces during May was severe. In June the PAVN and VC:

Main force units that remained outside SAIGON broke contact, dispersed and ex-filtrated west into (illegible) and northwest in WAR ZONE C [located along the Cambodian border in Tay Ninh province]. In executing this pull back the enemy avoided contact and when engaged was quick to disperse into smaller groups and disengage as quickly as possible. Intelligence sources clearly indicated the enemy's intent of withdrawing his depleted main force units to those traditional sanctuaries for replacements, resupply and retraining for future operations.[209]

As they did so, the division ended Operation TOAN THANG, Phase I and began execution of Operation TOAN THANG, Phase II.

TOAN THANG had become the division's primary operation and thus provided a framework for all other subordinate operations. While some elements of the division remained outside of Saigon, the remainder of its combat power was dispersed throughout its area of operations to "pursue the dispersed enemy and to seek out and destroy his concealed weapons, ammunition and supply caches."[210] As the operation developed, the subordinate units of the division were given further tasks and more specific guidance.

The 2d Brigade was designated to execute TOAN THANG, Phase II in Hau Nghia, Gia Dinh, Binh Duong, and Tay Ninh provinces. The brigade listed eight specific tasks under its mission statement for the operation. The first of which was to "frustrate enemy plans, locate and destroy VC/NVA forces, base camps and support areas."[211] This task represents no change from mission statements for operations before Tet. However, tasks four and five were to execute the pacification program and target the Viet Cong infrastructure.[212]

These tasks represented a partial shift in the focus of US ground force operations. Unfortunately, what exactly the unit was meant to do to execute them was not at all clear. There was no specific guidance on how the pacification program was to be supported and no direction on the means to target the Viet Cong infrastructure. The concept of operations statement provides a good idea of just how much emphasis the new tasks would actually receive. It stated that the brigade "conducted combined and unilateral offensive operations within the TAOI to pre-empt VC/NVA initiatives, to interdict his lines of communications and to counter enemy initiatives."[213]

It is revealing that the concept of operations statement makes reference to the enemy's initiatives twice in a short sentence. The Tet Offensive had been a severe shock to many in US ground units. Ron Hart, who served in a mechanized infantry unit that was part of the 25ID during Tet, recalled that "we all knew when we returned from the field in late January that things were going to be quiet in Tay Ninh base camp. After all, this was Tet, the Vietnamese new year celebration. We were wrong."[214] The division was determined not to be caught by surprise again and yet, most operations after Tet looked much like those before it.

The 2d Brigade conducted search and destroy operations or cordon and search operations throughout its four provinces relentlessly from June 1968 to January 1969. Such operations yielded large amounts of destroyed or captured supplies, including over 150 tons of rice and tens of thousands of pounds of munitions.[215] They produced little contact with large enemy forces, however. In the summary of nearly every month of the operation the brigade reported that enemy contact was limited or that the enemy avoided contact.[216]

While 2d Brigade continued to seek out battles with the enemy main force units, 3d Brigade conducted operations intended mainly to secure the lines of communication within the division's area of operations. Its report of operations demonstrates little change in operations between pre and post Tet. At the beginning of October 1968, the brigade's units conducted local reconnaissance operations or searches.[217] As October continued, they cleared and established observations posts along main supply routes and then executed Rome Plow operations to remove the vegetation from those same routes.[218]

Accelerated Pacification Campaign?

On 1 November 1968, the APC was launched across Vietnam. The campaign was intended to reverse the massive loss of GVN control in the rural areas of Vietnam that was produced by the movement of US and ARVN units to defeat the Tet Offensive. The Tropic Lightning supported the campaign by creating Operation COLORS UP, a subordinate operation to TOAN THANG, Phase II. The objective of Colors Up was to bring every hamlet in the division's area of operation under some measure of GVN control by the end of January 1969.[219]

Unfortunately, the division reports for this period are largely incomplete or unavailable. However, the fragments that are available call into question how the division was actually supporting the campaign. The

ORLL ending 31 January 1969[220] stated that "throughout the reporting period, all divisional resources and assets were committed to Operation TOAN THANG which is directed at the destruction of Viet Cong/North Vietnamese (VC/NVA) main force units and enemy political and guerrilla infrastructure (VCI) operating within the divisional tactical area of operational interest."[221]

The division assessed that PAVN and VC main force units had withdrawn to sanctuary areas "to reorganize, refit, and retrain following the offensive against TAY NINH City in the August-September time frame."[222] In response to the division's mission and priorities and

In view of this general enemy situation, the 25th Infantry Division was deployed in a manner in which it could maintain continuous surveillance of the recognized lines of communications (LOC) and avenues of approach for enemy main force units from their sanctuary areas to known target areas: namely, SAIGON and TAY NINH.[223]

No mention is made in the initial pages of the report about how the division was supporting execution of the APC, nor is any mention made of Operation COLORS UP. The operations of 3d Brigade did not change in November 1968.[224] The 2d Brigade, however, should have been conducting operations to support the APC given its mission to execute pacification as part of TOAN THANG, Phase II.

The brigade did not mention any operations specifically in support of the campaign in the main body of the AAR.[225] However, the commander reported that:

> During the TOAN THANG Campaign Phase II, intensified Civic Actions and Psychological Operations were conducted, particularly during the Accelerated Pacification Campaign from 1 November 1968-17 February 1969. The Civic Action Program was directed toward short range, high impact projects . . . and designed to involve the Vietnamese people in the effort on a self help basis. Our purpose was to improve the general well-being of the populace and to clearly demonstrate the interest of the GVN to the people.[226]

Of the civic actions that the brigade performed the commander assessed that MEDCAPs were the most effective.[227]

It is hard to determine just how effective such civic actions were in bringing the population under the government's control. A lieutenant who served with the 1st Battalion, 27th Infantry commented that in November 1968 "civic action was then in its good works phase–we bring you food, clothing medicine–and we convinced the inhabitants of Co

Trach [a hamlet in the district of Tri Tram] that it was in their interest to profess friendliness at least; the inhabitants of another hamlet were not so receptive."[228] This observation presents such operations as little more than a bribe that might or might not be accepted. Moreover, 25ID had been conducting similar actions since the very beginning of its time in country and the Tet Offensive revealed that these had not produced much in the way of government control of the population.

The 2d Brigade commander recognized the difficulty that the division was having with pacification operations. His final recommendation as a result of Toan Thang II was that:

> All operations must be oriented toward the existing pacification program. Pacification must not be overlooked even when the emphasis switches to strike rather than consolidation operations. Experience indicates that it is extremely difficult to reinforce a pacification program that has been supported then suddenly dropped for other tactical operations.[229]

This was the dilemma that was constantly presented to the Tropic Lightning. Pacification only worked if it was continuously supported, but doing so meant that the combat units dedicated to it could not be used to strike Communist units if and when they were located. As the war moved into 1969, the division tried to solve this dilemma and execute operations that would support all of its major objectives.

Tet 1969–1970

At the beginning of 1969, General Abrams, published a new campaign plan, the objective of which was protection of the population.[230] It was his assessment that the situation in Vietnam was now favorable to execute the one war strategy. Thus, pacification and the destruction of enemy main force units were no longer separate fights, but were officially part of a single campaign. The Nixon administration also introduced the strategy of Vietnamization in 1969.

The Pary and Front also adapted their strategy. As noted in the 25ID reports referenced above, the main force units had retreated to sanctuaries away from the operational areas of US units to rest, refit, and retrain after being badly hurt during the offensives in 1968. Despite the losses, they were determined to press ahead in their campaign and force the US to accept ceasefire conditions that required it to withdraw all forces from South Vietnam.[231]

To accomplish this goal meant that "both our military and political forces must be stronger than the remaining puppet army and administration, and this is possible only by annihilating, disintegrating and disrupting a major part of their infrastructure organization through the use of all forms of violence available in the hands of the masses."[232] In order to do so the Front leadership directed that "the basic task is to attack enemy posts, then gain control over the population. Control hamlets both in daytime and at night."[233]

The Tropic Lightning would have to change its operational pattern to support the new campaign from Abrams and the strategy of the new administration. It would also have to use its limited manpower across a larger area as time went on. Lastly, it had to do both of those while also defeating the coming PAVN and VC offensive which would test the division's ability to fight main forces and still provide protection to the population against attacks by local and guerrilla forces.

Operations in 1969

The initial thrust of the offensive began on 22 February 1969. Attacks were not nearly as spectacular as they had been during the previous year's offensive, but it cost 25ID a significant number of casualties and a large amount of embarrassment over the attack on its base camp at Cu Chi.[234] Nonetheless, the division reported several months later that it had defeated all of the enemy's attacks and inflicted heavy casualties in doing so.[235]

The enemy's renewed offensive focused the Tropic Lightning's operations in a new direction. Beginning in May 1969 the division recorded that it had:

Determined to pursue a three-fold objective aimed at preemption of any new enemy offensive moves. Through widespread reconnaissance missions and battlefield surveillance, the Division troops would detect, engage, and destroy enemy main force units through the rapid reinforcement of and application of massive firepower to every contact.[236]

Moreover, "pacification programs would be vigorously executed in order to further erode the enemy's physical and psychological strength. Special emphasis would be placed on the destruction of the Viet Cong Infrastructure."[237]

As the division adjusted to this new concept of operations, it continued to execute the missions that had been its basic means of population and resource control since arriving in Vietnam in 1966. The division reported that its operations during the month of May "were, for the most part, combat assaults, night combat patrols, counter VCI operations, reconnaissance-in-force, cordon and search, base camp defense and MEDCAPS."[238]

However, the effect of such operations improved because the decline in quality of Communist units as a result of losses in 1968 gave the division the opportunity to collect intelligence during such operations and act on it. It did so with deadly effect.

A combined cordon and search operation by 2d Brigade and ARVN in mid-May in Ap Giong hamlet led to the capture of a Front official from the Cu Chi district who disclosed the location of a VC local force company commander.[239] The brigade followed up on this information and conducted a raid on 26 May in which the C-20 local force company commander was killed. A document recovered on his body revealed the location of a meeting of all Viet Cong hamlet and district chiefs from Cu Chi set for 29 May. The resulting combined cordon and search killed 59 soldiers from the 3d Battalion, 268th NVA Regiment and "preempted the planned attack on the Trung Lap compound which was indicated by documents captured after the action."[240]

The effect of such operations on the Front's offensive was noticeable. In a document dated May 1969 the Current Affairs Committee C69 made exaggerated claims about the success of the spring offensive, especially against the Tropic Lightning.[241] However, it also observed significant weaknesses which were hampering the offensive. Specifically, it stated that "a number of local areas and units were unable to go into action when the climaxing phase started, and as a result, they failed to attack the enemy in time. We also failed to completely destroy enemy units."[242] Moreover, the committee noted that "very few enemy pacification personnel, Regional and Popular Forces troops, Village administrative officials, tyrants, or intelligence agents were eliminated."[243]

The committee blamed the weakness on a lack of comprehension of the importance of the spring offensive, a failure of fighting spirit, and local units relying on outside assistance.[244] It also stated that some local units did not:

Thoroughly understand the operating procedures and guidelines, such as concentrating forces to destroy enemy units, or dispersing troops to coordinate with guerrillas and the masses to frustrate the enemy pacification plan. The deployment and development of forces in districts and villages were not effective.[245]

Although the Communists blamed internal failings at the local level for the weakness of the 1969 spring offensive, the statements indicate that it may actually have been caused by the effectiveness of US and ARVN operations. The failure of fighting spirit was likely the result of the destruction that VC and PAVN units had been subjected to over the course of the last year and half. Local units expecting outside assistance could be an indicator that the supply system, which was reliant on local support, was under pressure because of pacification and population and resource control measures. Lastly, the failure of the offensive to eliminate members of the territorial security forces, pacification personnel, or government officials is potentially the result of increased security within the populated areas.

This assessment was confirmed in 25ID's area of operations by a document captured by the US 1st Infantry Division in June 1969. The document was signed by a cadre from the Rear Service Staff of the Party command for South Vietnam. The document recorded that:

> The activities of civilian labor teams, assault youth groups, and transportation units had been greatly reduced due to the large increase of allied operations and that the extensive use of armored vehicles, helicopters, air strikes and artillery by US/GVN forces had destroyed rice storage, animal and poultry and transportation and hospital areas. Pressure was also applied to these areas by a large number of successful ambushes.[246]

The effect of US and ARVN operations was not limited to the activities of PAVN and VC units, however. The increased security and isolation of the population, coupled with the death of many Viet Cong political cadre, had reduced the Front's control of the population. The captured document reported that Trang Bang district in Hau Nghia was an especially weak area and "the guerrilla movement had been slowly deteriorating due to a lack of cooperation by the local populace. The people refused to conceal troops, care for wounded soldiers, store rice or join civilian labor teams."[247]

Pacification appeared to be gaining momentum. The division recognized that its operations in May were somewhat out of balance and noted that it continued "to work towards a balanced mission of pacification, engagement of enemy main force units in heavy contact, and the continued upgrading of South Vietnamese units."[248] This desire, however, did not markedly alter the division's execution of operations or the population and resource control measures that it employed.

Terrain transformation and terrain denial operations continued. The division used Rome Plows to clear vegetation from major routes and to deny the enemy use of the Boi Loi Woods area.[249] The division also conducted 685 MEDCAPS and reported execution of a village festival in Trang Bang district during which it distributed, through its GVN partners, over 50,000 piasters and several thousand pounds of captured rice in a three day operation.[250] It subsequently observed that the village's security ratings had improved and believed that it would become secure during the coming months.[251]

While it is probably true that the village was more secure than it had been, it is unlikely that this three day operation had actually produced that effect. A document of instruction for VC cadre regarding the 1970 campaign noted that "spearhead elements and main force units in the sub-regions remained weak during combat.... The material resources problem has not yet been solved."[252] The Front assessed that these problems had allowed the GVN "to establish posts and watchtowers in a wide area. The enemy could not control the people, but he was able to recruit soldiers to replace his wounded and dead personnel and increase his troops strength. ... However, the enemy could accomplish a number of activities, and this made him more stubborn."[253]

Thus, GVN control over the countryside was improving because the Party and Front had been so badly hurt. Rural Vietnamese tended to support whichever side was stronger and offered the protection they desired. At this point during the war, that side appeared to be the GVN and its US allies. Exactly how much of this can be attributed to pacification and how much to the destruction of PAVN and VC elements is difficult to determine.

Operations in 1970

In response to the situation, 25ID focused on improving security in its area of operations in 1970. Its first ORLL during the new year noted that "while searching for main force units, Division elements sought every opportunity to annihilate local force units."[254] It also stated that it "stressed small unit operations, pacification, upgrading of ARVN/RF/PF/PSDF forces and security of lines of communications."[255]

While the emphasis on small unit actions represented a modest shift, the focus of operations remained the destruction of enemy units. Pacification and the improvement of the Vietnamese security forces were mentioned, but were presented as secondary to operations against PAVN and VC forces. Nonetheless, the division presented its actions as a new mode of operations, which it called protective reaction. The division stated that:

> Protective reaction refers to the type of combat operations used by Allied commanders against Communist forces in the Republic of Vietnam to provide for the security of his unit, his tactical area of operations and

the Vietnamese people. This is accomplished primarily by small unit reconnaissance patrols to locate the enemy, disrupt his movements and find his caches of arms, ammunition and rations.[256]

While this new mode of operations presents the protection of the Vietnamese people as part of its purpose, the actual operations themselves target enemy forces and supplies.

The small unit reconnaissance patrols cited above are in reality much the same as the operations the division previously conducted, but on a smaller scale. They focus on finding the enemy, akin to search and destroy, disrupting his movements, similar to Checkmates, and finding his supply stocks, the goal of a cordon and search. The division also recorded that "land clearing continued to be a valuable, viable means of denying the enemy his traditional sanctuaries and of destroying enemy booby traps while minimizing friendly losses. A total of 7,425 acres of land were cleared."[257] However, the division was forced to reduce its civic actions because of its expanded area of responsibility.[258]

The 25ID's emphasis on small unit operations and its employment of population and resource control measures was disrupted again when it participated in its last major operation of the war, the invasion of Cambodia in May 1970. It reported that "the 1st and 2d Brigades, 3d Brigade of the 9th Infantry Division and all maneuver battalions of the 25th Infantry Division played an integral part in the attack."[259] Bergerud characterizes participation in the invasion by US ground forces as a mistake despite its overall success.[260] However, the operation further changed the dynamic in 25ID's area of responsibility and completed the three phase approach that Westmoreland had envisioned for US ground combat forces in 1965.

After the invasion of Cambodia, division operations continued to follow the pattern established in previous reporting periods that did not include major combat operations. It was by now executing Operation TOAN THANG, Phase IV, and its report does not indicate a significant change to its standard operations. Though not explicitly stated, its operations appear to have consisted primarily of the small unit operations discussed above.

Moreover, the Tropic Lightning continued to employ the population and resource control measures that it had since arriving. Its engineer assets cleared several hundred acres in an abandoned village that contained booby traps and tunnels.[261] Its supporting artillery continued to fire tens of thousands of rounds in support of operations.[262] MEDCAPs remained the division's primary civic action program.

However, the results of the operations changed noticeably. It appeared that pacification was finally achieving great effect in Hau Nghia.[263] The division captured only 4.9 tons of rice in August and less than one ton in October.[264] Enemy activity was exceptionally low and the division reported that enemy forces "were experiencing severe difficulties in health and resupply operations and were forced to concentrate on the solution of these problems in lieu of combat operations."[265] It further recorded that its main contact was with PAVN and VC rear service elements and assessed that the enemy's main force units "appeared to be preoccupied with operations inside Cambodia."[266]

The huge reduction in captured supplies demonstrates that PAVN and VC supply points had finally been pushed out of the division's area of responsibility. However, it is not clear why this occurred. Certainly some of the reduction in supplies is the result of there no longer being large PAVN and VC units, whether main force or local force, in the area because of the division's successful operations during and after Tet and the invasion of Cambodia. The PAVN history of the war recounted that after the US campaign in the summer of 1969 "our main force army was forced to withdraw to our base areas to regroup. In the rural areas the strength of our local forces was seriously eroded."[267] It may also be the case that GVN control over the area had increased to the point where the population could no longer provide supplies in the quantities required to produce the massive stockpiles that were captured during 1966 and 1967. Again, the PAVN history of the war recounted that by September 1969 "they had only 2,000 tons of food in reserve. Units were forced to begin alternately eating rice for one meal and manioc for the next."[268] Moreover, it noted that the population was able to provide food, but not in significant quantities. It was only enough to "partially resolve their food supply shortage."[269] Which one of these two conditions is responsible for the greater part of the effect cannot be determined, however.

The Vietnamization strategy and the improving security situation allowed the 25ID and its subordinate units to begin withdrawing from Vietnam in the fall of 1970. The division's 1st and 3d Brigades returned to the US in November. The division handed over Cu Chi base camp to the ARVN 25th Division in December 1970. The 2d Brigade was the last to return home in 1971, but was under the control of IIFFORCEV after the division redeployed.[270]

As 25ID departed Vietnam it left behind an area of responsibility in which PAVN and VC main and local force units could no longer operate freely. ARVN and the territorial security forces seemed to be capable of continuing to secure the area given this condition. Outwardly, the GVN's control of the countryside appeared to be improving month by month. How deep this control went is not obvious, but the PAVN history of the war recorded that in the summer of the 1969 it had lost control of the majority of its supply areas in the lowlands of the Mekong Delta.[271] Moreover, the supply shortages noted above indicate that in some areas the GVN had assured at least the neutrality of the population through the pacification program. This was no small feat in an area that had heavily supported the insurgency before the arrival of the Tropic Lightning.[272]

Moreover, the area resisted Communist conquest right until the end of the war. The previously much derided ARVN 25th Division successfully counterattacked the 5th NVA Division in the fall of 1974 and drove it back across the Cambodian border.[273] The inheritors of the Tropic Lightning's base at Cu Chi were finally surrounded during the final drive for Saigon by the PAVN III Corps on 27 April 1975, just three days before the capital fell.[274] It is hard to believe that an area that had long been a major support area for PAVN and the VC could have resisted the onslaught for so long if the operations of the Tropic Lightning had not contributed to changing the conditions in it dramatically.

Analysis of 25ID Population and Resource Control Measures

The operations of the Tropic Lightning defy easy analysis. The division was constantly forced to decide how to allocate its scarce combat power between confronting the PAVN and VC main force units, which had come close to ending the war before the US intervention, and dedicating them to the support of pacification. Moreover, the US manuals and directives told the division that the primary way it supported the pacification effort was by destroying the main force units.

This dilemma, and the example of the division's operations, demonstrates how difficult it is to fight a counterinsurgency and a main force war simultaneously. Multiple times, during Tet 1968, Tet 1969, and again during the invasion of Cambodia, the division had to cease all other operations and concentrate its forces against the PAVN and VC main force elements. As a result, it suspended employment of population and resource control measures. This makes it difficult to know how well such measures would have succeeded if they had been executed continuously.

The record of the division's operations also makes clear how little its employment of such measures changed between 1966 and 1970. Although the number of battalion and larger operations diminished, the small unit operations that replaced them were nearly identical in mission and purpose. The division continued to conduct cordon and searches, terrain denial and terrain transformation, MEDCAPS and civic actions, and still sought to destroy PAVN and VC armed elements at every opportunity.

To some extent this is the result of guidance given to the division from above. Westmoreland decided as early as 1965 that US forces should not be used to conduct pacification directly and as late as 1971 US manuals were still telling ground combat forces that their primary mission was to protect the population from the threat of VC and PAVN main force units.[275] The lack of change in employment of population and resource control measures may also reflect the fact that they appeared to be working.

Protection and Isolation of the Population

The Tropic Lightning's operations from start to finish almost always included the purpose of finding and destroying the armed PAVN and VC elements to protect the population. Yet the division's early operations almost never brought them into sustained contact with such elements larger than a few men. The enemy's main force units assiduously avoided contact with the division's superior firepower despite the large operations that were intended to find them.

The inability to find and destroy the enemy's main, or even local, force units presented a major challenge to securing the population. Security of the population in areas undergoing pacification was supposed to be provided by Vietnamese territorial force units. These units were expected to be able to defeat small, lightly armed guerrilla forces. They could not defeat attacks by local force or main force units. This was to be done by ARVN or US units. However, these units were not in a position to reinforce territorial units that were attacked, because they were dedicated to the execution of anti-main force operations.

The division was able to secure the population when it combined cordon and search operations with other population and resource control measures such as Checkmates and saturation patrolling in one area. These operations were short in duration, however. Maili and Akumu lasted two and three weeks, respectively. While the division's consistent presence nearby improved the security of the population in the short term, it almost certainly degraded again as soon as the US units departed.

The division's early operations also failed to effectively isolate the population from main force units. It is true that when PAVN and VC main force units were avoiding contact with US units they were not in a position to threaten the population. However, the Tet Offensive demonstrated that this was only by choice. The offensive brought the Vietnamese population into sustained contact with these units throughout the country and produced a flood of refugees seeking to escape areas under their control.

The population was not isolated from the insurgency, either. The division was focused on destroying enemy main forces and was not targeting the local guerrilla forces or Front cadres within the hamlets and villages. Again, this was supposed to be done by Vietnamese elements, but the division's operations did not support their efforts. The division's movement control operations, terrain denial and transformation efforts, and its use of civic actions simply did not isolate the population from the Front cadres and guerrillas living among it.

The ability of PAVN and the VC to stockpile supplies, move units into position, and launch the Tet Offensive with near total surprise demonstrated how thoroughly their cadres were able to intimidate and control the population from this position. Government supporters and neutral members of the population were forced to accede to Front directives. Supporters of the insurgency could remain in contact with the cadres and provide materiel, intelligence, and other support as required without having to leave their hamlet or village.

After the Tet Offensive, the ability of the division to protect and isolate the population improved. However, whether this was because of the outcome of the Tet Offensive itself or was the result of the division's population and resource control measures is difficult to determine. Certainly, the destruction of a large portion of PAVN and VC armed elements improved the security situation in the division's area of operations. Moreover, the invasion of Cambodia forced PAVN and VC units into sanctuaries further from the population.

Once 25ID had forced most of the PAVN and VC armed elements out of the area, the small unit operations that they conducted in coordination with Vietnamese forces probably did improve security for the local population. The focus on maintaining a large number of patrols in a concentrated area likely prevented VC local and guerrilla force units from operating freely. Terrain denial and terrain transformation operations helped to continue to deny them access to areas that were closer to the population, thereby increasing their isolation from the insurgency.

However, the protection and isolation of the population was never total. Despite the noted decrease in the capture of supplies, the division did find stockpiles of weapons and food in the fall of 1970. Communist shelling, mining, and harassing attacks also continued through the end of the division's deployment.[276] The population was protected and isolated from PAVN and VC main forces, and possibly even VC local forces, but the guerrillas and cadres were active to the end. This would have presented a continued challenge to GVN control of the area had the Party not changed its strategy for conquering the country to one of all out conventional invasion by PAVN forces.

Focus on Behavior

The division was limited in its ability to focus on the behavior of the population during its operations because of the mission set that it had been given. Moreover, Vietnamese forces were supposed to be assisting the pacification effort which was intended to end support for the insurgency. As a result, the division's employment of population and resource control measures was not effectively focused on the behavior of the population.

Cordon and search operations theoretically presented the division's units with a means of preventing behavior that supported the insurgency. By conducting a thorough search of a hamlet, the division could identify who had stored caches of weapons, ammunition, rice, or other supplies and pass them on to Vietnamese or US interrogators for further screening. In practice, almost every Vietnamese household would have had some amount of supplies inside it that was designated for support of PAVN or VC forces.

A captured VC cadre from Duc Hoa stated that "people were also expected to keep one jar of rice for the village guerrillas and one bushel of paddy in reserve to sell to mobile units when necessary."[277] Therefore, nearly the entire hamlet would need to be questioned. Every single person in the hamlet, including the VC cadres and the Front's supporters, could plausibly claim to have been forced to maintain the cache. As the population was not protected or isolated from the insurgency they could not be expected to deny the Front support even if they wanted to.

Terrain denial and terrain transformation faced similar challenges. While terrain denial and transformation efforts probably kept the population out of those areas under normal circumstances, the armed elements could easily force them to go into them during supply operations. Guerrilla forces or cadres could collect rice from the population and then impress a work party to move it. The population had no way of refusing the VC's demands and the threat of some of the work party dying from the division's HI fires was probably acceptable to the VC and the cadres.

The division's movement controls were also poorly targeted to prevent behavior that supported the insurgency. The Checkmates consisting of random road blocks and searches clearly did not prevent the major movement of supplies that occurred in preparation for the Tet Offensive. The surveillance operations and saturation patrols may have prevented Front supporters or guerrillas within a hamlet from leaving, but if they were not under threat of being arrested during an accompanying cordon and search, they would have no reason to do so.

The division's operations did not facilitate behavior that supported the government either, particularly before the Tet Offensive. The division reported that MEDCAPS and civic actions were extremely effective at garnering support for the GVN. Yet, prior to Tet, the division gained very little actionable intelligence from the population. Its search and destroy and cordon and search operations repeatedly failed to make contact with large enemy units.

The division reported in its first ORLL after Tet that it had gained reliable intelligence during MEDCAPS about the location of booby traps, enemy units, and supply caches.[278] However, this may have been because the MEDCAPS were treating refugees from other areas who now felt comfortable disclosing information about the enemy because they were no longer under threat; not because the MEDCAP itself encouraged them to provide information. In its AAR on Toan Thang II, 2d Brigade reported that it received intelligence information from a total of 14 people.[279] This from an operation that lasted more than six months during which more than 600 MEDCAPS were conducted that treated over 50,000 people.[280]

The Tropic Lightning's operations also did not allow the neutral population to remain so. This stemmed primarily from the inability to protect and isolate the population discussed above. However, the division also did not, or could not, employ measures that would have made it impossible for the Front to coerce the population into providing them support. It is also the case that some of the division's actions during cordon and searches and terrain transformation operations probably did not endear it to the neutral population, and may have cost it some of their support. The Rome Plows tore down valuable fruit trees and units destroyed bunkers inside homes that were intended only for the safety of the individual residents.[281] Moreover, US soldiers viewed Vietnamese peasants as complicit with the VC even if they were being intimidated. A riflemen with the 25ID, Dan Vandenburg, recalled that:

> One of the biggest disappointment over there was the attitude of the Vietnamese peasants. None of them seemed to give a shit about us. The

feeling was mutual . . . There was never any warning of any kind, never one ounce of friendliness. On the other hand, I can understand why: If they'd have tipped us off, Charlie would have come that night and slit their throats but it would have been nice to have seen them take a small risk for us once."[282]

To prevent actions such as the destruction of valuable fruit trees and to improve the attitude of US forces towards the Vietnamese population would have required a major commitment to use US forces in close proximity to the rural population over an extended period of time. This also would have had to coincide with a definite commitment to protect the population from all threats, including Front intimidation and coercion. This may have been accomplished if the division had been operating under a holistic control mechanism that allowed it to focus better on the behavior of the population. This would have required the division to leverage a control mechanism that was as holistic, pervasive, and coercive as the Strategic Hamlet Program, which was anathema to the GVN and to its US supporters.

To effectively employ the measures contained in such a mechanism the division would have needed to concentrate its operations in a single area and to partner more closely with the Vietnamese forces than it did for most of its time in Vietnam. Giving US units specific areas of operations was resisted by many ARVN commanders who felt it would hurt the prestige of the GVN.[283] Moreover, because the 25ID did not have the power to legally enforce any measures that were put in place, it would have had to rely on its Vietnamese partners to do so.[284] Lastly, such operations require an extraordinary amount of manpower, probably more than was available to the 25th and its ARVN partners, to provide the enforcement capability. This was especially so because of the settlement pattern of the Vietnamese population in the division's area of operations.

Facilitate Targeting of the Armed and Subversive Element

The division's primary mission throughout its time in Vietnam was to target and destroy the armed elements, particularly the PAVN and VC main forces. It did not make targeting of the subversive element part of its mission until after the Tet Offensive. Despite the priority placed on it, the division's population and resource control measures generally failed to facilitate such targeting.

The division's early search and destroy operations made contact mostly with small elements. Its terrain transformation and cordon and search operations were often resisted only by harassing attacks designed to slow, not stop, them. In fact, the division did not begin to make sustained contact with large enemy main and local force units until the Tet Offensive. The offensive exposed them and presented the Tropic Lightning the opportunity to exercise its superior mobility and firepower against them. The PAVN and VC units also cooperated in their own destruction by continuing to press their attacks even after it was obvious that they were suffering a debilitating defeat.

After the Tet Offensive had ended, the division was able to maintain contact with large enemy units through May 1968, but then contact returned to its previous pattern. Outside of the two major enemy offensives and the invasion of Cambodia the division recorded very little success targeting and destroying large enemy elements. However, even during times of relatively sparse contact, such as October 1970 when it reported 101 enemy killed, the division did record a lot of PAVN and VC fatalities.[285]

These results were mainly due to PAVN and VC elements choosing to make contact. Throughout its time in Vietnam, 25ID had trouble gaining the initiative and making contact with the enemy. Enemy units, with knowledge of the terrain, the acquiescence, if not the support of, the population, and the ability to move quickly simply avoided the division's efforts to target it and the division's population and resource control measures did not force the enemy to confront it.

This failure again stems from the inability to effectively protect or isolate the population. The previous chapter noted how dangerous the Party and Front believed the Strategic Hamlet Program to be because it could effectively protect and isolate the population. The division's operations, however, did neither. So it was forced to chase the PAVN and VC units around the countryside rather than waiting for them to come to it.[286]

The division's operations also did not effectively target the subversive element. The Tet Offensive made this readily apparent. In fact, the division's mission statements do not even begin to mention targeting the Viet Cong infrastructure explicitly until it appears as part of 2d Brigade's mission statement during Operation TOAN THANG, Phase II. It was not explained how the brigade would do this and or with what assets it should try to do so.

It would have been difficult for a US unit to target the subversive element located within a Vietnamese hamlet, which is why such targeting was supposed to be done by the Vietnamese RD Cadre and the National Police Field Force.[287] For these groups to be successful, however, they required intelligence provided by the population, which would not be forthcoming unless the population was certain of its security. The inability to effectively protect and isolate the population thus prevented effective targeting of the infrastructure by these elements.

The division did experiment with Combined Reconnaissance Intelligence Platoons, a joint US-Vietnamese force with a US platoon as its nucleus, to target the infrastructure.[288] The division's reports contain no reference to their operations so it is impossible to assess whether or not they were effective. They would have needed to maintain a continuous presence in one area over a long period of time and this would not have occurred except for the periods outside of the major combat operations in 1968, 1969, and 1970.

It is true that the effectiveness of the Viet Cong infrastructure was greatly degraded from its high before the division's arrival in 1966 but this was more likely caused by the deaths of senior cadre during the Tet Offensive and its aftermath than the division's attempts to explicitly target them. Moreover, it remained active in the division's area of operations throughout its time in Vietnam. The division continued to capture infrastructure members into 1970 and it is unlikely that guerrilla units would have continued their harassing attacks against the division in the fall of 1970 without the presence of some cadres.

Overall, the Tropic Lightning's operations in Vietnam reduced the size, capability, and effectiveness of PAVN and VC forces in its area of responsibility. However, this was not the result of its employment of population and resource control measures, which were effective generally only in the short term. Rather, it was due to its ability to effectively prosecute the main force war against the enemy when presented the opportunity.

An improved set of population and control measures employed under a holistic control mechanism may have made the division's operations even more effective, but it is not certain. Moreover, implementing an improved set of measures would have required a number of changes to take place, most of which were outside the division's control. Regardless, they might not have changed the ultimate outcome of the war because of the ability of the Party, Front, and their armed forces to repeatedly respond to challenges to their operations with a change in strategy.

Notes

1. For more information about the campaign waged by Diem refer to the previous chapter.

2. Military History Institute of Vietnam, *Victory in Vietnam*, 124-126.

3. Westmoreland, "A Military War of Attrition," 58.

4. Military History Institute of Vietnam, *Victory in Vietnam*, 125.

5. Westmoreland, "A Military War of Attrition," 62.

6. Ibid., 62-63.

7. Bergerud, *The Dynamics of Defeat*, 114.

8. US Army units would also conduct operations in ICTZ beginning in 1968.

9. In US operational reports from the period operation names and many place names are written in all capital letters. In the text they will appear with the first letter of each word capitalized. However, when the original reports are quoted, they will be reproduced exactly as they appear in the report.

10. Bergerud, *The Dynamics of Defeat*, 126.

11. Operation Maili will be discussed in further detail below.

12. For more information on Combined Action Platoons and other units that executed the local security force mission see the thesis by CGSC Art of War Scholar Major Dustin Mitchell.

13. As will be shown later using the reports of the 25th Infantry Division, operations, such as Maili, which were intended to support pacification were often short in duration and employed very limited amounts of U.S. combat power.

14. Pacification will be discussed in more detail below.

15. Military History Institute of Vietnam, *Victory in Vietnam*, 206-207.

16. Ibid., 207.

17. Bergerud, *The Dynamics of Defeat*, 201.

18. Richard A. Hunt, *Pacification, The American Struggle for Vietnam's Hearts and Minds* (Boulder, CO: Westview Press, Inc., 1995), 157.

19. Bergerud, *The Dynamics of Defeat*, 241.

20. Willbanks, *Abandoning Vietnam*, 20.

21. Standing Committee of A. 26, "Matters to be Grasped when Performing the Ideological Task in the Party Body," in *Viet-Nam Documents and Research Notes, 'Decisive Victory': Step by Step, Bit by Bit*, TTU, 5.

22. Willbanks, *Abandoning Vietnam*, 44.

23. Tran Dinh Tho, *Pacification* (Washington, DC: Center for Military History, 1980), 17.

24. Bergerud, *The Dynamics of Defeat*, 286.

25. The PROVN study will be discussed further below. It should also be noted that General Abrams was part of the team that produced PROVN and therefore would have had a complete understanding of its conclusions and recommendations.

26. Tho, *Pacification*, 37.

27. Willbanks, *Abandoning Vietnam*, 48.

28. There is no clearly defined end date for the Strategic Hamlet Program. Some of the strategic hamlets remained in existence throughout the end of 1963 and 1964 and were subject to VC attacks against them during this time. However, as discussed in the previous chapter, the Vietnamese leaders who perpetrated the coup against Diem immediately disassociated themselves from the Strategic Hamlet Program so it can be concluded that its true end coincided with Diem's death.

29. The term pacification will be used in this paper to describe both the general control mechanism and the counterinsurgency strategy employed by the GVN and its allies after the Diem regime.

30. United States Military Assistance Command, Vietnam, *Handbook for Military Support of Pacification*, February 1968, Combined Arms Research Library, Fort Leavenworth, KS archives [hereafter cited as CARL], 1.

31. A full description and analysis of all of the elements of pacification is beyond the scope of this paper. The major component programs on both the U.S. and Vietnamese side, such as Chieu Hoi, Revolutionary Development, and CORDS, will be briefly described below, but will not be analyzed in depth. The focus will remain on the population and resource control measures employed by U.S. ground forces in support of the overall pacification effort.

32. MACV, *Handbook for Military Support of Pacification*, 1.

33. Andrew Krepinevich, *The Army and Vietnam* (Baltimore, MD: Johns Hopkins University Press, 1986), 166.

34. Tran Dinh Tho, *Pacification*, 15.

35. Pearce, *Evolution of a Vietnamese Village - Part I*, 18.

36. Ibid., 18-19.

37. Hunt, *Pacification*, 25.

38. Ibid., 26.

39. Robert Komer, *Bureaucracy at War: U.S. Performance in the Vietnam Conflict* (Boulder, CO: Westview Press, 1986), 140.

40. Hunt, *Pacification*, 36.

41. Tran Dinh Tho, *Pacification*, 4-5.

42. Ibid., 32-33.

43. Hunt, *Pacification*, 36.

44. Bergerud, *The Dynamics of Defeat*, 144.

45. Hunt, *Pacification*, 102.

46. Bergerud, *The Dynamics of Defeat*, 144.

47. Tran Dinh Tho, *Pacification*, 16.

48. MACV, *Handbook for Military Support of Pacification*, A-2.

49. Ibid., A-1.

50. Tran Dinh Tho, *Pacification*, 72.

51. Ibid., 31.

52. The role of CORDS in support of pacification will be discussed further below.

53. Hunt, *Pacification*, 137.

54. Bergerud, *The Dynamics of Defeat*, 223.

55. Tran Dinh Tho, *Pacification*, 23.

56. Ibid., 24.

57. Hunt, *Pacification*, 217.

58. Bergerud, *The Dynamics of Defeat*, 270.

59. Ibid., 270.

60. Robert Komer, *Impact of Pacification on Insurgency in South Vietnam* (Santa Monica, CA: RAND Corporation, 1970), 11.

61. Tran Dinh Tho, *Pacification*, 26.

62. Komer, *Impact of Pacification*, 19.

63. Military History Institute of Vietnam, *Victory in Vietnam*, 283.

64. Willbanks, *Abandoning Vietnam*, 188.

65. Ibid., 189-190.

66. Tran Dinh Tho, *Pacification*, 182.

67. Komer, *Bureaucracy at War*, 138.

68. Hunt, *Pacification*, 26-27.

69. Komer, *Bureaucracy at War*, 140.

70. Ibid., 142.

71. Krepinevich, *The Army and Vietnam*, 181-182. Also see Komer, *Bureaucracy at War*, 142.

72. Dale Andrade, "Westmoreland Was Right: Learning the Wrong Lessons from the Vietnam War," *Small Wars and Insurgencies* 19, no. 2 (June 2008): 158.

73. MACV, *Handbook for Military Support of Pacification*, 5.

74. Tran Dinh Tho, *Pacification*, 56.

75. Hunt, *Pacification*, 75-77.

76. Ibid., 82-85.

77. Ibid., 88.

78. MACV, *Handbook for Military Support of Pacification*, 27-28.

79. Ibid., 5.

80. Hunt, *Pacification*, 93.

81. One of the major reports involved was the Hamlet Evaluation System (HES). The HES was and remains a controversial means of gauging the security and pacification status of a hamlet. Responsibility for gathering and inputting the data into the HES lay with the district advisers and not the US units on the ground and so its usefulness will not be analyzed as part of this paper. See Hunt, *Pacification* 95-96.

82. BH060, Vietnam Political and Military Analyst, Interview by Mark Battjes, Ben Boardman, Robert Green, and Dustin Mitchell, 22 March 2011, Williamsburg, VA.

83. Hunt, *Pacification*, 106.

84. Bergerud, *The Dynamics of Defeat*, 223-225.

85. This will be discussed further below. Also see II Field Force Vietnam, "Combat Operations After Action Report, Tet Offensive," Bud Harton Collection, TTU, 25.

86. Headquarters, 25th Infantry Division, "Operational Report - Lessons Learned, Period Ending 31 July 1968," 27 January 1969, Bud Harton Collection, TTU, 29.

87. Krepinevich, *The Army and Vietnam*, 253.

88. Headquarters, 25th Infantry Division, "Operational Report - Lessons Learned, Period Ending 30 April 1970," Bud Harton Collection, TTU, 1-2.

89. Hunt, *Pacification*, 273.

90. Ibid., 274.

91. Willbanks, *Abandoning Vietnam*, 187.

92. Hunt, *Pacification*, 274.

93. Willbanks, *Abandoning Vietnam*, 213-216.

94. Westmoreland, "A Military War of Attrition," 62-63.

95. MACV, *Handbook for Military Support of Pacification*, 5.

96. MACCORDS, *Territorial Security in Vietnam*, 1 January 1971, CARL, 37.

97. David W. P. Elliot and W. A. Stewart, *Pacification and the Viet Cong System in Dinh Tuong: 1966-1967* (Santa Monica, CA: RAND Corporation, 1969), 64.

98. Ibid., 32-33.

99. MACV, *Handbook for Military Support of Pacification*, 6.

100. Department of Defense, *DoD GEN-25, Handbook for U.S. Forces in Vietnam*, 1966, CARL, 102.

101. Ibid., 104.

102. MACV, *Handbook for Military Support of Pacification*, 43.

103. Ibid., 43.

104. DOD, *Handbook for U.S. Forces in Vietnam*, 105-106.

105. Elliot and Stewart, *Pacification and the Viet Cong System*, 64.

106. Tran Dinh Tho, *Pacification*, 37.

107. Bergerud, *The Dynamics of Defeat*, 286-287.

108. Tran Dinh Tho, *Pacification*, 166.

109. Komer, *Impact of Pacification*, 11.

110. Elliot and Stewart, *Pacification and the Viet Cong System*, xi.

111. VC Cadre from Duc Hoa District, quoted in Bergerud, *The Dynamics of Defeat*, 96.

112. CORDS, *The Vietnamese Village 1970 Handbook for Advisors*, 2 May 1970, CARL, 77-79.

113. In this section, each tactic and technique will be described briefly and its use as a population and resource control measure established. The efficacy of the tactics and techniques will be examined below through their employment by the U.S. 25th Infantry Division.

114. DOD, *Handbook for U.S. Forces in Vietnam*, 103.

115. U.S. Army, Field Manual 31-16, *Counterguerrilla Operations* (Washington, DC: Department of the Army, 1963), 40. Although this manual was focused on countering guerrilla operations, which is primarily a military task, it also directs units to conduct activities more generally associated with counterinsurgency. This includes being prepared to provide humanitarian assistance and support local governance. Moreover, the population and resource control measures described in the manual for protecting and isolating the population and denying supplies to the guerrillas were relevant to the situation that U.S. units confronted in Vietnam. As the manual was issued in 1963 it can be assumed that US units preparing to deploy to Vietnam in 1965 and later would have been familiar with the manual and the tactics and techniques that were described within it. Although the manual does not discuss the operations of the British Army in Malaya explicitly, it has clearly been

influenced by them. The manual discusses classifiying areas into red, yellow, and green based on the amount of guerrilla activity and their relative security, similar to the system employed by Templer. It also discussed using techniques such as food control which had not been used recently by the US Army.

116. Ibid., 40.

117. MACV, *Handbook for Military Support of Pacification*, 50-52.

118. Ibid., 51.

119. Ibid., 51.

120. Air strikes, including those by B-52 strategic bombers, referred to as Arc Light strikes were also used in this manner. BH060. Also see Bergerud, *The Dynamics of Defeat*, 243.

121. Bergerud, *The Dynamics of Defeat*, 135.

122. US Army, FM 31-16, *Counterguerrilla Operations*, 40.

123. Tran Dinh Tho, *Pacification*, 97.

124. Ibid., 97.

125. Headquarters, 25th Infantry Division, "Operational Report - Lessons Learned, Period Ending 31 October 1967," 5 March 1968, Bud Harton Collection, TTU, 5.

126. MACV, *Handbook for Military Support of Pacification*, 43.

127. Ibid., 21 and 49. However, nearly every 25ID ORLL examined by the author contains reference to MEDCAPs. Such operations were a regular feature of 25ID operations and have also been a regular feature of U.S. operations in Iraq and Afghanistan.

128. Bergerud, *The Dynamics of Defeat*, 165.

129. U.S. Army, FM 31-16, *Counterguerrilla Operations*, 107.

130. As much as possible, the operations of the 25th Infantry Division will be examined by using the division's original operational reports. Not all of the operational reports from the period were available to the researcher. However, enough reports are available during each of the critical periods to present a thorough examination of the division's operations.

131. Headquarters, 25th Infantry Division, "Operational Report on Lessons Learned for Period Ending 30 April 1966," Bud Harton Collection, TTU, 2.

132. The operations presented in this section will primarily be in Hau Nghia province. However, some will occur outside of Hau Nghia or in areas that are contiguous to it in order to allow a thorough examination of the division's use of population and resource control measures.

133. Pearce, *Evolution of a Vietnamese Village-Part I*, 6.

134. Ibid., 8.

135. Bergerud, *The Dynamics of Defeat*, 116.

136. Pearce, *Evolution of a Vietnamese Village-Part I*, 5.

137. Bergerud, *The Dynamics of Defeat*, 118.

138. 25ID, "ORLL Ending 30 April 1966," 6.

139. Ibid., 7.

140. Ibid., 7.

141. Robert Conner, quoted in Eric M. Bergerud, *Red Thunder, Tropic Lightning* (Boulder, CO: Westview Press, Inc., 1993), 96.

142. Ibid., 96.

143. 25ID, "ORLL Ending 30 April 1966," 3-4.

144. Ibid., 6.

145. Ibid., 9.

146. Ibid., 9.

147. Bergerud, *The Dynamics of Defeat*, 117.

148. The term major operation in Vietnam usually refers to an operation of battalion size and higher. The term small unit operations was reserved for operations at the company and below. This paper follows the same convention.

149. 25ID, "ORLL Ending 30 April 1966," 10.

150. Ibid., 10.

151. Bergerud, *The Dynamics of Defeat*, 117.

152. Ibid., 149.

153. 25ID, "ORLL Ending 30 April 1966," 12.

154. Ibid., 12.

155. Ibid., 12.

156. Ibid., 25.

157. Headquarters, 25th Infantry Division, "Operational Report for Quarterly Period Ending 30 April 1967," 19 May 1967, Bud Harton Collection, TTU, 1-8.

158. Ibid., 5.

159. Ibid., 10.

160. Ibid., 30.

161. Ibid., 30.

162. A Rome Plow is "a bulldozer with a sharpened blade set at an angle, constructed to be used in jungle clearing operations." See 25ID, "ORLL Ending 31 October 1967," 5 March 1968, Bud Harton Collection, TTU, 5.

163. Headquarters, 25th Infantry Division, "Operational Report for Quarterly Period Ending 31 July 1967," 19 August 1967, Bud Harton Collection, Texas Tech University Vietnam Archives, 3.

164. Ibid., 3.

165. Ibid., 6.

166. Ibid., 6-7.

167. Bergerud, *The Dynamics of Defeat*, 164.

168. 25ID, "ORLL Ending 31 July 1967," 8.

169. Ibid., 8.

170. Ibid., 9.

171. Ibid., 6.

172. Ibid., 6.

173. Headquarters, 25th Infantry Division, "Operational Report - Lessons Learned, Period Ending 31 January 1968," 15 May 1968, Bud Harton Collection, Texas Tech University Vietnam Archive, 3.

174. 25ID, "ORLL Ending 31 October 1967," 7.

175. 25ID, "ORLL Ending 31 January 1968," 4.

176. Ibid., 17.

177. 25ID, "ORLL Ending 31 October 1967," 21.

178. Ibid., 21.

179. Tran Dinh Tho, *Pacification*, 128.

180 25ID, "ORLL Ending 31 October 1967," 48. The report cautions that US personnel should not be conducting these operations, but should allow Vietnamese officials to do so in order to improve their popularity.

181. Bergerud, *The Dynamics of Defeat*, 173.

182. 25ID, "ORLL Ending 31 October 1967," 21.

183. Ibid., 8.

184. 25ID, "ORLL Ending 31 January 1968," 4.

185. 25ID, "ORLL Ending 31 October 1967," 6.

186. Ibid., 19.

187. Ibid., 8.

188. 25ID "ORLL Ending 31 July 1968," 29.

189. II Field Force Vietnam, "Combat Operations After Action Report, Tet Offensive," 25.

190. Ibid., 27.

191. Ibid., 2.

192. No author, "Viet Cong Loss of Population Control Evidence from Captured Documents," 1968, TTU, 1-3.

193. Ibid., 8.

194. 25ID, "ORLL Ending 31 January 1968," 5.

195. Ibid., 2.

196. Ibid., 2.

197. Headquarters, 25th Infantry Division, "Operational Report - Lessons Learned, Period Ending 30 April 1968," 31 July 1968, Bud Harton Collection, TTU, 3.

198. Bergerud, *The Dynamics of Defeat*, 201.

199. 25ID, "ORLL Ending 30 April 1968," 5.

200. Ibid., 6.

201. Ibid., 7.

202. Ibid., 7.

203. Bergerud, *The Dynamics of Defeat*, 209.

204. 25ID, "ORLL Ending 30 April 1968," 3.

205. 25ID "ORLL Ending 31 July 1968," 10.

206. Ibid., 10.

207. Ibid., 10-13.

208. Ibid., 2.

209. Ibid., 4.

210. Ibid., 4.

211. Headquarters, 2d Brigade, 25th Infantry Division, "Combat Operations After Action Report, Operation TOAN THANG, Phase II," 10 March 1969, Bud Harton Collection, TTU, 6.

212. Ibid., 6.

213. Ibid., 6.

214. Ron Hart, quoted in Bergerud, *Red Thunder, Tropic Lightning*, 173.

215. 2-25ID, "Combat Operations AAR–TOAN THANG, Phase II," 9-10.

216. Ibid., 7-8.

217. Headquarters, 3rd Brigade, 25th Infantry Division, "TOAN-THANG Phase II Execution, 1 OCT 68–30 NOV 68," 31 March 1969, Bud Harton Collection, TTU, 2.

218. Ibid., 3-4.

219. Bergerud, *The Dynamics of Defeat*, 225.

220. The digital copy of this document located by the author contains only the first three pages. However, it is those pages of the report in which the division is expected to record its major operations during the reporting period and therefore a conclusion can be drawn about what the division's priorities during the period were.

221. Headquarters, 25th Infantry Division, "Operational Report Period Ending 31 January 1969," 1 February 1969, 1st Battalion, 8th Artillery, 25th Infantry Association Collection, TTU, 1.

222. Ibid., 2.

223. Ibid., 2.

224. 3-25 ID, "TOAN-THANG Phase II Execution," 16-43.

225. The AAR indicates that two enclosures contain detailed execution summaries for different periods of the operation, but these are not part of the document located by the author. However, the main body of the AAR provides some sense of the brigade's priorities.

226. 2-25ID, "Combat Operations AAR–TOAN THANG, Phase II," 16.

227. Ibid., 16.

228. Alfred S. Bradford, *Some Even Volunteered* (Westport, CT: Praeger Publishers, 1994), 36.

229. Ibid., 20.

230. Bergerud, *The Dynamics of Defeat*, 241.

231. Standing Committee of A. 26, "Matters to be Grasped when Performing the Ideological Task in the Party Body," in *Viet-Nam Documents and Research Notes, 'Decisive Victory': Step by Step, Bit by Bit*, TTU, 5.

232. Ibid., 5.

233. "Study of Directive 81 of 5 [Nam] Truong [COSVN] Opening of Phase H," in *Viet-Nam Documents and Research Notes, 'Decisive Victory': Step by Step, Bit by Bit*, TTU, 11.

234. Bergerud, *The Dynamics of Defeat*, 245.

235. Headquarters, 25th Infantry Division, "Operational Report - Lessons Learned, Period Ending 31 July 1969," 18 December 1969, Bud Harton Collection, Texas Tech University Vietnam Archive, 1.

236. Ibid., 1.

237. Ibid., 1.

238. Ibid., 11.

239. Ibid., 8.

240. Ibid., 8.

241. Current Affairs Committee C69, "Directive No. 78/CTNT, An Order to Continued to Take Advantage of our Success, Develop the Overall Attack, and Accomplish the 1969 Spring Plan," 14 May 1969, TTU, 2.

242. Ibid., 5.

243. Ibid., 5.

244. Ibid., 5.

245. Ibid., 5.

246. 25ID, "ORLL Ending 31 July 1969," 31.

247. Ibid., 31.

248. Ibid., 12.

249. Ibid., 42.

250. Ibid., 78-79.

251. Ibid., 79.

252. SVN People's Liberation Army, Political Department, "Outline of the Reorientation of Forthcoming Missions in 1970 (For Elementary and Intermediate Cadre)," 14 January 1970, TTU, 11.

253. Ibid., 11-12.

254. 25ID, "ORLL Ending 30 April 1970," TTU, 2.

255. Ibid., 2.

256. Ibid., 42.

257. Ibid., 64.

258. Ibid., 16.

259. Headquarters, 25th Infantry Division, "Operational Report - Lessons Learned, Period Ending 31 October 1970," 30 April 1971, Bud Harton Collection, TTU, 1.

260. Bergerud, *The Dynamics of Defeat*, 287.

261. 25ID, "ORLL Ending 31 October 1970," 20.

262. Ibid., 21. It is not clear how many of these rounds were fired in support of HI missions, however. The division's earlier reports directly state how many rounds were fired for these missions but those in later years do not. Given the relative lack of contact and the high number of rounds expended, though, it could be concluded that many such missions were still occurring.

263. Bergerud, *The Dynamics of Defeat*, 293.

264. 25ID, "ORLL Ending 31 October 1970," 6, 14.

265. Ibid., 17.

266. Ibid., 17.

267. Military History Institute of Vietnam, *Victory in Vietnam*, 246.

268. Ibid., 247.

269. Ibid., 249.

270. Bergerud, *The Dynamics of Defeat*, 289.

271. Military History Institute of Vietnam, *Victory in Vietnam*, 246.

272. Pearce, *Evolution of a Vietnamese Village-Part I*, 6-8.

273. Willbanks, *Abandoning Vietnam*, 212.

274. Ibid., 273.

275. MACCORDS, *Territorial Security in Vietnam*, 37.

276. 25ID, "ORLL Ending 31 October 1970," 13.

277. VC Cadre from Duc Hoa District, quoted in Bergerud, *The Dynamics of Defeat*, 96.

278. 25ID, "ORLL Ending 31 July 1968," 44.

279. 2-25ID, "Combat Operations AAR–TOAN THANG, Phase II," 19.

280. Ibid., 17.

281. Bergerud, *The Dynamics of Defeat*, 233-234.

282. Dan Vandenburg, quoted in Bergerud, *Red Thunder, Tropic Lightning*, 221.

283. Bergerud, *The Dynamics of Defeat*, 232.

284. Ibid., 232.

285. 25ID, "ORLL Ending 31 October 1970," 14.

286. This, however, would have been viewed negatively by Westmoreland who observed after the war that "one can point to few cases, if any, in military history where victory was achieved by passive defense." Westmoreland, "A Military War of Attrition," 65.

287. MACV, *Handbook for Military Support of Pacification*, 17-19.

288. Bergerud, *The Dynamics of Defeat*, 224.

Chapter 6
Iraq, 2003–2011

I never knew how much murder and intimidation was going on. When we got the COP [Combat Out Post] in and finally broke the intimidation that was the real turning point. They needed that sense of security in order to give us or the ISF [International Security Force] the information that we needed.

—A US Army Battalion Commander, Interview with author

The US campaign in Iraq has only recently ended with the withdrawal of all US combat forces in December 2011 and it will be many years before any judgment can be made about its ultimate outcome or its affect on the national security of the US At the same time, the length of the campaign, the large number of different units that participated in it, and the changing strategy employed by the US presents an opportunity to examine US operations in depth. This is especially true with respect to population and resource control measures. Throughout the campaign, US forces employed such measures and altered them as the strategy changed.

Initial efforts to control the population suffered from a lack of understanding of the threat, insufficient numbers of security forces, and a desire to reduce the presence of US forces among the population. However, once the US developed a better understanding of the situation that it was confronted with and determined that it needed to operate closer to the population the efforts improved. Moreover, a large increase in the number of security forces available, US and especially Iraqi, facilitated these efforts and dramatically curtailed the insurgency.

Overview

Operation IRAQI FREEDOM began on 19 March 2003 when President Bush ordered the execution of a "decapitation strike" to kill the senior leaders of Saddam Hussein's regime in an attempt to immediately destabilize it.[1] Less than 24 hours later, the US ground invasion began as the US Army's 3d Infantry Division (3ID) and the USMC's I Marine Expeditionary Force (MEF), supported by the British Army's 1st Division, attacked north from Kuwait. 3ID attacked to seize the Iraqi air base at Tallil while I MEF and the British attacked to secure the southern oil fields, the city of Basra, and seize the port at Umm Qasr.[2]

The initiation of ground operations with a relatively small force, especially when compared with the size of the force used during Operation DESERT STORM, was part of a plan developed by US Central Command

(CENTCOM) that was referred to as the "Running Start."[3] The Running Start concept aimed to avoid a lengthy build up of forces in Kuwait in order to surprise the Iraqi regime.[4] The attack would begin with only the forces immediately available and before the remainder of the assault force was ready to begin operations. In fact, 3ID was the only US Army division available for combat when the invasion began.[5]

The Running Start plan was also part of a deliberate effort by Secretary of Defense Donald Rumsfeld to limit the number of US forces used in the invasion. The previous CENTCOM plan for invading Iraq, Operational Plan 1003-98, required as many as 500,000 US troops.[6] Rumsfeld felt that this number was far too high and indicated that he thought only 125,000 would be necessary.[7] The limited number of troops did allow the invasion to begin more quickly and achieve strategic, operational, and tactical surprise. However, it also reduced the amount of US and coalition forces that were available to control Iraq in the wake of the invasion.

After the seizure of the air base at Tallil, the southern oil fields, and the port at Umm Qasr, the invasion force continued its advance north. The resistance offered by the Iraqi Army was light but they also did not surrender in large numbers as had been expected.[8] However, this did not mean that there was no resistance. Heavy fighting occurred around An Nasiriyah and As Samawah which cost 3ID a number of casualties. The Ba'ath party paramilitary force, the Fedayeen Saddam, carried out these attacks.[9]

The Fedayeen Saddam were a major component of the regime's survival mechanism. They were a lightly armed paramilitary force that would be used to contain uprisings in a city for long enough to allow the regime's ultimate defenders, the Republican Guard, to arrive.[10] Their attacks did not significantly disrupt the invasion force operations but they did provide a prelude of the hard fight that the US and coalition forces would confront when the insurgency began later.

The US drive to Baghdad continued rapidly as 3ID in the west and I MEF in the east aggressively carried out their attacks. Despite the heavy fighting in As Samawah, An Najaf, and other cities, they were not cleared by the initial force that encountered them. Rather, they were contained and bypassed to allow the main body of the attack to continue north. However, the bypassed cities provided staging areas for the Fedayeen Saddam to attack the invasion force's LOCs.[11] As a result, V Corps altered its initial plan and used the 101st Airborne Division (Air Assault) (101 ABN) and the 82d Airborne Division (82 ABN) forces that were available to begin securing the areas that had been bypassed.¹² This action recognized the need to assert control over territory and population and, in effect, began the occupation of Iraq.

These operations were successful. The entire 1st BCT of the 101 ABN, and 2d Battalion, 70th Armor, were dedicated to clear and secure An Najaf.¹³ The force rapidly gained control over the city and ended the Fedayeen Saddam attacks on the LOCs. However, as 3ID moved north, the forces of the 101 ABN and 82 ABN would have to secure more cities, leaving fewer forces in each to control them. The dedication of combat power to these efforts also left fewer forces available to occupy and control Baghdad.

This situation, however, was part of the pre-war plan. In order to reduce the number of forces required for the invasion, the CENTCOM planners anticipated being able to use Iraqi resources, such as the police and the Army, to maintain control.¹⁴ Moreover, at a political level, it was believed that it would be better for an Iraqi authority to assume control of the country.¹⁵ It was hoped that this would allow the US to avoid being viewed as an occupying power. However, as soon as US forces began securing and holding territory, that is precisely what they were.

The rapid advance of 3ID and the I MEF ended with the fall of Baghdad on 9 April 2003. This followed two raids into Baghdad, referred to as "Thunder Runs," that were conducted by elements of 2BCT, 3ID on 5 and 7 April 2003.¹⁶ With the fall of the regime, the US Army, Marine, and British forces began a transition to stability and support operations that were intended to re-establish some measure of civil control.¹⁷ However, there was not a civilian authority to turn control over to.

The US had created the Office of Reconstruction and Humanitarian Assistance in January 2003 to serve as an adjunct to the CENTCOM staff and provide support to its efforts to establish a new Iraqi government after the invasion.¹⁸ The office was headed by Lieutenant General (R) Jay Garner, who had very little time and few resources to establish the new office. In late April 2003, Garner began the task of creating an Interim Iraqi Authority, which would ultimately become a provisional government of Iraq.¹⁹ A conference of Iraqi exiles had taken place in London in December 2002 to begin development of a means to govern post-invasion Iraq but the conference did not produce a governing structure that could be inserted into Baghdad to control the country.²⁰ Thus, with the collapse of the regime there was no civilian governing authority in Iraq. Moreover, "just after the 3d ID and other Coalition elements arrived in Baghdad, Saddam's army, the Iraqi police, and other institutions of authority dissolved. Concurrently, looters began stealing from buildings and facilities across the capital."[21] 3ID and the other coalition elements did not have clear guidance about how to react to such a situation and some commanders allowed the looting to continue unchecked.[22]

In May 2003, the Bush administration created the Coalition Provisional Authority (CPA) and endowed it with sovereign political power in Iraq.[23] The CPA was intended to be a short-lived body which would hand control over to an Iraqi governing entity, being developed by Garner, as soon as possible. However, the head of the CPA, L. Paul Bremer, decided to indefinitely postpone such a handover and delay the formation of an Interim Iraqi Government (IIG).[24] Although a postponement was necessary, as the process of forming such a government had begun in earnest less than a year earlier outside of Iraq, it undermined the work done by Garner and created a sense in some communities in Iraq that the coalition would remain for longer than expected. It also did not improve the coalition's ability to control Iraq, which required a greater number of forces and more coordination between the military and the CPA. It would be more than a year before the IIG was formed and during that time an insurgency[25] developed that would challenge not only coalition control, but would also present a challenge to the newly formed government.

An insurgency had not been anticipated by the war's planners, despite what was known about the capabilities of the Fedayeen Saddam and other paramilitary bodies in Iraq at the time of the invasion. As a result, when insurgent attacks began during the summer of 2003, each of the divisions in Iraq reacted differently.[26] The insurgency remained at a relatively low level throughout 2003. However, it became increasingly clear that it was composed of a number of disparate elements including a Sunni Arab nationalist insurgency and a Sunni Arab Islamic extremist insurgency led by Abu Musab Al Zarqawi which ultimately became Al Qaeda in Iraq (AQI).[27] A major blow against the insurgency, or so it was believed at the time, occurred when Saddam Hussein was captured in December 2003.

Subsequently, far fewer attacks were recorded during the first three months of 2004.[28] But, the insurgency intensified in early 2004 with near simultaneous events in Fallujah, Najaf and other areas across southern Iraq, and the Baghdad slum, Sadr City.[29] The murder of US contractors in late March 2004 led the Bush administration to order an offensive to clear Fallujah, which drew Sunni insurgents from across Iraq to defend the city.[30] The USMC and US Army forces conducting the attack encountered heavy resistance. The administration ended the assault less than two weeks after it began, leaving the insurgency effectively in control of Fallujah.[31]

The Shi'a population of Iraq,[32] concentrated in the areas south of Baghdad and in some neighborhoods of Baghdad itself, had not opposed the initial US invasion. However, many Shi'a were opposed to the ongoing occupation of Iraq and some of them united under the leadership of Muqtada al Sadr to form the *Jaysh al Mahdi* (JAM), the Army of the Mahdi.[33] Sadr used CPA actions directed against him to initiate an uprising across southern Iraq and in Sadr City.[34] Fighting was heaviest in Najaf and Sadr City but was largely confined by the summer.

The summer of 2004 included two major events that would shape the future of Operation IRAQI FREEDOM. The first was the transfer of sovereignty from the CPA to the IIG in late June 2004. The second was the creation of the Multi-National Force Iraq (MNF-I) headquarters and the appointment of General George Casey to serve as its first commander.[35] These two events gave shape to a new strategy for the campaign in Iraq.

The IIG was established under the conditions of the Transitional Administrative Law (TAL) and was intended to govern Iraq until elections in January 2005 to select a Transitional National Assembly (TNA).[36] The TNA would produce a new Iraqi constitution to be confirmed by a national referendum in October 2005. This would lead to a second national election to select a permanent government in December 2005. Thus, the strategy at the political level was to gradually produce a permanent government of Iraq that would be broadly representative of the population.

Casey inaugurated a military strategy whose goal was to transition responsibility for security from US and coalition forces to Iraqi forces in every province.[37] The transition strategy also envisioned a reduction of US presence among the Iraqi population and a consolidation of U.S forces on as few bases as possible by the end of 2005.[38] This strategy also meant that US forces would gradually withdraw, leaving fewer to conduct operations and control areas in Iraq. At the beginning of 2005 there were three US BCTs operating in the eastern half of Baghdad; only one remained at the end of 2005.[39]

The parallel political and military strategies achieved what appeared to be significant successes in 2005. All three Iraqi national elections were held with minimal disruption by insurgents. Operations in Tal Afar and Al Qaim pacified cities that had previously been centers of insurgent activity.[40] The Iraqi Army (IA) grew rapidly and participated in operations throughout the country. However, these successes were largely on the surface.

Sunni Arabs boycotted the January 2005 election which ultimately produced a constitution that might deprive them of access to political power and their share of the resources under federalization.[41] They were granted some representation and did help draft the constitution, which included a set, but limited, number of seats for Sunni areas regardless of turnout.[42] Sunnis voted heavily in the December 2005 election, but this was only for the set number of seats that they had been granted by the constitution, and thus it did not greatly improve their representation and power in the government.[43] Moreover, the IA, while capable of conducting combined operations, was not capable of quelling the insurgency, especially in Sunni areas where it was viewed as a Shi'a occupation army.[44] The IA was largely recruited from Shi'a communities and because it was a national army this naturally required a mostly Shi'a force to be deployed to Sunni populated areas.[45] The inability of the IA and the other security forces to control the insurgency and deal even handedly with the Sunni population was illustrated dramatically in the aftermath of the bombing of the Askariya (Golden) Mosque[46] in Samarra.

The bombing of the Golden Mosque in February 2006 by AQI initiated a cycle of retaliatory violence between the Sunni and Shi'a Arab populations in Iraq, which was especially acute in Baghdad.[47] Some US officers have stated that the bombing of the mosque was not a trigger of the violence, but was only an indicator of the failure of the US approach.[48] However, it is clear that the level of violence between Sunni and Shi'a in Iraq dramatically increased after the bombing occurred.

Despite the massive increase in violence and the inability of the IA, the Iraqi Police (IP), or any of the paramilitary police organizations of the Ministry of Interior[49] to control it, the US transition strategy moved forward. One BCT (Brigade Combat Team) was off ramped[50] during 2005 and instead of deploying to Iraq was sent to Kuwait to serve as a theater reserve.[51] A second BCT was off ramped during 2006 and instructed to remain in Germany and begin a training cycle that included the conduct of gunnery on its mechanized platforms.[52]

The worsening violence, which has been characterized as a civil war, continued nearly unabated, especially in Baghdad.[53] In an attempt to halt the violence, US and Iraqi forces in Baghdad executed two major operations during the late summer of 2006 called Operation TOGETHER FORWARD I and Operation TOGETHER FORWARD II. The concept for both operations was for US forces to clear areas of the city, behind which Iraqi forces would erect new checkpoints, enforce curfews, and secure the population in the cleared areas.[54] Although security improved immediately following US clearing operations, Iraqi forces were unable to maintain security and the operations failed to achieve their objectives.

This prompted the US to end the transition strategy. Of the two BCTs that had been off ramped the first was already deployed to Iraq and the second was ordered to execute an accelerated deployment.[55] This presaged an even greater increase in the number of US forces in Iraq that is commonly referred to as the surge. President Bush announced in January 2007 that an additional five US Army BCTs and two USMC infantry battalions would be deployed to Iraq to reinforce the US forces already operating in the country.[56]

The change in force levels was accompanied by a change in US strategy and a new command team in Baghdad. The new command team consisted of Lieutenant General Raymond Odierno, who assumed command of the Multi-National Corps Iraq (MNC-I) in late 2006, General David Petraeus the new MNF-I commander who arrived in February 2007, and Ambassador Ryan Crocker who assumed his post in March 2007. The new strategy temporarily ended the transition of security responsibility to Iraqi forces and focused on the protection of the population using both US and Iraqi forces.[57] Petraeus believed that a reduction in violence could produce space for political reconciliation to occur.[58]

The surge forces deployed to Iraq at the rate of approximately one BCT per month between February and June 2007. Although initially intended to be used primarily in Baghdad, Odierno also directed surge forces to Anbar province and the areas surrounding Baghdad. The increased force levels initially produced an increase in US casualties, but were accompanied by a dramatic reduction in violence against Iraqi citizens.[59] Moreover, by the end of 2007, attacks and casualties of all kinds had significantly decreased.[60]

The increase in US forces represented by the surge was but one of the causes of the reduction in violence, however. In 2005, tribal leaders in Al Qaim in western Anbar province partnered with USMC forces to drive Al Qaeda out of the city.[61] In September 2006, in the city of Ramadi in Anbar province, a group of Sunni Arab tribal leaders, inspired by the actions in Al Qaim, agreed to partner with US forces to fight AQI.[62] Key to this agreement was that the tribal leaders' forces would ultimately become IPs in order to connect them to the Government of Iraq (GOI).[63] The movement of Sunni Arabs to partner with US forces and become part of the security apparatus in Iraq eventually became known as the Sahwa, or Awakening, movement. Following its success in Anbar, the Awakening spread to Baghdad in late spring 2007.[64]

The Awakening greatly increased the number of security forces available to the US and the GOI to protect the population. In neighborhoods across Baghdad and in the areas surrounding Baghdad, US forces partnered with the Awakening movement to create irregular security forces that would later become known as the Sons of Iraq.[65] Not all of these forces were destined to become IPs, and in some areas there were far more than could ever be integrated into the Iraqi security force structure.[66] However, their temporary inclusion in the security force structure, coupled with their removal from the pool of available insurgent forces, enabled the US and GOI to control a greater amount of territory and reduce violence throughout the country.

The security situation continued to improve throughout Iraq during the remainder of 2007 and into 2008. However, in the spring of 2008 the Shi'a insurgency presented a renewed challenge to the GOI and coalition forces, despite Sadr having been forced to declare a cease fire in the fall of 2007 because of the pressure applied by the coalition as a result of operations targeting the leadership of JAM.[67] The trouble began in the southern Iraqi city of Basra, which was the responsibility of British Army forces.

British forces, with agreement from MNF-I, began to withdraw from Iraq in 2007 and wanted to transition control of Basra to the GOI.[68] To facilitate this transition, British forces entered into an "accommodation" with JAM elements in Basra to cease operations in the city in return for an end to attacks against British soldiers.[69] The withdrawal of British forces from Basra prevented them from having a good understanding of the situation, but they were convinced that the IA division in charge of the city was "sufficiently mature to underpin PIC [Provincial Iraqi Control] by December 2007."[70] They were not.

Violence increased throughout Basra and shortly after the last JAM prisoner was released by British forces in accordance with the Accommodation, attacks against British forces resumed as well.[71] Basra was effectively under the control of JAM. The IA division commander wanted to regain control of the city deliberately, but he was overruled by the Iraqi Prime Minister, Nouri al Maliki, who ordered two brigades to the city to confront JAM in a poorly planned operation.[72] Ultimately, Operation CHARGE OF THE KNIGHTS was supported by US Army, USMC, and British forces. It regained control of the city, achieving the original objective of the British to transition control of Basra to the GOI, though not in the way that they had originally intended.[73]

The operation instigated additional JAM attacks in cities throughout Iraq but especially in Baghdad. Attacks increased significantly throughout the city and US Army forces were redeployed away from the relatively peaceful Sunni neighborhoods of Baghdad to fight against JAM in Shula, Sadr City, and other neighborhoods.[74] Sadr was again forced to declare a cease fire but not before the GOI had regained control of Baghdad and a significant portion of Sadr City.

The security situation continued to improve following the end of Charge Of The Knights and the violence perpetrated by JAM in the spring of 2008. The US surge forces withdrew and were not replaced. In January 2009, the US and Iraq signed a security agreement that established a series of milestones for the withdrawal of US forces and the transition of responsibility for security to Iraqi forces. US forces ended unilateral operations in urban areas on June 30, 2009.[75]

The transition of responsibility continued throughout 2009 and into 2010. In 2010, US BCTs began operating primarily as advisers to ISF and assumed responsibility for greater and greater amounts of territory as the withdrawal continued. By the summer of 2010, only one US BCT remained in Baghdad where it was partnered with six different division-size ISF elements and the IPs.[76] In July 2011, the US had just six BCTs and three division headquarters remaining in Iraq. All of these forces withdrew from Iraq by mid-December 2011 in accordance with the security agreement.[77]

Control Mechanism

It might appear that there never existed a holistic control mechanism in Iraq. However, Iraq was governed, and therefore controlled, by civil law for almost the entire period of the campaign. Unfortunately, it was not always clear to commanders on the ground or to the Iraqi people what the law said and how it could be applied. As a result, the control mechanism of civil law was less effective than it could have been.[78]

While the invasion was ongoing, control of Iraq was exercised by multiple authorities. In areas where the Saddam regime was still in power, it exercised control. In areas which the US and its coalition partners occupied, they exercised control. In areas where the regime no longer was in control but which had not been secured and occupied, it could be said that no one was in control.

While the US wished to avoid being characterized as an occupying force, the US Army field manual on the law of land warfare identifies that:

> Military occupation is a question of fact. It presupposes a hostile invasion, resisted or unresisted, as a result of which the invader has rendered the

invaded government incapable of publicly exercising its authority, and that the invader has successfully substituted its own authority for that of the legitimate government in the territory invaded.[79]

Therefore, as soon as the US military began securing and holding Iraqi cities, such as An Najaf and As Samawah, they were occupied and should have been subject to military government. Nor was it necessary to issue a proclamation declaring occupation.

Moreover, occupation is not permanent. Rather, "military occupation confers upon the invading force the means of exercising control for the period of occupation. It does not transfer the sovereignty to the occupant, but simply the authority or power to exercise some of the rights of sovereignty."[80] This meant that, by recognized international law, the US and its coalition allies' occupation of Iraq would had to have been only temporary. The occupation and the exercise of some rights of the Iraqi state, though, were necessary to "maintaining law and order, indispensable both to the inhabitants and to the occupying force."[81]

However, even if the US had made the decision to control Iraq through a military government it still would have needed sufficient forces to do so. The situation in Baghdad demonstrated that the US did not have enough forces on the ground to maintain control. The 3ID had around 1,200 dismounted infantry to conduct patrols and were spread thin trying to cover the vast number of critical sites in the capital city.[82] Moreover, the collapse of the police meant that US forces could not use them to assist in the maintenance of law and order.[83]

The looting in Baghdad and other cities disillusioned many Iraqis, even those who may have had a favorable view of the US invasion. The power vacuum created by "the regime's collapse was far more vivid to Iraqis, who often did not comprehend why Coalition forces would not immediately fill that void."[84] Lawlessness, the collapse of power grids, and general insecurity, when combined with a society in which nearly everyone had access to firearms, produced a situation that was nearly impossible for the US and coalition forces to control.[85] This was especially so without clear guidance about what powers the military could exercise and which laws it should enforce.

In May 2003, the administration established the CPA. Though not required to do so, the United States and Great Britain sought legal recognition for the new body from the United Nations Security Council (UNSC). In late May 2003, UNSC Resolution 1483 recognized the "specific authorities, responsibilities, and obligations under applicable international law of these states [the United States and the United Kingdom] as occupying powers."[86] Furthermore, the UNSC directed the CPA "to promote the welfare of the Iraqi people through the effective administration of the territory, including in particular working towards the restoration of conditions of security and stability and the creation of conditions in which the Iraqi people can freely determine their own political future."[87]

Recognition by the UNSC and the broad authority that it provided gave the CPA tremendous power to shape conditions in Iraq. In truth, the CPA had already begun exercising such authority. It issued CPA Order No. 1 on 16 May 2003, entitled a "De-Baathfication of Iraqi Society."[88] The order immediately removed all "Senior Party Members" of the Baath from government and directed that managers in the top three levels of all government agencies be investigated and removed from their positions if determined to be full party members, even those junior in rank.[89]

The CPA followed up this order by issuing Order No. 2, "Dissolution of Entities," on 23 May 2003.[90] The specific entities dissolved were listed in an annex to the order and included the Ministry of Defense, the Iraqi Intelligence Service, the National Security Bureau, the Directorate of National Security, the Special Security Organization, and all of the military services.[91] Also dissolved were all agencies subordinate to those specifically named. The plan to utilize Iraqi resources, especially those of the military, to help control the country was now impossible.

The first two orders of the CPA can be interpreted as the first major effort to implement population and resource control measures by the US and its coalition partners. They did so poorly, however. While it was not wrong to ban the Baath party per se, it was far more embedded in Iraqi society, and its rank structure more inflated, than was understood at the time.[92] One Iraqi recalled that the Baath party "had become part of the fabric of Iraqi society, a complex, interrelated pyramid of economic, political, religious, and tribal links. .. but to dismantle the Party, the Army, and the other structure of the state was only to replace them with chaos."[93]

Thus, the combination of the two orders ended up depriving the US of many tools that could have helped it control the population. The De-Baathfication order banned from government even some low level civil servants who could have helped the US administer the country. The dissolution of the army and the other elements of the security apparatus prevented the US and coalition forces from leveraging their manpower as had been intended in the original plan.

At the same time, the CPA did not, and probably could not, direct US and coalition military forces to enforce the law. CPA Regulation No. 1 stated that "the Commander of US Central Command shall directly support the CPA by deterring hostilities; maintaining Iraq's territorial integrity and security; searching for, securing and destroying weapons of mass destruction; and assisting in carrying out Coalition policy generally."[94] Deterring hostilities and carrying out policy generally could mean that US military forces should enforce the law but they were not directed to do so.

Coalition Provisional Authority Order No. 7, issued in early June, re-emphasized this point. This order established the 1969 version of the Iraqi penal code as the basis of maintaining law and order. It further directed that "all judges, police and prosecutors shall perform their duties in accordance with CPA Regulation No.1."[95] However, no mention is made of the ability of coalition military forces to enforce the law or what power they could exercise to control the population.

This lack of guidance was critical, especially as later orders begin to establish population and resource control measures under law. An example is CPA Order No. 3., originally issued 23 May 2003, but later amended and revised. Order No. 3 prohibited Iraqi citizens from carrying weapons and required them to register small arms weapons to keep in their home or business.[96] It also provided that "firearms or Military Weapons, including Special Category Weapons, possession or use of which is unauthorized, are subject to confiscation by Coalition Forces and other relevant authorities."[97]

The order also allowed for those in violation of it to be arrested and prosecuted but it did not specifically say that this would or could be done by coalition military forces.[98] Thus, one interpretation of the order is that US and coalition forces were allowed to confiscate weapons that they found in violation of the order, but were not allowed to arrest those violators. This had to be done by an Iraqi authority.

Further clarification of the powers of US, coalition, and Iraqi military forces was not forthcoming as the situation developed. UNSC Resolution 1511 reaffirmed the status of the CPA as the governing authority within Iraq and directed that it transfer sovereignty to an Iraqi governing body as soon as possible.[99] It further authorized "a multinational force under unified command to take all necessary measures to contribute to the maintenance of security and stability in Iraq."[100] Therefore, the UNSC provided the military forces within Iraq a broad mandate to implement control measures to ensure security, but the CPA regulations and orders that they were operating under did not specifically direct them about how they could do so.

The Iraqi Governing Council, formed under the CPA's guidance, produced the TAL in the spring of 2004 to govern the country when sovereignty was transferred.[101] The UNSC endorsed this law and the IIG that would form as a result of it in Resolution 1546.[102] The resolution also specifically reauthorized the multinational force presence codified in Resolution 1511 and decided that the:

> Multinational force shall have the authority to take all necessary measures to contribute to the maintenance of security and stability in Iraq in accordance with the letters annexed to this resolution expressing, inter alia, the Iraqi request for the continued presence of the multinational force and setting out its tasks, including by preventing and deterring terrorism.[103]

Thus, the military forces within Iraq, to include US, coalition, and Iraqi forces, again received broad guidance to control violence in Iraq. Their specific authority to do so, however, was limited by the TAL itself. The TAL stipulated that all laws in force on June 30, 2004, would remain in effect, which meant that all the previous CPA orders were still valid.[104] However, it also proscribed certain actions that impeded the ability of security forces to conduct counterinsurgency operations.

The TAL placed the Iraqi military under civilian control and subject to the restrictions contained within it.[105] One such restriction regarded search and seizure. The TAL stated that "police, investigators, or other governmental authorities may not violate the sanctity of private residences, whether these authorities belong to the federal or regional governments, governorates, municipalities, or local administrations, unless a judge or investigating magistrate has issued a search warrant."[106] The TAL also granted Iraqis "the right of free movement in all parts of Iraq."[107]

Taken together, the three provisions referenced above could be interpreted to mean that the Iraqi military could not employ population and resource control measures to counter violence, despite the broad authority granted by the UNSC resolution. However, the text of the TAL provided one further complication. It stated that until a permanent constitution was adopted "the Iraqi Armed Forces will be a principal partner in the multinational force operating in Iraq under unified command pursuant to the provisions of United Nations Security Council Resolution 1511."[108] It was therefore still not clear how much authority the US, coalition, and Iraqi forces actually had to control the population and what specific powers they could use to do so.

Thus, despite the existence of a number of laws that could be used to employ population and resource control measures, it was not clear to commanders on the ground what they could actually do. Moreover, the laws were relatively limited in scope. No mention is made in any specific directive of the ability to enforce curfews, impose movement restrictions, or conduct unannounced searches for weapons, munitions, or other materiel. In fact, the text of the TAL made it appear that such measures were prohibited. Some US commanders employed these measures anyway.[109]

The TAL remained in effect until the Iraqi Constitution was approved by a national referendum in October 2005. The new law did little to clarify the set of authorities and powers that could be used to confront the insurgency. It stated that "the Iraqi Armed Forces shall defend Iraq and shall not be used as an instrument of oppression against the Iraqi people."[110] This clause, interpreted broadly, could restrict the IA's ability to execute counterinsurgency operations. The new constitution also contained a number of restrictions similar to those contained in the TAL.

It directed that "the sanctity of the homes is inviolable and homes may not be entered, searched, or put in danger, except by a judicial decision, and in accordance with the law."[111] It further identified that "each Iraqi enjoys the right of free movement, travel, and residence inside and outside Iraq."[112] Once again, these articles appeared to deny the security forces the ability to employ population and resource control measures in an effort to counter the insurgency.

However, the constitution did allow the Council of Representatives to ratify the declaration of a state of emergency if requested by both the President and the Prime Minister.[113] Once the state of emergency was in place, "the Prime Minister shall be authorized with the necessary powers that enable him to manage the affairs of the country within the period of the state of emergency."[114] The ability to impose a state of emergency therefore provided the Iraqi government with the flexibility to confront the insurgency. It was still unclear what measures the Prime Minister could authorize the security forces to use, however.

Moreover, the new constitution did not specify how the Iraqi security forces would cooperate with the US and coalition forces to confront the insurgency. In fact, the text of the constitution makes no reference to the presence of foreign militaries on Iraqi soil. A series of UNSC resolutions provided the authorization for the continued presence of US and coalition forces within the country.

The first reauthorized coalition presence through 2006.[115] The next permitted the coalition to remain until the end of 2007.[116] Resolution 1790 then extended the mandate through 2008.[117] While these resolutions directed that the multinational force undertake certain additional tasks, each also reaffirmed "the authorization for the multinational force as set forth in Resolution 1546."[118] Thus, the UNSC resolutions provided the coalition with broad authority to take action to maintain security within Iraq, but how it should do so under the restrictions of the new Iraqi constitution was not specified.

Again, this produced a situation where the powers and authorities of the various governments, commanders, and their security forces were not clear. The text of the Iraqi constitution proscribed narrow limits of authority, but then provided flexibility through the mechanism of a state of emergency. The UNSC resolutions gave MNF-I broad authority, but also directed that it should be used in accordance with the wishes of the Iraqi government. These contradictions undermined the civil law control mechanism.

US Counterinsurgency Campaign in Iraq

The US counterinsurgency campaign in Iraq evolved over time and met with many setbacks. It was also plagued by inconsistencies within the US military community about the nature of the insurgency and the proper response to it. As early as July 2003, the commander of CENTCOM, GEN John Abizaid, commented that the US confronted a classic guerrilla campaign.[119] However, at the strategic level a former member of the Army staff recalled that in December 2003, "we were actually told to take the word insurgency out of the National Military Strategy and take all reference to Iraq out of it."[120]

The debate about the nature of the opposition that the US was confronting would continue for a number of years. The former Army staff member observed that "there starts to be some debate in 2005 as folks try to determine is this really an insurgency or not."[121] The debate was not limited to whether or not the US was confronting an insurgency, but also how best to counter any insurgency in Iraq.

Abizaid, a highly educated Arabic speaking American of Lebanese descent, believed that US forces were an anti-body to the Iraqi state and therefore their presence inflamed the insurgency.[122] This assessment seemed plausible at the time and partially drove the decision to adopt the transition strategy. A US Army field grade officer who served in Iraq during 2004 recalled that "the strategy was get out of the cities. It was very in line with GEN Abizaid's anti-body thoughts."[123]

Moreover, the US Army lacked a comprehensive doctrine on counterinsurgency to guide how commanders responded to the threats that they faced. A US Army history of the campaign written at the Combined Arms Center at Fort Leavenworth noted that:

> Instead of relying on institutional experience or well-established doctrine, each American unit in Iraq in the summer of 2003 tended to focus on their immediate challenges and ultimately each took a unique approach to the problems it perceived in their area of responsibility (AOR). In many cases, the commander's perception of the threat became the most important factor driving the unit's approach.[124]

As will be shown, this did not mean that US units did not execute counterinsurgency operations or did not employ classic counterinsurgency tactics and techniques. What it did mean, however, was that unit operations were not synchronized across the theater. A US Army field grade officer recounted that one battalion was allowed to continue to operate in the city of Tikrit in 2004 while another battalion from the same BCT was forced to leave the city of Samarra.[125]

The US military did attempt to improve the understanding of counterinsurgency tactics and techniques and their application in Iraq. In 2005, Casey established a counterinsurgency academy at Camp Taji, Iraq. All incoming commanders and staffs had to attend the one-week course before assuming responsibility for their area of operations.[126] The course provided the incoming commanders and staffs with examples of tactics and techniques that had been successful, but it did not improve operational synchronization. A US Army company commander who served in Iraq in 2005 recalled that "every unit over there was going as hard as they could in their own direction. We all had a mission and we all were plowing ahead as hard as we could, doing our own thing."[127] That is to say, some units were executing counterinsurgency tactically within their own battlespace, but these actions were not synchronized to produce operational effects across the theater.

The synchronization of operations improved when the transition strategy was abandoned and the new command team arrived at the end of 2006 and the beginning of 2007. Critically, they did not direct all units to execute their operations in the same way tactically. Rather, they designed the campaign to coordinate unit operations across the battlespace to achieve operational success. The same company commander stated that in 2007 "we were all pulling together. ... I knew the guys in my sister battalions in the north of Baghdad were doing the same thing I was doing in southern Baghdad."[128] The synchronization of operations would prove critical to the effectiveness of the entire campaign.

Also in 2006 the US Army and USMC issued an updated manual on counterinsurgency. Its affect on US military operations in Iraq is not certain, however. Some units that were in Iraq in late 2006 had not received the manual before they deployed. Nonetheless, they understood counterinsurgency tactics and techniques. As a US Army field grade officer recalled, "we all knew what the options were out there ... and you knew what had to be done, even at the soldier, platoon, company level ... but we finally got the 'let's do it' guidance."[129]

This guidance allowed commanders to confront problems that they had identified in their area of operations and provided them the resources to do so.[130] It also ensured that within the framework of the broader campaign all units would execute operations that were mutually supportive. Moreover, it reflected an abandonment of the anti-body theory of the insurgency and led US units to conduct operations to secure the population in much closer proximity to the population than had been done before.

The changing nature of the campaign described above can be illustrated by examining the employment of population and resource control measures by US units. Throughout the campaign, US units implemented such measures with varying degrees of success. As the campaign evolved so did the use of population and resource control measures. This section will examine the use of population and resource control measures during two portions of the campaign.

The first portion of the campaign that will be examined is the period immediately following the invasion until the implementation of the Baghdad Security Plan in early 2007.[131] Then the period between the implementation of the Baghdad Security Plan until the end of 2008 will be considered. Although US units have continued to employ population and resource control measures in partnership with Iraqi forces since the beginning of 2009, the reduced threat and the changed nature of the relationship between these forces makes it less valuable to study for the purpose of this paper.

Post Invasion–Implementation of the Baghdad Security Plan

Following the fall of the regime and the end of major combat operations, US units were deployed across Iraq to secure and assume control of the vast territory. 1AD assumed control of Baghdad, 101 ABN was sent north to Mosul, 4ID assumed responsibility for much of the Sunni triangle in the area north of Baghdad, including around Saddam's hometown of Tikrit, and 3ID and 3ACR took control of Anbar province.[132] Each division confronted an unique set of circumstances and executed operations differently as a result.

These varying approaches were manifest not just during the early period immediately following the invasion, but were prevalent throughout the campaign, at least until the implementation of the Baghdad Security Plan. As a result, US units employed population and resource control measures in order to confront the specific problems that they identified, but in general did not synchronize such efforts across the battlespace. These individual efforts were often tactically successful but they did not translate into operational and strategic success.

Early Employment of Population and Resource Control Measures

Population and resource control measures were common place early in the campaign. One of the very first CPA orders issued concerned the possession of weapons. Many units responded by issuing weapons cards under the commander's authority as the occupying military officer.[133] These cards provided authorization for the Iraqi populace to maintain a weapon in their home or place of business but did not allow them to carry such weapons. It was difficult for such measures to be effective, however, as the number of weapons and their penetration within the population was so great.[134]

Restricting the possession of weapons was a relatively even-handed response to the insurgency. Not all of the early population and resource control measures were so restrained. Some units responded to insurgent attacks by imposing population and resource control measures punitively. In his personal account, Lieutenant Colonel Nathan Sassaman recalled that after an attack against his battalion in November 2003 he detained about two dozen local sheiks.[135] He asserted that the primary reason for doing so was to gather intelligence but also noted that "that there was a punitive purpose as well."[136]

Sassaman's battalion then imposed a restrictive population and resource control regime on the town of Albu Hishma, which was near the site of the attack. The day after the attack, "we began to wrap the entire village in barbed wire, and closed all but one entrance and exit."[137] The battalion also issued identification cards to adult males and imposed a curfew. These measures were not, however, to protect the population from the insurgency, but to protect Sassaman's own unit. He recalled that "the Iraqi citizens, not surprisingly responded with anger and hostility of their own."[138] Similar actions occurred elsewhere in Iraq as towns that were viewed as uncooperative were wired in.[139]

As the campaign evolved the employment of population and resource control measures by US units became more nuanced, however. In the summer of 2004, the 1st Infantry Division (1ID) conducted Operation BATON ROUGE to regain control of the city of Samarra. After clearing the city, a curfew was imposed, but violence continued. A US Army field grade officer recalled that "after a week or two of this contact, we realized that it was cyclic in nature. We set up a vehicular curfew that started at 1800 and the pedestrian curfew at 1900. The mines were going out between the two because there were no Iraqi cars on the road at that time."[140] The battalion responded by adjusting "the curfew so that the vehicle and pedestrian curfew [were] on at the same time."[141]

Employing population and resource control measures to react to specific enemy actions also occurred in Tikrit during the same time frame. A US Army battalion commander recalled that "we had a period of time where it seemed like every VBIED [Vehicle Borne Improvised Explosive Device] that took place was a taxi cab. So I did a program called ORANGE CRUSH,[142] registration of every taxi cab. We pull them over, queue them up, make sure that we have water for them, give them a few dinar when we register them."[143]

To conduct this operation, the battalion partnered with the local Iraqi forces to establish checkpoints to stop every taxi cab, photograph the driver with the cab, and then place a shipping label that the battalion had printed out on each one.[144] Although there were a large number of such vehicles in the city and the battalion did not have the ability to track each one, this measure was still effective. The battalion commander noted that "it pulled the taxi cabs off the grid."[145] One of his field grade officers observed that "the insurgents had no idea what the hell we were doing, but they stayed away from taxis."[146]

Although the disruption to the insurgency as a result of such operations was only short term, it provided units time and space to adjust and continue to target the insurgency. Moreover, they helped to protect the population as attacks by VBIEDs often resulted in more Iraqi than American casualties. In a large city such as Tikrit it would have been difficult to completely control vehicular movement but in smaller towns units did exactly that.

The town of Haqlaniyah is near Haditha in western Anbar province. In 2005 this area was the responsibility of Multi-National Force West, the USMC command in Iraq. The Marine unit responsible for the area had seen heavy fighting and did not have enough combat power to control every town within the area. As a result, the town of Haqlaniyah had not had any US presence for an extended period of time.[147] In preparation for the constitutional referendum and national elections in late 2005, a US Army battalion was deployed to regain control of the town.

The battalion executed a night attack to secure the town. The night time assault gave the battalion a number of advantages over the insurgents in the town but the commander recalled that:

> Those advantages kind of disappeared when the sun came up and people started walking around and our momentum slows down. We decided not to stop the momentum and we shut down all vehicle traffic through PSYOP [psychological operations] broadcast teams and every method possible. I made it very clear that no one was going to move a vehicle, and no one did.[148]

This proved feasible for a few days, but then the battalion had to adjust.

The commander remembered that:

> It would start to be a pain in the ass because sooner or later people needed to start going places: food needed to be delivered, fuel needed to be delivered, people needed to go to the hospital. Things needed to happen. We started a vehicle registration program. I directed that everyone in town who owned a car had to present their ID and register their car and we would provide them a pass ... to put in their windshield and that would allow them to move their vehicle.[149]

The battalion employed this measure to deter attacks by car, including VBIED attacks, but also was able to use it to target the insurgency. The battalion commander noted that during the registration process several people on its targeting list came with their cars and were detained on the spot.[150] The battalion combined the vehicle registration operations with patrols, observation posts, and sniper positions to deter movement of any kind. The commander recalled that the operations "suppressed the enemy's freedom of movement because of the vehicle ban, the aggressive patrolling, and the use of snipers, even if they weren't snipers. The feedback we got from the enemy talking was that Haqlaniyah was a very inhospitable place to be."[151]

The battalion's employment of population and resource control measures, in concert with standard operations such as patrolling, was tactically very effective. The battalion did not remain in the area beyond the execution of the elections, however. The population and resource control measures and level of patrolling could not be maintained. Therefore, the tactical success that the battalion achieved did not translate into broader operational success, despite the low level of violence across Iraq during the elections.

Baghdad

US units were also employing population and resource control measures in response to specific enemy actions in Baghdad, though the enormity of the city made this difficult.[152] The two most significant threats to the population and US forces in Baghdad were VBIED attacks by Sunni insurgents and Explosively Formed Penetrator (EFP)[153] Improvised Explosive Device (IED) attacks by Shi'a insurgents. The former, though they were sometimes used to attack US forces, were more often employed to cause large numbers of casualties among the Shi'a population of Baghdad; the latter exclusively targeted US forces.

During late summer of 2005 there were a large number of VBIED attacks in Baghdad, including one day which AQI dubbed the "day of a thousand VBIEDs." In response to these attacks, Iraqi security forces, particularly the Public Order Battalions from the Ministry of Interior, established vehicle checkpoints throughout the city. Iraqi security forces also wanted to establish a berm or wall around Baghdad and control all movement into the city. Checkpoints on roads leading into the capital were established, but a berm was not.[154] These checkpoints were often insufficiently manned and protected, and failed to prevent VBIED attacks in the city.

Other measures did, however. In preparation for the referendum and national elections in the fall of 2005, US forces emplaced concrete barriers around polling sites.[155] These sites were then secured by IA or Public Order Battalion units to deny VBIED attacks on election day. The GOI also imposed a night-time curfew and imposed a total ban on vehicle movement in the days prior to the elections. Few attacks were conducted during the elections and this allowed a fairly high participation rate. So the measures did produce tactical success. Once they were lifted, however, the effects disappeared.

EFP attacks were especially difficult to counter. During 2004 and 2005 the sophistication of EFPs advanced significantly. By the fall, multiple penetrators were being combined into a single device that could be rapidly emplaced and easily camouflaged. In an effort to combat this, the unit responsible for securing many of the routes in east Baghdad conducted operations to deny insurgents the terrain that was most favorable to the employment of EFPs. They did so using a variety of methods.

The first method was to simply use random patrols of armored vehicles along the routes to deny insurgents the opportunity to emplace them. They also established temporary observation posts with patrols to surveil one intersection that had been used in a number of EFP attacks. Moreover, the unit utilized a camera mounted on a large tower to persistently observe the intersection from a nearby US base. If insurgents were identified a patrol could be diverted to the location.

The battalion also conducted an operation to remove all potential camouflage along Route Brewers.[156] First, the battalion secured large armored bulldozers which pushed all of the trash and debris away from the shoulders of the road. The battalion then removed the metal guard rails from the highway, which had been used to conceal EFPs. Finally, the battalion employed a specialized vehicle which combined a spray of a flammable mixture and an ignition source to burn all of the vegetation remaining along the side of the road.

These operations did deny Shi'a insurgents the ability to use this terrain for EFP attacks, but only for a short period of time. Eventually, the patrols became less effective as the insurgents lessened the time needed to emplace the devices. Persistent observation and occupation of the intersection was consistently effective, but consumed a large amount of combat power. Removing camouflage reduced attacks for a short period of time, but EFPs were soon emplaced among new camouflage.[157]

Similar operations were occurring across Baghdad with similar results. US forces, the GOI, and Iraqi forces would implement a new measure and attacks would recede. Once the measure was lifted, or the insurgents had determined a means to respond to it, the attacks returned. This pattern was seen during Operations Together Forward I and II. US forces searched an area, Iraqi forces temporarily secured it, but attacks resumed soon after the clearance concluded.

The measures were not synchronized in a way to produce lasting effects. Moreover, operations of individual units, such as the terrain denial operations described above, were not supported by those of other units. However, outside of Baghdad, US units in 2005 and 2006 began to employ population and resource control measures and synchronize operations in ways that produced long term effects.

Tal Afar and Ramadi

The city of Tal Afar lies west of Mosul in the Ninewah province of Iraq and has a mixed Sunni and Shi'a population. The city had been cleared by US forces in 2004, but soon after their departure the city was under the control of Sunni insurgents who were using it to support their operations in the rest of Iraq.[158] The security situation was so poor that the Iraqi police commander of the region could not find an officer to become the chief of police in the city. The man who eventually did so recalled that:

> No one wanted to take this position. He [the regional police commander] asked many, many officers to take this position and no one would accept the position in Tal Afar. Tal Afar was tough city and the population was mixed–Sunni, Shi'a, Turkomen–and it was very dangerous. He told me he asked 64 officers and they all turned him down.[159]

To regain control of the city, Casey deployed the 3ACR under the command of Colonel H.R. McMaster to Tal Afar in late spring 2005 to conduct Operation RESTORING RIGHTS. Rather than simply clearing the city as had been done previously, 3ACR conducted a deliberate campaign to remove the insurgent presence and ensure that it did not return. The unit began by conducting cordon and search operations in the surrounding villages to force the insurgents out of them and isolate Tal Afar.[160]

The unit then entered into a partnership with the Iraqi forces in the city, led by the mayor/police chief, to continue the campaign into the city. As part of this plan, the unit employed a number of population control measures. The former mayor remembered that:

> We had checkpoints in the city on the road to Mosul on the Sinjar road, the Muhallahbiya road but that didn't prohibit terrorists from entering the city. They would come at night easily into the city in cars. Or they would use sheep to pretend to be shepherds. So we found a way to stop it. What we did is we had checkpoints around the city but it is a big city and would need a lot of checkpoints to stop everything. The terrorists could also attack those CPs at night. It wasn't very effective. So we saw that it would be better, especially since the 3d Iraqi Army Division had a

lot of cranes, that they make a berm that it would be difficult for cars to pass. So it would make the cars that wanted to get to the city, they could only go through the checkpoints.[161]

After isolating the city, 3ACR was able to conduct a clearing operation of the city and establish combat outposts (COPs) that US and Iraqi forces jointly occupied inside it.[162] The commander of a battalion attached to 3ACR during the operation stated that his "battalion task force moved into the violent Sarai neighborhood and transitioned to stability operations within 72 hours."[163] The employment of population and resource controls did not end there, however.

The same battalion commander noted that his battalion collected census information as part of the process of settling claims for damages done during operations. The commander observed that:

> The census helped us gain situational awareness because it documented identities, afforded a means of cross-checking stories and histories, and provided pictures of suspected insurgents that we could use to test the veracity and accuracy of our intelligence sources. After we had established the credibility of an intelligence source, we could then ask him to identify insurgents from among the census photos and to provide detailed witness statements of violent acts by those insurgents. Altogether, the census enhanced our targeting and thus our ability to defeat insurgent cells.[164]

Although the berm, the checkpoints, and the large number of US forces living in the city severely disrupted the daily life of the population, this was welcomed. The former mayor remembered that "the Shi'a liked it. They knew the reason why. The Sunnis, the tribal leaders that were loyal to us told their people it was OK. ... The people who want security, they have to sacrifice. Everyone has to sacrifice if you want security."[165] The anti-body theory of the insurgency did not prove true in Tal Afar. US units, partnered with Iraqi forces and taking steps to secure the population, successfully eliminated the Sunni insurgency in the city.

Operation RESTORING RIGHTS eliminated a base of support for the Sunni insurgency and facilitated permanent GOI control of the city. This was made possible by 3ACR's large amount of combat power and the manner in which it synchronized its operations and its employment of population and resource control measures. Shaping operations outside of the city removed potential support areas for the insurgency before operations in the city began. Population and resource control measures within the city denied insurgents freedom of movement and facilitated the unit's targeting of them.

The operations in Tal Afar demonstrated that synchronized population and resource control measures could help US forces achieve more than just short term tactical effects. This lesson was absorbed by the unit which replaced 3ACR, the 1st BCT from 1AD, which applied and expanded on them to achieve another significant success in the city of Ramadi.

The successful operations in Al Qaim in late 2005-early 2006 had begun to improve the situation in Anbar province as Al Qaeda was denied the use of a critical base of support near the Syrian border and along the main route leading east to Ramadi, Fallujah, and then Baghdad. However, the Sunni insurgency was still deeply embedded in the city of Ramadi. In fact, an August 2006 assessment from a USMC intelligence officer from I MEF concluded that *"the social and political situation has deteriorated to a point that MNF and ISF are no longer capable of militarily defeating the insurgency in al-Anbar."*[166] A battalion commander who served in Ramadi in 2006 recalled that the BCT commander he served under was ordered to retake Ramadi "but don't make it like Fallujah."[167]

In other words, do not conduct a direct assault on the city that will destroy it and cost significant US casualties. 1BCT, 1AD did not; rather, it executed synchronized operations that employed population and resource control measures. A US Army BCT commander noted that initially the five battalions in Ramadi were conducting largely independent operations.[168] To rectify this situation and confront the insurgency the BCT "had to develop a series of mutually supporting operations that would systematically deprive the enemy of his safe havens."[169]

The unit did this by systematically clearing areas, establishing COPs in them, and then building up local security forces to help protect the population. The unit also conducted a census operation. A battalion commander in Ramadi recalled that "my goal was that every house in Anbar was numbered. What I wanted to get done was that they could tell us who lived in every house before you went in. We were trying to figure out who was who."[170] The BCT combined census information from all of its subordinate battalions into a database that was created by a junior enlisted intelligence analyst in one of the battalions.[171]

The BCT also employed other population and resource control measures. In coordination with the Iraqi forces in the town it imposed a curfew, established "gated communities" that had access control and patrols, and "tried to get to the point where we had windshield stickers and register vehicles."[172] The unit also conducted terrain denial operations. The unit "did all kinds of terrain denial: kinetic/non-kinetic, direct fire, indirect fire, fast movers [fixed wing aircraft], UAVs off set" in order to deny the insurgents the ability to use a particular area or draw them to an area and target them with lethal fires.[173]

As the effects of these operations accumulated it produced a profound change in the population. The BCT commander stated that "as we took the fight to the enemy and deprived him of more and more resources and control over parts of the population some of the local sheikhs took heart from that and that coupled with our presence in combat outposts in their tribal areas encouraged them to stand up and form the Awakening Movement."[174] One of the battalion commanders recalled that the improved security provided by the unit's operations and establishment of COPs "broke the intimidation. That was the real turning point. They needed that sense of security in order to give us or the ISF the information that we needed."[175]

As in Tal Afar, the operations of 1BCT, 1AD in Ramadi produced not just tactical effects, but contributed to operational and strategic effects. Ramadi lies along the main highway leading from Anbar into Baghdad. So by denying the Sunni insurgency control of the city, US forces removed a critical support base from which it had been supporting operations in Baghdad. Moreover, by controlling this city that lied along a crucial LOC for the insurgents, it allowed units operating both west and east of Ramadi to better target their own operations, because it was no longer supplying Sunni insurgent attacks in them.

The other major effect of the operations in Ramadi was to provide additional momentum to the Awakening movement. Because the US unit's operations and population and resource control measures effectively protected and isolated the population from the insurgency it allowed the population, now free from intimidation, to choose to protect itself, and in the process support US forces and the GOI.[176] They did so on a tactical level by providing intelligence information. On an operational and strategic level, they joined the Iraqi Police and began a process by which a greater number of Sunni Arab Iraqis would become part of the security force structure.

The US operations in Tal Afar and Ramadi proved that the anti-body theory of the insurgency was a fallacy. They also showed that if US forces synchronized their operations to target the enemy's support areas that they could defeat the Sunni insurgency in that area. Moreover, they demonstrated that by using population and resource control measures as part of those synchronized operations, US forces could better protect and isolate the population, giving them the ability to support the counterinsurgents without fear of intimidation or murder. US forces would apply these lessons during 2007 and 2008 in operations in Baghdad and the surrounding areas.

Baghdad Security Plan–2008

The operations in Ramadi were beginning to show significant success in the fall of 2006. At the same time, the US was undergoing a major review of its strategy and force structure in Iraq. In the new year, the US announced that it would increase its force structure by an additional five US Army BCTs and two USMC infantry battalions. However, these forces would not arrive immediately and their deployment would actually occur throughout the first six months of the year.

What did change dramatically at the end of 2006 and the beginning of 2007 was the US strategy in Iraq. While the change has generally been credited to General Petraeus, Lieutenant General Odierno actually developed and began implementing a new operational plan in late 2006 and early 2007, prior to Petraeus' arrival. A field grade officer on the MNF-I staff during the time period recalled that Odierno and Colonel Hickey developed an operational concept for the campaign that "was all about locating the enemy's safe havens and sanctuaries and then disrupting those."[177]

Once a safe haven or sanctuary was identified, MNC-I would use the incoming surge forces and "put a unit right on top of that place. ... If they are disrupted there, where will they go next? Then put another unit down there."[178] The officer recalled that this concept was how "the Battle of the Belts[179] was conducted."[180] Denying the Sunni insurgency their supply bases in the areas surrounding Baghdad could potentially slow the violence in Baghdad itself, which was raging essentially unchecked in late 2006.

This idea was reflected in a briefing that Odierno gave Petraeus in early February 2007. In it Odierno described his intent for MNC-I's operations, key to which was that "militarily, we must interdict accelerants of Baghdad sectarian violence emerging from Southern Salah ad Din, Eastern Diyala, and Western Anbar, exploiting recent successes in these areas."[181] To accomplish this, Odierno would use some of the surge forces in Baghdad itself to increase the security of the population, the rest would be used in an offensive operation to secure the Baghdad Belts and deny AQI use of these areas.[182]

Also critical to Odierno's plan were population and resource control measures. In the same briefing to Petraeus, he indicated that one of the conditions for beginning his operations was that the GOI needed to extend the "existing state of emergency, with measures including at a minimum: banning vehicles from selected locations; controlling access into, and internal to, the city as required; random searches of vehicles, people, businesses, and homes; full enforcement of weapons ban."[183]

Thus, Odierno sought to ensure, through the GOI, that all of the measures that he wanted to employ with both US and Iraqi forces were legal in accordance with the Iraqi constitution. This action allowed him to give the "let's go" guidance to commanders that they had needed to begin employing such measures on a large scale. Moreover, by establishing it as a criterion to begin operations he ensured that it would be more difficult for the GOI to end the employment of such measures prematurely.

Battle of the Belts

Notwithstanding the original plan to use the majority of the surge forces inside of Baghdad itself, many of the surge BCTs were actually deployed to areas surrounding Baghdad to deny these areas as safe havens and bases of support for the Sunni insurgency. They conducted operations to prevent the movement of weapons, munitions, and fighters into Baghdad to assist in halting the cycle of retaliatory violence that gripped the city. The BCT commander responsible for the area east of Baghdad recalled that "our task was to block accelerants, bad people, Sunni extremists, Shi'a extremists, and foreign fighters in the Mada'in Qada[184] to prevent them from getting into Baghdad."[185]

In order to accomplish this task the unit created a framework operation called Operation NEW JERSEY TURNPIKE, "that was a series of CPs [checkpoints] on known routes of infiltration ... It started out with just us and then partnered with the Iraqis. ... We picked certain locations on certain MSRs where we put these and then we would change them out."[186] Although the checkpoints rarely captured materials bound for Baghdad, they disrupted the flow of such materials and were a means of "trying to control things and also deter bad things from happening."[187]

The unit employed additional population control measures. They conducted census operations to "map out who lived where and how many Sunnis and Shi'as."[188] In the process of collecting this information, the units were able to build relationships with the population which could later be leveraged to gain intelligence information about the enemy. The relationship also facilitated the unit's ability to explain the actions that it was taking.

This proved critical when the unit conducted terrain denial operations. The BCT commander recounted that he fired artillery on locations that had been used by insurgents to shoot mortars at coalition bases.[189] Though this often upset the population in the area, he was able to use relationships with the sheiks to explain why he was conducting these actions and told them that "I will stop firing those fires as soon as you stop people from going into your backyard and firing mortars."[190]

On the other side of the Tigris River, another BCT was conducting similar operations in the farmland south of Baghdad. This area had seen very little US presence during the campaign and the Sunni insurgency was using it as a support base for attacks in Baghdad when the BCT arrived in the summer of 2007. The BCT commander recalled that:

> Our job was to go in and clear out the insurgents. When you look at a map, along the Tigris there was a route, it was called Route Gnat, it was basically a hardball, intermittent dirt road that ran all the way from Sayifia right into Baghdad. ... homegrown Al Qaeda were using that, and other insurgents were using that, as a means to get into the city, and also transit further out to the west, because they could just go around Baghdad off that route and it had to be blocked. So, we had to block the insurgents, defeat the enemy threat in the region, and protect the population. Those were the three missions.[191]

To accomplish these missions, the BCT executed a deliberate plan to systematically clear areas of the Sunni insurgents, establish COPs, and then build local security forces to maintain security. A major component of this plan was the employment of population and resource control measures. The BCT recognized that the limited road networks in the area were all essential LOCs for the insurgents. This led the unit to establish movement controls on the routes. The BCT commander stated that:

> We physically blocked the roads coming into Baghdad. In the south ...we physically blocked that exit of the southern portion of the battle space and put our checkpoints out, our patrols, until we could get others to come out and to man those checkpoints. Curfews, no vehicles moving; no vehicles moving on that road unless we clear it and, at night time, no vehicles moving.[192]

Physically blocking the insurgent LOCs produced immediate effects. A company commander in the BCT reported that "there were three Tier 1 hotspots[193] on Route Tampa that died after I took crossing point Whiskey 1 over the Bismarck Canal and blocked it so that they couldn't get out there anymore. Within a month, three Tier 1 hotspots on Tampa were gone."[194] The unit did not limit its movement controls to the road, however.

The BCT also identified that Sunni insurgents were using the Tigris River to transport supplies. As a result, the BCT prohibited all river traffic and the commander made it "very clear, to every leader in the area, 'You will not be on the water; and, if you're on the water, you will be deemed as hostile.'"[195] To make this restriction effective, the BCT coordinated with the unit on the other side of the river to help them enforce it.[196]

Like its sister unit across the river, the BCT also employed terrain denial fires, shooting artillery onto historical insurgent mortar firing points. The BCT fired the artillery onto these sites "to force them into areas where we could engage them. That was the key."[197] The BCT also conducted census operations and enrolled the Iraqi populace in a biometric database using the Biometric Automated Tool Set (BATS) and Handheld Interagency Identity Detection Equipment (HIIDE).[198][199]

Despite the invasive, coercive, and restrictive nature of the measures, the population was generally positive about their effects. The BCT commander recalled that "we presented it to them that, 'this is to secure you.' ... they had movement; they just didn't have freedom of movement to where they could go anytime they wanted to, day or night."[200] He also noted that once an area was cleared and the restrictions were in place that the populace would work with his units to identify caches of weapons, munitions, and other supplies.[201]

Similar operations were being conducted to the northwest of Baghdad in the area around the town of Sab al Boor. The US Army battalion commander in that area recounted that:

> We did an operation where we looked at all the LOCs coming into Sab al Boor and we routed everybody through a checkpoint or a series of checkpoints that were integrated. So we now had at least control of access or for people leaving the city as well. So we could put a stranglehold on supplies and things going in. We did cache clearances and other things because we had a lot of unpopulated areas in the city.[202]

What is critical to note about these operations is that they were being conducted not only to improve security in the areas where they took place, but also to support operations in Baghdad itself. This was despite the fact that the BCTs conducting operations in the Baghdad Belts were not under the control of Multi-National Division, Baghdad (MND-B). They were also, in the case of the first two BCTs described, mutually supportive of one another.

This synchronization of operations across the battlespace, both in method and in purpose, allowed each of the unit's population and resource control measures to be more effective. Previously, if one US unit interdicted a LOC being used by the insurgency, it could easily transfer its supplies to another that went to the same location. This was especially true for Baghdad. However, with US units interdicting all of the LOCs into Baghdad, it made it much more difficult for the insurgency, particularly the Sunni insurgency, to resource attacks in the capital.

Baghdad

While US forces in the Baghdad Belts were interdicting the movement of fighters and supplies, what Odierno had called "accelerants", into the city, the units in the city were confronted by a battle between Sunni and Shi'a insurgents for control of the city. One BCT commander who served in Baghdad recalled that "the real problem, however, when we got there, was the cycle of violence between Sunni and Shi'a. We had AQI, but Shi'a extremists were in the northern part of our AO, but were trying to expand their control over physical territory."[203] A member of the MNF-I staff noted that "the militants who ran Sadr City were trying to project power into West Baghdad and then the militants who held sway in Dora and a couple of other spots in West Baghdad were trying to project power into East Baghdad."[204]

Another issue was that the Sunni and Shi'a insurgents were presenting themselves as protectors of their own populations against attacks by the other. A US Army field grade officer recounted that Sunnis in Baghdad felt that they had to "rely on Al Qaeda and other Sunni extremists as the only recourse against the Shi'a expansion."[205] The presence of AQI was used "as an excuse" by the Shi'a community to justify attacking Sunnis as a "way to get at AQ."[206]

The battle between Sunni and Shi'a insurgents created a situation where units in different parts of Baghdad confronted similar but opposite problems. One BCT commander stated that his unit had to "deny the access of the Shi'a extremists to the Sunni populated areas and we had to defeat Al Qaeda."[207] Another BCT commander recounted that he "wanted to separate them [Al Qaeda in Iraq] from the Shi'a neighborhoods and protect the people, to keep the flow of insurgents from going in freely and coming out freely, and hiding among the populace."[208]

The overarching operation that would guide and facilitate all unit operations in Baghdad was the Baghdad Security Plan, officially called Operation FARDH AL QANOON (Enforcing The Law). The Baghdad Security Plan was similar in concept to Operations Together Forward I and

II which had failed to create a lasting security improvement in Baghdad. There were major differences between the first two operations and the new Baghdad Security Plan, however.

The previous two operations had combined clearance of neighborhoods by US forces with long term security provided by Iraqi forces after the US unit departed the neighborhood but, the Baghdad Security Plan, as described by the MND-B commander, consisted of:

> Three basic parts: clear, control and retain. The first objective within each of the security districts in the Iraqi capital is to clear out extremist elements neighborhood by neighborhood in an effort to protect the population and after an area is cleared, we're moving to what we call the control operation. Together with our Iraqi counterparts, we'll maintain a full-time presence on the streets, and we'll do this by building and maintaining joint security stations throughout the city.[209]

Moreover, rather than relying on Iraqi forces, primarily IPs, to provide security to the population after the clearance operation was completed, the plan involved "the application of military force to ensure that the security of the people of Baghdad is solidly established and sustained."[210] This was critical because the IP, IA, and Iraqi National Police (INP) had failed to secure the population during previous operations.

US units also employed far more population and resource control measures than had been used to this point in the campaign. In fact, senior staff at MNC-I asserted that "population control is a key part of Operation FARDH AL QANOON."[211] The baseline of which was the set of security measures outlined by Odierno in his briefing to Petraeus. As previously discussed, US and Iraqi forces had regularly enforced such measures in Baghdad for limited periods of time. During the Baghdad Security Plan, the measures would be combined and maintained to break the cycle of violence. At the center of these measures was the establishment of safe neighborhoods, also called gated communities.

The concept behind the safe neighborhoods was simple: completely surround a single neighborhood[212] with a solid set of concrete walls, create a limited number of access points to the neighborhood, and then conduct searches of and enforce movement restrictions on all traffic, vehicular and foot, moving in and out of the neighborhood. The walls denied the insurgent groups' freedom of movement in the city, protected and isolated the population from them, and facilitated US and Iraqi targeting operations. Moreover, the walls could address either problem set described above: they could secure a Sunni community from Shi'a insurgent attacks and allow them to disavow AQI or they could secure a Shi'a community from Sunni insurgent attacks and allow them to disassociate from JAM and other Shi'a extremists.

While some units established walls unilaterally, others emplaced them very deliberately in consultation with the local community. One BCT commander recounted that the local neighborhood leader "explained to us where best to put the walls ... and then we took up on that and drew out a plan, which included the barriers along the MSR [main supply route], all the way to the MSR overpass. That would be the only way in."[213] Moreover, the emplacement of walls "was based on risk assessment and was tied to the placement of combat outposts."[214]

As the walls started to go in around Baghdad some communities began asking for them. One US Army battalion commander remembered that "we actually had a neighborhood that asked for concrete. ... We did an operation at the request of the leadership of one of the neighborhoods and we walled in a neighborhood because they wanted us to wall them in."[215] Even in neighborhoods where the population initially viewed the walls negatively, the attitude changed once the population recognized a tangible improvement in their security.[216]

Emplacement of the walls often resulted in a rapid reduction of violence. One US Army BCT commander recalled that the walls "dramatically stopped the flow of violence and lethal aid into the neighborhood."[217] A US Army battalion commander in another part of the city observed that after the walls were in place, "we didn't see the attacks on the Sunni population coming from the Shi'a. We saw a reduction of the SVBIED [Suicide VBIED] attacks."[218] The security and isolation provided by the safe neighborhoods also allowed the population to begin supporting US forces and the GOI.

The Sunni Awakening movement that had begun in Al Qaim and Ramadi spread into Baghdad in the late spring of 2007. Once walls were established around some neighborhoods of Baghdad, local leaders came forward and offered to form local security forces to reinforce the protection provided by US and Iraqi units.[219] The local Iraqi populace also then felt secure enough to provide intelligence to US and Iraqi forces. A BCT commander stated that after the emplacement of walls "exponential tips came into company commanders."[220]

The safe neighborhood program did not entirely account for the reduction in violence, however. The level of violence had been so high for so long that many neighborhoods which had once been mixed were entirely segregated by the time the program began. A senior civilian serving at MNC-I remarked that the walls were:

> not stopping anything, the worst of the violence [had] run its course and the communities had been separated. People had swapped houses. So then you're making these enclaves and these enclaves, at a certain stage, people feel safer. Initially there's a sense that 'I feel safe in my neighborhood,' but then there comes a time of 'but it's not my neighborhood really, and I can't go back where I am really from.' It started to cement divisions in a society which had been very mixed.[221]

This is a valid criticism of the program and many of the walls were still in place as of 2010.[222] However, it is not true that all of the violence had run its course. The BCT and battalion commanders interviewed noted significant reductions in violence. In June 2007, after the safe neighborhood program had been executed in many neighborhoods, units were still finding the bodies of Iraqi civilians who had been murdered by Sunni or Shi'a insurgents.[223] Moreover, the walls did not just target the Sunni-Shi'a violence itself, they also served to interdict the flow of weapons, munitions and materials and facilitated the targeting of insurgents by US and Iraqi forces.

The safe neighborhood program was not the only population and resource control measure employed in Baghdad. Units also reinforced the actions of the BCTs in the Baghdad Belts by interdicting the flow of supplies into their neighborhoods. A US Army field grade officer recounted that "we knew where the Al Qaeda lines were coming from Anbar. Let's make it difficult, the first time they approach Baghdad, the Sunni terrorists, let's make it difficult for them to get into those neighborhoods."[224]

In order to make it difficult, the BCT extended the walls associated with the safe neighborhood program west along the main road leading into Baghdad from Anbar province. The BCT commander stated that "we put nine foot barriers on both sides of the MSR. Once you got into there you couldn't get off into the farmlands and infiltrate into the city. Once you got into the pipe you had to go through a series of CPs [checkpoints] manned by the Iraqi Army."[225] Other units in Baghdad were interdicting supply bases by using terrain denial fires.

One BCT Commander recounted that "on that far eastern edge along the river there was a perfect rectangular palm grove region and the [main supply route] ran right along that. So you had a major confluence of major high speed avenues of approach."[226] He recalled that Sunni insurgents "would camp out and stage and cache" supplies in the palm grove.[227] In response he fired artillery and mortars "on preplanned targets and denied that area because I couldn't patrol it. Area denial."[228] The commander noted that once he began conducting terrain denial operations "it dramatically cut down the numbers of IED incidents I was having ... Eventually they just stopped going in there."[229]

Units within Baghdad supported their interdiction efforts by conducting cordon and searches of neighborhoods to capture or destroy enemy supplies. Large cache finds consisting of several IEDs or hundreds of pounds of homemade explosive were common in Baghdad through the summer of 2007.[230] As operations continued into the fall of 2007 and winter of 2008, cache finds occurred less often and contained fewer weapons and munitions.

However, it is hard to assess precisely the effects that all of these operations achieved. Those interviewed believed that they reduced violence and the flow of weapons and munitions into Baghdad. Yet, attacks continued to occur in Baghdad, though at a greatly diminished rate. Moreover, it is difficult to separate and isolate the effects of the operations in Baghdad from the operations in the Baghdad Belts. Nor is it possible to determine how much of the reduction in violence and the flow of supplies was the result of the Awakening movement and the corresponding reduction in the number of Sunnis who provided support to the Sunni insurgency.

This is not necessarily a major concern. The employment of population and resource control measures by US units early in the campaign was often done in isolation. It was therefore easier to assess their effects. Yet, this isolation also meant that any success that was achieved was necessarily limited and did not produce lasting operational and strategic effects. This problem was recognized at MNC-I.

Senior members of the MNC-I staff wrote in the summer of 2007 that "population control, however, cannot be solely focused on actions at the tactical level that center on restricting movement or acquiring data on the population. Strategic and operational-level leaders must plan, coordinate, and execute activities that set the conditions for success at the tactical level."[231] This analysis facilitated the synchronization and coordination of population and resource control measures throughout the theater and therefore they produced more significant effects over a longer period of time. It could be said that the whole effect was greater than the sum of the individual effects.

Analysis

It is clear that the employment of population and resource control measures by US forces evolved significantly during the campaign. Early efforts to do so were sometimes ineffective and almost always isolated in time and space. As the nature of the conflict changed, so did the employment of population and resource control measures. Units began to employ them comprehensively, aligning the purpose of the measures with the units' objectives. Moreover, at an operational level the measures were synchronized across the battlespace so that unit operations would mutually reinforce one another.

Protection and Isolation of the Population

It is perhaps on this count in which US units' employment of population and resource control measures evolved the most. Many of the early examples discussed above were not used to protect the population; rather, their focus was on increasing the protection of US forces. Although they sometimes also resulted in improved security for the population, as happened during ORANGE CRUSH in Tikrit, this effect was ancillary and transient in nature.

Some of the measures employed did isolate the population, as in the case of the town of Albu Hishma but they did not do so from the insurgency itself. Little analysis was done regarding where the insurgency was receiving support from and whether or not such support was being willingly supplied by the population or supplied as a result of coercion. Moreover, because the measures did not produce increased security for the population, the isolation only served to anger them and potentially contributed to an increase in support for the insurgents in the area.

Beginning with Operation RESTORING RIGHTS in Tal Afar, US forces' employment of population and resource control measures began to improve in this regard. The operations in Tal Afar were deliberately planned to remove bases of support from the control of Sunni insurgents and then permanently transfer that control to the GOI. This systematic isolation of the insurgency allowed 3ACR and its Iraqi partners to consistently improve the security of the population.

Furthermore, by isolating the city with berms and controlling movement into and around it with checkpoints, the US and Iraqi forces were able to assure the population that if the insurgents in their midst were removed they would no longer be able to intimidate or coerce them. Thus, the isolation and security provided by the population and resource control measures mutually supported one another and produced lasting effects.

A similar situation occurred in Ramadi. US forces synchronized their operations to target the bases of support for the insurgency both in and outside the city. As these were secured and brought under the control of US and Iraqi forces, it allowed them to continue to clear other parts of the city. Once residents of Ramadi realized that the Sunni insurgents could no longer execute their campaign of murder and intimidation, they supported the US effort by joining local Iraqi security forces in large numbers. Again, isolation and security reinforced one another.

The cycle of retaliatory violence between Sunni and Shi'a in Baghdad produced a situation where almost every person in the city had to side with extremists on one side or the other. As a result, the neutral population was reduced to an extremely low level and both the Sunni and Shi'a insurgencies were deeply embedded in the city. Moreover, because the insurgents and the population were so closely tied together, it was difficult for US forces to separate them. As one BCT commander recalled "we didn't have a controlled environment. We didn't know who was going in and was going out and who lived there. ... We knew that was a bad AQ spot. We also knew there were some good people in there who needed to be protected."[232] However, once the population and resource controls were employed, particularly the safe neighborhood program, they effectively isolated and secured the population from the insurgents that were attacking them. This meant that they could now renounce their alignment with the extremists within the neighborhood, facilitating the ability of US and Iraqi forces to target them.

Even if the population did not become openly supportive of US forces and the GOI, their neutrality reduced support for the insurgency. However, in many neighborhoods the population did openly support the counterinsurgent effort, if not necessarily the GOI, by joining the Awakening movement and becoming SOI. This enabled them to protect their own families and neighborhoods and produced an additional increase in the number of forces available, reinforcing the security and isolation of the population.

Baghdad involved isolation and security not only at a tactical level in individual neighborhoods but operationally as the actions of units in Baghdad itself and in the Belts were synchronized and mutually supporting. Units were deployed into areas that were known support bases for the insurgency and ordered to interdict the flow of weapons and munitions into Baghdad that supported the insurgency. Movement restrictions, curfews, terrain denial, and cordon and search operations were employed in combination and resulted in a major reduction in the amount of accelerants that reached Baghdad. This further improved the security of the population in Baghdad and isolated those living in the Belts from the insurgency.

Legitimacy

The belief that US forces represented an anti-body in the Iraqi state and would inflame the insurgency probably also contributed to a reluctance to employ population and resource control measures because of a fear about their legitimacy. If US forces employed population and resource control measures it might reinforce the view of the population that they were occupiers and not liberators. Moreover, the confusing nature of the civil law control mechanism denied US commanders a clear understanding of what they could and could not do to control violence in their areas. Therefore, actions that might be perfectly legitimate in terms of providing security to the population may not have been strictly legal.

The US and the administration should never have been concerned about appearing to be occupiers. Not because it wasn't a valid concern, but because occupation is a question of fact. After having invaded Iraq, deposed the Saddam regime, established a security presence in most major cities, and dissolved all elements of the state that could be used to control the population, the US and its allies were occupiers. It was at that point more important to implement measures to maintain control than it was to worry about how such actions would be perceived.

Recall that many Iraqis were incredulous that the US had disbanded all elements of the state control apparatus and then failed to fill the void thus created. The gap between the existing capability of the fledging Iraqi state and its security forces to exert control and the capability it required was vast, and remained so for many years. Odierno proposed to fill that gap with US forces in late 2006 and 2007 in order to provide space for the GOI to develop its own capability.[233]

Moreover, by failing to exert control the US allowed the situation to get so bad that it led to a civil war, particularly in Baghdad. A senior civilian with MNC-I stated that "it started as soon as 2003. As soon as the regime fell and security forces dissolved, people were forming their own neighborhood groups."[234] Then when the US did finally start to assert control in order to end the civil war it was "almost a conceit in a way because we created these problems. They have a civil war and then we come in as if we'd never been there and the past had nothing to do with us."[235]

The anti-body theory was also thoroughly disproved in many areas of the country. While it is true that some Shi'a insurgents solely targeted US forces, they facilitated such targeting by coercing and intimidating the population. Thus, even if the outward effects of violence were only observable as attacks on US forces, there remained an underlying issue of security. This denied the population the ability to be neutral, they had to support the insurgents or they would be intimidated or killed.

It is also probably the case that the US would not have been able to legitimately execute the safe neighborhood program early during the campaign. However, other measures should have been used to maintain control and prevent the widespread lawlessness and insecurity that was prevalent in Iraq. This would best have been done in combination with Iraqi forces, but, as they were dissolved in the wake of the invasion, none were available until much later in the campaign.

This last point is probably the most important regarding legitimacy. Although US units did unilaterally employ restrictive population and resource control measures that were viewed legitimately by the Iraqi populace, they were most effective when done in partnership with local forces. This is especially true of local police. Areas, such as Ramadi and many neighborhoods of Baghdad, where US units employed such restrictive measures and then formed local security forces to become police witnessed a much greater decrease in violence than where US forces employed them unilaterally or even in combination with the Iraqi Army.

Facilitate the Targeting of the Armed and Subversive Element

It is difficult to assess just how well the employment of population and resource control measures supported the targeting of the armed and subversive element of the insurgency. The commanders that were interviewed could not provide the level of detail necessary to make any such analysis valid. A precise analysis will have to await the declassification of US operational reports in the coming years. Moreover, many upper level Sunni and Shi'a insurgents were targeted by US and Iraqi special operations forces, and how control measures supported their targeting may never fully be known.

It does appear, anecdotally, that such measures supported targeting of the insurgency to some extent. Commanders recalled that they were able to arrest suspected members of the insurgency in their areas during the implementation of population and resource control measures. Census operations provided greater information on who actually lived in the area and gave units pictures of the population in the area. After some controls were applied and security improved, units received additional intelligence from the population. Thus, population and resource control measures may have improved the ability of US forces to target members of the insurgency, but how much so is not clear.

However, these measures were effective at targeting the insurgents' bases of support. In Tal Afar, Ramadi, the Baghdad Belts, and Baghdad itself, the US deliberately applied combat power and population and resource control measures to assert control over such areas and deny the insurgency the ability to use them. Additionally, the US applied the control measures systematically to the insurgents' LOCs. Such actions forced the insurgents to either locate a different support base and LOC or, once the controls were synchronized across the battlespace, openly fight US and Iraqi forces to control them.

Targeting insurgent bases of support and LOCs was effective not only because it denied the insurgency free access to specific areas, but also because the insurgency was road bound.[236] The vast expanses of desert and minimal numbers of roads through them created a situation where insurgents had to utilize the road networks to transport weapons, materiel, and fighters. Furthermore, even in areas where they might have walked, such as Baghdad, they could not if they wanted to conduct the dramatic attacks that had become the norm, which required large explosive devices weighing hundreds of pounds.

When US forces employed measures that denied insurgents the use of vehicles it sometimes reduced violence dramatically, even if the attacks did not need to be conducted by vehicle. One BCT commander recalled that "we put in a series of barriers ... just Jersey barriers [about 3 feet high], and we cut the murder rate in there in one week by 50 percent because the death squads couldn't come in."[237] Thus, even if the population and resource control measures did not facilitate targeting individual members of the insurgency, they did enable US forces to target the support structure of the insurgency and limit the number and type of attacks the groups could conduct.

The effectiveness of the population and resource control measures at targeting the insurgency has had one significant unintended consequence, however. US officers that served in Baghdad in 2010 reported that Iraqi forces were reluctant to remove the controls for fear of being held accountable if an attack subsequently occurred.[238] The security forces have become reliant on the population and resource control measures to provide security. A US Army company commander observed that "if you are going to take the t-walls down that means you really have to have a connection to the people."[239] How long the Iraqi populace is willing to tolerate such invasive control measures and how well the GOI and its security forces will respond when they are forced to remove them remains to be seen.

Population and resource control measures were not the answer to the challenges that the US and GOI confronted in Iraq. However, they did form a critical part of the campaign, especially during late 2005 and after once they were employed in a deliberate and synchronized manner across the battlespace. They helped to protect the population, isolate the insurgency, and target the insurgents' bases of support. Moreover, by enabling the US and GOI to finally exert control over the population and provide them the security they desired, they were viewed legitimately by the population.

Notes

1. Gregory Fontenot, E. J. Degan, and David Tohn, *On Point, The United States Army in Operation IRAQI FREEDOM* (Fort Leavenworth, KS: Combat Studies Institute Press, 2004), 86.

2. Ibid., 88-89.

3. Michael R. Gordon and Bernard E. Trainor, *Cobra II* (New York: Pantheon Books, 2006), 50.

4. Ibid., 50.

5. Fontenot, Degan, and Tohn, *On Point*, 94.

6. Gordon and Trainor, *Cobra II*, 4.

7. Ibid., 4.

8. Fontenot, Degan, and Tohn, *On Point*, 102.

9. Ibid., 102.

10. Gordon and Trainor, *Cobra II*, 62.

11. Fontenot, Degan, and Tohn, *On Point*, 209.

12. Ibid., 210-218.

13. Ibid., 217.

14. Gordon and Trainor, *Cobra II*, 68.

15. Douglas J. Feith, *War and Decision* (New York: Harper Collins Publishers, 2008), 374.

16. Fontenot, Degan, and Tohn, *On Point*, 336.

17. Ibid., 339.

18. Feith, *War and Decision*, 349-50.

19. Ibid., 422-25.

20. Ibid., 379-81.

21. Donald P. Wright and Timothy R. Reese, *On Point II: Transition to the New Campaign* (Fort Leavenworth, KS: Combat Studies Institute Press, 2008), 90.

22. Bing West, *The Strongest Tribe* (New York: Random House, 2009), 5.

23. Wright and Reese, *On Point II*, 26.

24. Ibid., 27.

25. The insurgency in Iraq is not, and never has been, a single, well-defined insurgency. Multiple insurgent groups with diverse objectives have formed, fought, disbanded, re-formed, and changed names and objectives during the campaign. Throughout this paper the author will attempt to identify the specific insurgent group being referred to, however a certain amount of generalization will

be necessary. If the term "insurgency" is used without any modifiers or descriptors it is used to refer generically to the violent campaign conducted by the multiple groups against US/Coalition forces and the Government of Iraq.

26. Malkasian, "Counterinsurgency in Iraq," 289.

27. Wright and Reese, *On Point II*, 101-103.

28. Wright and Reese, *On Point II*, 36.

29. At the time of the invasion, this area of Baghdad was called Saddam City. However, after the regime fell it was renamed in honor of a Shi'a Grand Ayatollah, Muhammed Sadiq al-Sadr, who was assassinated in Najaf in 1999 with two of his sons. One of Muhammed Sadiq's other sons, Muqtada al Sadr, would eventually become a major leader of the Shi'a insurgency in Iraq. See Wright and Reese, *On Point II*, 34-35.

30. Malkasian, "Counterinsurgency in Iraq," 290-291.

31. This is generally referred to as the First Battle of Fallujah. For more information about Fallujah, see West, *The Strongest Tribe*, 29-36. The city was eventually brought under coalition control following the Second Battle of Fallujah, Operation AL FAJR, in November 2004. These two actions profoundly affected Sunni perceptions regarding the coalition. See Malkasian, "The Role of Perceptions and Political Reform in Counterinsurgency."

32. This paper will not examine in depth the divisions within Iraqi society. Broadly, two major divisions exist: an ethnic division between Arabs and Kurds (and other minority populations such as the Turkomans), and a sectarian division between Sunni Muslims (which include Sunni Arabs and the majority of the Kurdish population) and Shi'a Muslims. The Arabs form the ethnic majority and the Shi'a Muslims are the sectarian majority. These divisions produce three major population groups around which the narrative of the insurgency in Iraq can be constructed with reasonable accuracy: Sunni Arabs, Shi'a Arabs, and the Kurds.

33. The Mahdi is a central figure in Twelver Shi'a ideology, which is prevalent in Iraq. Twelver Shi'as believe that the 12th Imam of the Muslim faith disappeared and that his return would herald the coming of the Mahdi. The Mahdi is a divine redeemer who will rid the world of evil upon his return. See Karen Armstrong, *A History of God* (New York: Ballantine Books, 1993), 160-162. This book also provides good information on the origin of the schism in Islam between Sunni and Shi'a and how it has evolved over time.

34. Wright and Reese, *On Point II*, 39.

35. Malkasian, "Counterinsurgency in Iraq," 294.

36. Wright and Reese, *On Point II*, 41.

37. Malkasian, "Counterinsurgency in Iraq," 294.

38. West, *The Strongest Tribe*, 79.

39. Author's personal experience serving in 2BCT, 3ID in eastern Baghdad in 2005.

40. Malkasian, "Counterinsurgency in Iraq," 298-299.

41. Ibid., 301.

42. Malkasian, "The Role of Perceptions and Political Reform in Counterinsurgency," 385-86.

43. Malkasian, "Counterinsurgency in Iraq," 301.

44. Ibid., 301.

45. The Ministry of Defense did make an effort to recruit more Sunnis into the Army in 2005, but this measure was largely unsuccessful. The previous incarnations of the Iraqi Army, the Iraqi Civil Defense Corps and the Iraqi National Guard, had been recruited to serve in their home areas which would have allowed Sunnis to protect Sunni areas and Shi'a to protect Shi'a areas.

46. The Golden Mosque is an important site in Twelver Shi'a ideology. It is the place where the 12th Imam is believed to have been taken into hiding by Allah and many believe it is also the place where he will reappear. Additionally, the site is the burial place of the 10th and 11th imams.

47. BH020, BCT Commander, Interview by Mark Battjes, Ben Boardman, Robert Green, Richard Johnson, Aaron Kaufman, Dustin Mitchell, Nathan Springer, and Thomas Walton, 21 March 2011, Washington, DC.

48. Thomas E. Ricks, *The Gamble* (New York: The Penguin Press, 2009), 33.

49. The name, composition, and purpose of these paramilitary police units have changed a number of times during the campaign. In their initial iteration they consisted of Public Order Battalions, which mostly executed static security operations, and Police Commando units, which conducted raids against suspected terrorists. These organizations were later disbanded and combined into Iraqi National Police units which were organized similarly to Iraqi Army infantry battalions, but not as heavily armed. Presently, such units are called Iraqi Federal Police.

50. The term "off ramped" is used by US planners to indicate that a unit will no longer deploy according to its original timeline.

51. BA020, Battalion Commander, Interview by Mark Battjes and Benjamin Boardman, 23 February 2011, Fort Leavenworth, KS.

52. BB010, Battalion Commander, Interview by Mark Battjes and Nathan Springer, 2 March 2011, Fort Bliss, TX.

53. Malkasian, "Counterinsurgency in Iraq," 304.

54. West, *The Strongest Tribe*, 79. Also see Ricks, *The Gamble*, 49-50.

55. BA020 and BB010.

56. Malkasian, "Counterinsurgency in Iraq," 304.

57. There has been some disagreement within the US military about whether or not the new strategy represented a real change in the mission of US forces. See

Ricks, *The Gamble*, 217-219. In an interview conducted by the author, a former member of the Army staff recalled that "particularly under GEN Casey the focus was on transition." He also noted that "if you look at GEN Casey's strategic assessment in the winter of 2006 it says that the strategy has failed to achieve its objectives under the security, development, economic and political lines of operation." One of the key objectives under the security line of operation was the protection of the population. BH030, Iraq Veterans Panel, Interview by Mark Battjes, Robert Green, Aaron Kaufman, and Dustin Mitchell, 22 March 2011, Washington, DC.

58. Malkasian, "Counterinsurgency in Iraq," 304.

59. Ricks, *The Gamble*, 248-249.

60. Ricks has reproduced an MNF-I chart that shows the number of security incidents per week in Iraq from January 2004 to October 2008. It is included on page 13 of the photographic insert in *The Gamble*.

61. BH040, Afghanistan Veterans Panel, Interview by Richard Johnson, Aaron Kaufman, Nathan Springer, and Thomas Walton, 24 March 2011, Washington, DC. Also see West, *The Strongest Tribe*, 101-02.

62. BH040. Also see Neil Smith and Sean McFarland, "Anbar Awakens: The Tipping Point," *Military Review* (March-April 2008): 49.

63. Interview BA020.

64. Dale Kuehl, "Testing Galula in Ameriyah, The People are the Key," *Military Review* (March-April 2009): 76.

65. BA090, Brigade Commander, Interview by Mark Battjes and Benjamin Boardman, 24 February 2011, Fort Riley, KS. BG090, Battalion Commander, Interview by Mark Battjes and Nathan Springer, 16 March 2011, Fort Stewart, GA.

66. BE060, Brigade Commander, Interview by Mark Battjes and Thomas Walton, 9 March 2011, Fort Irwin, CA.

67. West, *The Strongest Tribe*, 319.

68. United Kingdom, Ministry of Defence, "Operation TELIC Lessons Learned Compendium," http://www.mod.uk/NR/rdonlyres/F0282A90-99E5-415E-B3BC-97EAD7D7873A/0/operation_telic_lessons_compendium.pdf (accessed 1 May 2011), 9.

69. Malkasian, "Counterinsurgency in Iraq," 306.

70. UK MOD, "Operation TELIC Lessons Learned," 9.

71. Malkasian, "Counterinsurgency in Iraq," 307.

72. West, *The Strongest Tribe*, 351.

73. UK MOD, "Operation TELIC Lessons Learned," 9.

74. Author's personal experience while serving as a company commander in Baghdad during 2007-2008.

75. Malkasian, "Counterinsurgency in Iraq," 309.

76. BG020, Brigade Commander, Interview by Mark Battjes and Thomas Walton, 14 March 2011, Fort Stewart, GA.

77. One of the US BCTs that was withdrawn from Iraq in December 2011 was reassigned to Kuwait under the control of US Army Central Command (ARCENT).

78. This section will describe the body of civil law that governed Iraq during the campaign. It will mention the broad authorities of and the limitations that were imposed on the security forces within Iraq. It will demonstrate how unclear the overlapping provisions were and this will contribute to the later analysis of the effectiveness of the employment of population and resource control measures. Despite the lack of clarity, US forces, as will be shown, employed population and resource control measures throughout the campaign.

79. Department of the Army, Field Manual 27-10, *The Law of Land Warfare* (Washington, DC: Department of the Army, 1956), A-90–A-91.

80. Ibid., A-91.

81. Ibid., A-91.

82. Gordon and Trainor, *Cobra II*, 469.

83. Ibid., 465-466.

84. Wright and Reese, *On Point II*, 91.

85. Gordon and Trainor, *Cobra II*, 469-470.

86. United Nations Security Council, "Resolution 1483," 22 May 2003 http://www.un.org/Docs/sc/unsc_resolutions03.html (accessed 1 May 2011), 2.

87. Ibid., 2.

88. Wright and Reese, *On Point II*, 26.

89. Coalition Provisional Authority, "Order No. 1, De'Ba'athification of Iraqi Society," in Wright and Reese, *On Point II*, 593-594.

90. Wright and Reese, *On Point II*, 26.

91. Coalition Provisional Authority, "Order No. 2, "Dissolution of Entities," in Wright and Reese, *On Point II*, 598.

92. West, *The Strongest Tribe*, 7.

93. Quoted in Wright and Reese, *On Point II*, 96.

94. Coalition Provisional Authority, "Regulation No. 1," 16 May 2003, http://www.iraqcoalition.org/regulations/20030516_CPAREG_1_The_Coalition_Provisional_Authority_.pdf (accessed 1 May 2011), 1.

95. Coalition Provisional Authority, "Order No. 7," 9 June 2003, http://www.iraqcoalition.org/regulations/20030610_CPAORD_7_Penal_Code.pdf (accessed May 1, 2011), 1.

96. Coalition Provisional Authority, "Order No. 3, (Revised) (Amended)," 31 December 2003, http://www.iraqcoalition.org/regulations/20031231_CPAORD3_REV__AMD_.pdf (accessed 1 May 2011), 3.

97. Ibid., 4.

98. Ibid., 4.

99. United Nations Security Council, "Resolution 1511," 16 October 2003 http://www.un.org/Docs/sc/unsc_resolutions03.html (accessed 1 May 2011), 2.

100. Ibid., 3.

101. Wright and Reese, *On Point II*, 37.

102. United Nations Security Council, "Resolution 1546," 8 June 2004 http://www.un.org/Docs/sc/unsc_resolutions04.html (accessed 1 May 2011), 1.

103. Ibid., 4.

104. Iraqi Governing Council, "Transitional Administrative Law," 8 March 2004 http://www.constitution.org/cons/iraq/TAL.html (accessed 1 May 2011), Article 26.

105. Ibid., Article 5.

106. Ibid., Article 15(B).

107. Ibid., Article 13(D).

108. Ibid., Article 59(B).

109. BB030, Brigade Commander, Interview by Mark Battjes and Nathan Springer, 3 March 2011, Fort Bliss, TX.

110. Transitional National Assembly, "Iraqi Constitution," retrieved from http://www.uniraq.org/documents/iraqi_constitution.pdf (accessed 1 May 2011), Article 9(A).

111. Ibid., Article 17.

112. Ibid., Article 42.

113. Ibid., Article 58(9)(A).

114. Ibid., Article 58(9)(C).

115. United Nations Security Council, "Resolution 1637," 8 November 2005 http://www.un.org/Docs/sc/unsc_resolutions05.htm (accessed 1 May 2011), 3.

116. United Nations Security Council, "Resolution 1723," 28 November 2006 http://www.un.org/Docs/sc/unsc_resolutions06.htm (accessed 1 May 2011), 3.

117. United Nations Security Council, "Resolution 1790," 18 December 2007 http://www.un.org/Docs/sc/unsc_resolutions07.htm (accessed 1 May 2011), 4.

118. Ibid., 3-4.

119. West, *The Strongest Tribe*, 10.

120. BH030.

121. Ibid.

122. West, *The Strongest Tribe*, 20.

123. BH030.

124. Wright and Reese, *On Point II*, 113.

125. BH030.

126. Ricks, *The Gamble*, 12.

127. BA070, Battery Commander, Interview by Richard Johnson and Thomas Walton, 24 February 2011, Fort Leavenworth, KS.

128. Ibid.

129. BD010, Field Grade Officer, Interview by Benjamin Boardman and Dustin Mitchell, 14 March 2011, Fort Knox, KY.

130. Ibid.

131. Dividing the Iraq campaign is decidedly difficult. Even determining when the surge began is difficult because of the phased nature of the deployment of surge forces. However, the Baghdad Security Plan provides a clear dividing line. It is implemented after President Bush has announced the surge and Generals Petraeus and Odierno have taken command and therefore the period after it clearly includes the change to US strategy and force posture.

132. Wright and Reese, *On Point II*, 28.

133. Author's personal experience serving as a battalion staff officer in 2003.

134. Gordon and Trainor, *Cobra II*, 469-470.

135. Nathan Sassaman with Joe Layden, *Warrior King* (New York: St. Martin's Press, 2008), 183.

136. Ibid., 183.

137. Ibid., 184.

138. Ibid., 184.

139. West, *The Strongest Tribe*, 23.

140. BD010.

141. Ibid.

142. At the time of the invasion and the period immediately following it, most Iraqi taxi cabs were orange and white. Later in the campaign, just about any Iraqi car could potentially serve as a taxi.

143. BC020, Brigade Commander, Interview by Robert Green and Aaron Kaufman, 2 March 2011, Fort Bragg, NC.

144. BH030.

145. BC020.

146. BH030.

147. BB030.

148. Ibid.

149. Ibid.

150. Ibid.

151. Ibid.

152. Unless otherwise noted the accounts in this section are based on the author's personal experience serving in Baghdad during 2005 as a BCT planner and later a battalion Assistant Operations Officer.

153. EFPs are also referred to as Explosively Formed Projectiles. However, the term penetrator is more accurate as the purpose of the metal slug formed by the explosive is to penetrate armor.

154. At the time, I recall that this idea seemed particularly ill conceived. However, the Baghdad Security Plan and accompanying operations in the areas surrounding Baghdad did almost exactly that.

155. BD020, Commander, Interview by Benjamin Boardman and Dustin Mitchell, 14 March 2011, Fort Knox, KY.

156. Route Brewers runs generally NW to SE in the eastern half of Baghdad. It terminates next to the then American Forward Operating Base Rustamiyah and connects to the Main Supply Route across the river from west Baghdad. Therefore, it had a high volume of combat logistics patrols along it which provided a large number of targets for EFPs.

157. The proliferation of trash was an especially difficult problem. The city government of Baghdad was not yet capable of consistently picking up trash in every neighborhood so Baghdadis would dispose of their trash along the sides of the roads. RTE Brewers was a favored spot to do so.

158. Jay B. Baker, "Tal Afar 2005: Laying the Counterinsurgency Framework," *Army* (June 2009): 62.

159. BH070, Iraqi Mayor, Interview by Mark Battjes and Robert Green, 25 March 2011, Washington, DC.

160. West, *The Strongest Tribe*, 84.

161. BH070.

162. Ibid.

163. Chris Gibson, "Battlefield Victories and Strategic Success: The Path Forward in Iraq," *Military Review* (September-October 2006): 48.

164. Ibid., 50.

165. BH070.

166. I Marine Expeditionary Force, "State of the Insurgency in al-Anbar," 17 August 2006, reprinted in Ricks, *The Gamble*, A-1.

167. BA020.

168. BA010, Brigade Commander, Interview by Richard Johnson and Thomas Walton, 22 February 2011, Fort Leavenworth, KS.

169. Ibid.

170. BA020.

171. BA010.

172. Ibid.

173. Ibid.

174. Ibid.

175. BA020.

176. Some Iraqi commentators have noted that while Sunnis in Anbar did ally with the Americans, it was the ability of their men to join the security forces that really created the feeling of safety and security within the population. It is likely that, as in many other instances discussed in this paper, the two actions were mutually reinforcing. See Najim Abed al-Jabouri and Sterling Jensen, "The Iraqi and AQI Roles in the Sunni Awakening," *Prism* 2, no. 1 (2010): 11.

177. BH030.

178. Ibid.

179. The Baghdad Belts are the generally rural areas that surround the city itself. The US had failed to control them for most of the campaign and they had become prime support areas for the city itself. A captured AQI document indicated that the belts were a critical part of the supply lines for Baghdad.

180. BH030.

181. Multi-national Corps Iraq, "MNC-I Inbrief GEN Petraeus," 8 February 2007, reprinted in Ricks, *The Gamble*, C-13.

182. West, *The Strongest Tribe*, 327.

183. MNC-I, "MNC-I Inbrief," C16.

184. A Qada is an administrative area in Iraq that is roughly analogous to a U.S. county.

185. BA040, Brigade Commander, Interview by Aaron Kaufman and Dustin Mitchell, 23 February 2011, Fort Leavenworth, KS.

186. Ibid.

187. Ibid.

188. Ibid.

189. Ibid.

190. Ibid.

191. BE060, Brigade Commander, Interview by Mark Battjes and Thomas Walton, 9 March 2011, Fort Irwin, CA.

192. Ibid.

193. A "Tier 1 hotspot" refers to a location that has been historically used by the insurgency to conduct attacks, in this case IED attacks. It is called a "hotspot" because when groups of attacks are analyzed and differentiated by various color shades on a map, those areas with the highest concentration of attacks appear to be hot – i.e. red. A Tier 1 hotspot is an area with an extremely high concentration of attacks.

194. BA070.

195. BE060.

196. Ibid.

197. Ibid.

198. The BATS and HIIDE are two complementary pieces of equipment used by U.S. forces to collect biometric data. The centerpiece of the BATS is a laptop that can be used to upload and link biometric data to a centralized served. It can also be used to enter biometric data and print out identification cards based on the data entered. The HIIDEs is a device that can be carried by an individual soldier and is capable of uploading fingerprints, iris scans, and facial recognition pictures of individuals. The process of enrolling people in the system is commonly referred to by U.S. forces as "BATS/HIIDESing" or another variation.

199. BA070.

200. Ibid.

201. Ibid.

202. BE080, Battalion Commander, Interview by Robert Green and Aaron Kaufman, 7 March 2011, Fort Irwin, CA.

203. BH020

204. BH030.

205. BD010.

206. Ibid.

207. BH020.

208. BA090.

209. Joseph F. Fil, quoted in Kimberly Kagan, "Enforcing the Law: The Baghdad Security Plan Begins," *Iraq Report* (10 February-5 March 2007): 3.

210. Kagan, "Enforcing the Law: The Baghdad Security Plan Begins," 4.

211. Joseph Anderson and Gary Volesky, "A Synchronized Approach to Population Control," *Military Review* (July-August 2007): 145.

212. Defining what constituted a single neighborhood proved to be a challenge as the views of US forces, Iraqi forces, the GOI, and the Iraqi populace that actually lived in an area about what was a single neighborhood did not always correspond.

213. BH020.

214. Ibid.

215. BG090.

216. BB010. Also BG090.

217. BA090.

218. BB010.

219. BH020.

220. BA090.

221. BF020, Civilian Advisor to MNF-I, Interview by Richard Johnson and Aaron Kaufman, 11 March 2011, Boston, MA.

222. BG030, Troop Commander, Interview by Mark Battjes, Nathan Springer, and Thomas Walton, 14 March 2011, Fort Stewart, GA.

223. Author's personal experience as a company commander serving in Baghdad in 2007-2008.

224. BD010.

225. BH020.

226. BA090.

227. Ibid.

228. Ibid.

229. Ibid.

230. Author's personal experience as a company commander serving in Baghdad in 2007-2008.

231. Anderson and Volesky, "A Synchronized Approach to Population Control," 146.

232. BH020.

233. MNC-I, "MNC-I Inbrief," C-2.

234. BF020.

235. Ibid.

236. West, *The Strongest Tribe*, 53. West asserts that the Iraqi insurgency was the world's first "vehicle-based guerrilla movement." Whether this statement is historically accurate is debatable, but it does illustrate the point that the Iraqi insurgency, both Sunni and Shi'a, was extremely reliant on the use of roads.

237. BH020.

238. BG010, Battalion Commander, Interview by Nathan Springer, 14 March 2011, Fort Stewart, GA.

239. BG030.

Chapter 7
Conclusions and Recommendations

The next and perhaps overlapping step in mobilizing the masses must be to give the population the security it needs to escape reprisals by the revolutionaries. This security affords to the population the opportunity to choose other alternatives besides that of supporting the revolutionary cause. The security must be apparent, effective, and stable so that the people recognize its existence, can depend on it, and will be confident of the future.

—John J. McCuen, *The Art of Counter-Revolutionary War*

Conclusions

This study examined the employment of population and resource control measures by counterinsurgent forces during three unique conflicts and some conclusions can be drawn from this examination. However, before any conclusions are discussed, a note of caution is in order. Population and resource control measures are not a panacea for addressing the problems caused by an insurgency. They should form a part of the solution and are a valuable tool for counterinsurgents but they should not be relied upon in all circumstances. Moreover, while almost every instance of their employment produced short-term tactical success, it is only when employed appropriately as part of a holistic control mechanism that they are able to facilitate long-term operational success.

Some such measures are harsh and invasive and should be employed only when, and for as long as, is absolutely necessary. When the existence and nature of the state is at stake, however, government leaders should not hesitate to employ them. It should also be recognized that some population and resource control measures are a part of the control mechanism which modern states use to protect their populations and secure them from violent actors day in and day out. Identification cards, address lists, and restrictions on firearms and munitions are all features of liberal democratic states. The more effectively these measures are employed before a crisis begins, the less likely it is that the harsher and more restrictive measures will be necessary.

Evaluating the Framework

The second chapter posited a framework for population and resource control measure regimes composed of six critical components. Those critical components are: legitimacy, enforcement provisions, protection of the population, isolation of the population, a focus on behavior, and the destruction of the armed and subversive elements. The employment of population and resource control measures in the case studies reveals that this framework is valid. However, it also revealed that the framework is incomplete and needs to be adjusted.

Protection and Isolation are Most Important

The first adjustment is that protection and isolation of the population must be emphasized as the most important components of any population and resource control measure regime. Observations in each of the case studies reveal that if the population is not protected from insurgent violence and subsequently isolated from the insurgency, then all other components of the framework will fail. This is, perhaps, intuitive. However, it was not always obvious to the practitioners involved in the conflicts.

As discussed in Chapter 3, the measures employed in the Philippines, especially reconcentration, were consistently able to protect and isolate the population from the insurgency. As a result, the counterinsurgent forces, whether US Army or Philippines Constabulary, were able to control the behavior of the population and deny further support to the insurgency. Moreover, it facilitated their targeting of the insurgent armed forces and they were able to restore control of violence to the state quickly.

In Vietnam, during both the Diem regime and the US ground force intervention, the counterinsurgent forces were never able to consistently protect, isolate, or control the population. Where they were able to do so, the population and resource control measures were effective. Once Viet Cong forces were again able to contact and threaten the population, however, the regime broke down. The Front and Party recognized this and responded to Government of Vietnam success in pacification with renewed offensives. A South Vietnamese brigadier general recalled after the war that "the most discernible pattern in pacification was that progress depended entirely on security ... This pointed to another significant pattern: a major enemy spoiling action could always be expected when pacification seemed to attain a reasonable degree of success."[1]

In Iraq, as was shown in Chapter 6, the employment of population and resource control measures by US forces early in the campaign was often limited and not directed at protecting and isolating the population. Thus, the measures produced some tactical success, such as those in Tikrit and Haqlaniyah, but never achieved lasting effects in terms of countering the insurgency. However, as the campaign evolved, US forces improved their employment of such measures and directed them towards protecting and isolating the population. Where this was done in Al Qaim, Tal Afar, Ramadi, and Baghdad, it achieved not only tactical success but more enduring operational success.[2]

Control Mechanism

Another adjustment that must be made is an explicit recognition that the population and resource control measures must be employed within a holistic control mechanism. While components of the framework, notably legal enforcement by counterinsurgent forces, might lead to this conclusion, it is important enough that it should be explicitly stated. This control mechanism may take the form of a body of laws, as in the Philippines and Iraq, or it may be a comprehensive counterinsurgency strategy such as the Strategic Hamlet Program or Pacification.

The control mechanism identifies to all of the actors in the campaign–the insurgents, the counterinsurgents, and the population–what measures will be employed, how they will be enforced, and what legal sanctions will accompany violations. This leads to clear enforcement powers for the counterinsurgent forces, which improves their ability to employ them. In the Philippines, US Army and Constabulary forces were never burdened by trying to separate ordinary criminals from true insurgents. The control mechanisms, first military law and then civil law, simply defined certain actions as criminal with a low burden of proof, and this gave the counterinsurgents the ability to detain and punish any who violated them, insurgent or not.

This was not the case for US forces in Vietnam or Iraq. As there was no clear ability for these forces to legally enforce population and control measures, it constantly put young Soldiers and Marines in a position where they had to differentiate between an insurgent, who could be detained, or a simple violator, who might be questioned but could not be detained. This led to extremely negative situations. Just one example is the conduct of Soldiers in Lieutenant Colonel Sassaman's battalion in Iraq who temporarily detained two Iraqi men for violating curfew and then forced them to jump off a bridge into a river.[3]

The control mechanism also provides the population the ability to deny insurgent demands for support on the basis that they will be imprisoned or otherwise sanctioned. While this may or may not prevent the insurgents from coercing the population, it does make it more difficult. This was especially true in the Philippines but it was also true in Vietnam. Party leaders directed their cadres to "ensure a legal standing for the masses."[4]

Cadres who had required the population to tear up their identification cards were thoroughly admonished.[5] In Iraq, vehicle registration enabled the population to deny insurgents the use of their vehicles.[6]

Moreover, the control mechanism synchronizes the efforts of all of the counterinsurgent forces across the theater. This synchronization ensures that when population and control measures are employed that they are mutually supporting. Bell's employment of such measures would have been far less effective if Malvar and his guerrillas could have received support from other communities outside of Batangas province. However, because the US Army was in control of these areas and operating under the same control mechanism as Bell's forces, it would have been simple to extend the employment of such measures to other communities and further Malvar's isolation.

In Vietnam, US operations were intended to support pacification by defeating the threat presented by People's Army of Vietnam and VC main force units. They were therefore somewhat synchronized with the pacification control mechanism. Unfortunately, the movement of US and ARVN forces around the battlefield to confront the PAVN and VC main forces exposed the weakness of the security forces assigned to hold areas undergoing pacification. The Vietnamese brigadier general recalled that:

> The great number of military forces employed in support of pacification never seemed to keep up with the requirements occasioned by the necessity to deploy a permanent occupation force to every hamlet. The situation was such that when protection forces were deployed from a certain area considered 'secure,' that area might relapse into insecurity and the local population would lose confidence in the GVN.[7]

Only after the PAVN and VC main forces had been forced out of South Vietnam in the aftermath of the 1968 Offensive, 1969 Tet Offensive, and the invasion of Cambodia would this problem be rectified.

The US campaign in Iraq decidedly suffered from a lack of synchronization through 2006. Individual units employed population and resource control measures but these only achieved short-term tactical success against the insurgency in their area. They had no effect, and possibly even a negative effect, on the insurgency beyond their boundaries. Only later in the campaign when such measures were synchronized and mutually supportive did their employment facilitate long-term operational success against the insurgency across the battlespace.

Targeting the Armed and Subversive Element

The case studies also demonstrate that a population and resource control measure regime is most effective when all components support the targeting of the armed and subversive element of the insurgency. This could be taken to mean that the regime should target only the insurgents themselves. However, the case studies indicate that targeting the insurgency's support bases and lines of communication is also effective.

In Batangas province, Bell did this by simply removing all possible means of support from the insurgency through reconcentration. Malvar's guerrillas had no other available means of supply and so were denied the ability to continue operating. In Vietnam, US ground forces consistently used terrain denial and terrain transformation operations. Unfortunately, these were not PAVN's and the VC's only bases of support in the area so targeting them was not decisive. Tal Afar, Ramadi, the Baghdad Belts, and Baghdad all demonstrate that removing bases of support and interdicting lines of communication can significantly weaken the insurgency.

It could be argued that such an approach will not work when there are significant bases of support external to the state. It is true that such a situation makes this approach more difficult but it does not mean that targeting bases of support and lines of communication within the state is worthless. There existed major bases of support for the Sunni insurgency outside of Iraq. Nonetheless, by removing internal supply bases from the control of the Sunni insurgency, MNC-I [Multi-National Corps-Iraq] severely degraded its ability to support operations, especially in Baghdad.[8]

It is also not certain how well such an approach could be applied to the war in Afghanistan. A member of the MNF-I [Multi-National Force-Iraq] staff during the surge commented that "we have never applied the same approach [Odierno's targeting of bases of support with surge forces] at the operational level in Afghanistan."[9] It could be argued, however, that recent coalition efforts in Afghanistan to regain control of Marja do represent a similar approach. What is clear is that the insurgency in Afghanistan, like that in Iraq, is not monolithic and therefore targeting bases of support and lines of communication can only be done with an accurate and thorough assessment of each threat group and its means, methods, and bases of supply.

Neutrality of the Population

Another adjustment to the framework concerns the ability of the population to be neutral. This is a minor adjustment but an important one.

The original framework states that the counterinsurgent should employ population and resource control measures in order to prevent behavior that supports the insurgents and enable behavior that supports the government. However, such measures should also make it possible for the population to simply remain neutral.[10]

This is important because a neutral population is, in general, an advantage for the counterinsurgent. The counterinsurgent usually has greater capabilities and therefore the insurgent has to leverage the support of the population in order to challenge the government's control. If the insurgent is unable to leverage the population, because they are protected and isolated from him, then he will remain at a disadvantage vis-a-vis the government. A population that is not forced to support either side is in essence supporting the government.

It should also be recognized that in preventing behavior that supports the insurgent, the government is actually coercing the population to remain neutral. In other words, if the population intends to support the insurgents, but the government's population and resource control measures prevent them from doing so, their behavior is now neutral. If they do not contest this situation, they have acquiesced to the government's control. Therefore, it is important for the government to both enable neutrality and to enforce it.

Temporary in Nature-Sliding Scale of Control

The final adjustment to the framework is to recognize that population and resource control measures represent a means for the government to increase and decrease its control over the population. That is to say, they do not have to be employed in an all or nothing fashion, but can be increased or decreased as the situation requires. Many of the measures discussed, such as identification cards, censuses, registration of vehicles, and control over the purchase and use of arms, ammunition, and other materials, can and should be employed by the government at all times. However, harsher measures, such as curfews, movement restrictions, barriers, and resettlement, must be used only as long as the situation requires them to be.

This allows the government and the counterinsurgent to increase its control from a baseline state in response to an insurgent threat and clearly inform the population of the reason for its actions. The government may not wish to set a deadline for removing the restrictions but should indicate that once the threat from the insurgency is over that they will be lifted. This contributes to the legitimacy of the measures and also indicates to the population that the counterinsurgent intends to return the situation to a relative state of normalcy as quickly as possible. The other reason to emphasize their temporary nature is to prevent the security forces from becoming reliant upon them.

In the Philippines, as shown in Chapter 3, the temporary nature of reconcentration was highlighted by the actions of Bell, Baker, and Bandholtz, all of whom ended the harsh measures of control as soon as they were no longer necessary. Emphasizing the temporary nature of the Strategic Hamlet Program may have helped Diem's efforts against the VC, though how much so is not obvious. How the Iraqi populace will react if the most invasive measures used during that campaign are not lifted remains to be seen but the current uprisings across the Arab world indicate that they are unlikely to tolerate them for much longer.

Control

The case studies also lead to the conclusion that control, of territory and population, is of central importance to any counterinsurgency campaign. This seems to be intuitive and the theorists all made this point. However, there is often in contemporary writing on insurgency, an intense focus on winning the support of the population and a corresponding degradation of the importance of physical control over territory and population.[11] Yet, physical control over territory and population can give the counterinsurgent a tremendous advantage as it denies the insurgents' freedom of maneuver and facilitates the targeting of their bases of support and lines of communication.

The other reason control is so important is because when it is lost, it is often very difficult to regain. The case studies illustrate this point very well. The US Army was unable to occupy and control southern Luzon during the early phase of its campaign in the Philippines. As a result, the insurgency became entrenched there, particularly in Batangas. Malvar's forces were able to resist two years of persistent effort by the US Army and were only defeated after Bell imposed an exceptionally restrictive and coercive population and resource control regime. Later on under civilian control, insurgencies were defeated much more rapidly because the Constabulary was able to maintain persistent control over the archipelago.

Diem was severely disadvantaged compared to the Party, PAVN, and the VC because of the terms of the 1954 Geneva Agreement. He did not immediately have control over the instruments of state power and his government lacked a presence in many rural areas for a number of years.[12]

Thus, he was denied control over the country and the rural population. As a result he had constantly to engage in operations to regain and maintain that control over the coming years. All of his successors, and his US allies, faced the same challenge. Despite massive efforts during his regime and later, the GVN never really had full control over its territory and population and this hampered the war effort. Moreover, the VC and the Front realized how important such control was. A report by US researchers concluded that "the objective of the Viet Cong system in Dinh Tuong province, at least to the time when active field research on this study ended in November 1967, was to establish control over *both* territory and people."[13]

In Iraq, the failure of the US and its partners to control the territory of Iraq in the wake of the invasion was nearly catastrophic. Although the insurgency built slowly over time, it was raging in many parts of Iraq by the spring of 2004. Operations to regain control, such as in Fallujah and Najaf, were costly in terms of casualties and legitimacy. Moreover, the need to control Baghdad ultimately required a massive influx of US manpower and the extension of US Army tours in Iraq to 15 months.

A US Army battalion commander commented that:

If you really go back and look at the force requirements that were laid out initially, which was a half a million, we never would have lost control and by losing control because we had a smaller force and we tried to do it with the minimal force, similar to what we set off to do in Afghanistan. We probably would have saved ourselves a number of years and a number of lives.

His words are echoed by a British Army Battle Group commander who noted that "you get one shot at this [controlling territory and population] and if you get it wrong from the outset you must accept your own consequences and say 'It will take me a long time to get it back.'"[14]

Recommendations

The conclusions above regarding the framework naturally lead into a set of recommendations. The first recommendation is that counterinsurgents use the framework outlined, with the modifications listed, to design population and resource control measure regimes when they are to be employed. This is not meant to be limiting in any way. The framework is sufficiently flexible that it can be applied in a variety of situations and allows for the use of almost any measure which may be legitimate and enforceable by the counterinsurgent forces. If such measures are to be employed, however, a thorough understanding of the threat, the environment, the population, and the society are required in order to make them successful.

The next recommendation concerns the concept of occupation and the role the military plays in it. There was a lot of concern within the US administration in the run up to the Iraq war that the invading coalition forces would be perceived as occupiers. This led to decisions concerning force structure and roles and responsibilities that exacerbated the insurgency which ultimately began. As already discussed, concerns about perception are ridiculous as occupation is a question of fact.

Moreover, occupation includes moral and legal obligations to protect the noncombatants within the occupied territory. In the immediate aftermath of an invasion these moral and legal obligations are the responsibility of the military. It is highly unlikely that the US or any of its allies will in the near future develop a paramilitary security force to serve in this capacity. Therefore, the military, especially the US Army and USMC, must be prepared to perform the roles associated with occupation; it is an integral part of war.

The next recommendation is less a recommendation than a caution not to become overly reliant on technology to support population and resource control measures. In recent decades the US military has grown fond of seeking technological solutions to problems. This was true as far back as Vietnam where the helicopter and starlight scope were viewed as technologies that could change the nature of the war. It was even more so in the campaign in Iraq, during which a variety of new technologies were rapidly designed, fielded, and deployed to respond to insurgent challenges.

These technologies were often used to support the employment of population and resource control measures. US units used x-ray and other scanning technologies at check points, hand held devices to capture biometric identity data, and surveillance cameras mounted on blimps and masts. The hunger for improved technology has even infected our Iraqi partners and may have encouraged them to purchase and rely on devices with dubious credibility.[15]

Population and resource control measures are manpower intensive. The best technology for finding weapons, munitions, and other contraband is the same now as it was in the Philippines: well trained, disciplined soldiers. Even the biometric devices, which have yielded valuable captures, may be impeding US units from conducting census operations rapidly.[16] Consider that in the Philippines, US units collected information on potential insurgents by hand and sent it to a single office in Manila for processing which was then able to disseminate accurate intelligence information to over 450 posts across the archipelago.[17]

Notes

1. Tho, *Pacification*, 164.

2. While this thesis was being written a new book was released which contains more information on the campaigns in Al Qaim, Tal Afar, and other locations in Iraq during the pre-surge period. Readers should see James A. Russel, *Innovation, Transformation, and War: Counterinsurgency Operations in Anbar and Ninewah, Iraq, 2005-2007* (Stanford, CA: Stanford Security Studies, 2011).

3. Sassaman, *Warrior King*, 240-41. Regardless of whether either of the men drowned as was later alleged, the example illustrates how easy it is for young Soldiers and leaders to make bad decisions when not provided clear guidance about how to enforce population and resource control measures. If, for example, curfew violation was always to be punished by detention for a certain period of time–a week say–then there would not have been any need for the young leaders involved in this incident to apply their judgment. They would have detained the men knowing full well that they would be in detention for a certain period of time. Moreover, if this were also clear to the population itself, they would know that failure to return home on time would always result in detention and therefore should be avoided as much as practicable.

4. Nam Bo Regional Committee, "Letter from the Regional Committee," 6.

5. Ibid., 2.

6. BC020.

7. Tho, *Pacification*, 56.

8. Such a situation was also present in the campaign in Dhofar, which this paper did not consider in depth. However, in Dhofar the Sultan's Armed Forces established a series of fortified lines across the desert to interdict the flow of supplies from Yemen to the insurgents. These lines did not halt the flow of supplies, but did severely degrade it and facilitated the end of the insurgency. BI050, Dhofar Veterans Panel, Interview by Mark Battjes, Ben Boardman, Robert Green, Richard Johnson, Aaron Kaufman, Dustin Mitchell, Nathan Springer, and Thomas Walton, 28 March 2011, United Kingdom.

9. BH030.

10. It should be noted here that "neutral" does not mean that the population is not providing support to the government in any manner. This is especially true in the case of the payment of taxes. A government that collects taxes in any form from its citizens will not allow those under its control to not pay taxes just because they consider themselves to be "neutral." In reality, neutral behavior is acquiescence to government control and this includes support that is required by law. One can easily imagine many citizens in modern democracies (US, Canada, UK, etc.) that do not support their government and would not voluntarily assist

it any way. However, at almost every level of government such states collect taxes from their citizens automatically. It would in most cases be quite difficult for citizens of modern states to completely deny their governments support of any kind.

11. Mackinlay, Hoffman, and Metz all aver in some fashion that physical control of population and territory is not as important as winning the battle of ideas. Mackinlay does so because he believes that coercive control measures are not feasible for interventionist forces, Hoffman because he believes that the ability of insurgent's to gain external support overmatches the ability of the government to control its territory, and Metz because he believes only a complete alteration of society can end an insurgency. See Chapter 2 for a more in depth discussion of the views of modern COIN writers.

12. Chapter 4 details how Diem systematically gained control over the instruments of power within the GVN and then attempted to gain control over the rural areas of the country. As he did so, the Party, PAVN, and the VC changed their strategy to counter his actions resulting in a constant battle for control over the population.

13. Elliot and Stewart, *Pacification and the Viet Cong System in Dinh Tuong: 1966-1967*, x.

14. BI110, Battalion Commander, Interview by Mark Battjes, Richard Johnson, and Dustin Mitchell, 8 April 2011, United Kingdom.

15. Rod Norland, "Iraq Swears by Bomb Detector U.S. Sees as Useless," *The New York Times*, November 3, 2009.

16. Fully enrolling someone in the device is a laborious process. Even if only some of the data is collected, say thumb and index finger fingerprints, photograph, and name, a single entry could take 10 minutes. Furthermore, the biometric data must be stored on a server, updating which is an uncertain prospect given the instability of secure broadband networks in austere conditions. However, recording name, address, occupation, and taking a digital photograph requires less than 1 minute and can easily be cataloged and stored locally on a laptop computer.

17. McCoy, *Policing America's Empire*, 76-82.

Further Research

There are also a number of topics concerning the employment of population and resource control measures that merit further research. The first is whether and how such measures can be employed to support all of the lines of operation in a campaign. They are primarily associated with the security line of operation, but if properly employed they might also support the governance and economic development lines of operation.*

Another promising line of research concerns the difference between legitimacy and legality in the employment of population and resource control measures. The case studies illustrate that measures which are legal may not be legitimate. Conversely, measures that are legitimate may not be strictly legal. This is a line of inquiry that the author wanted to pursue but did not feel able to properly complete given constraints on time and access to sufficient primary resources. While the legality of any measure is a matter of fact, its legitimacy is not. Moreover, legitimacy must be examined from the perspective of three different groups: the population of the state where the campaign is being conducted, the counterinsurgent forces, and the populations of the intervening powers. Gaining insight on these perspectives requires access to a large number of primary sources, especially those which capture the attitudes of these groups at the time of the conflict.

Further research is also needed on how population and resource control measures should be employed differently when confronting a truly local insurgency versus an externally supported insurgency. That was not the focus of this paper and so any conclusions drawn regarding this topic from the case studies would be shallow. This line of research would be especially relevant for operations in Afghanistan as some in the panoply of different insurgencies there may truly be local.

Note

*One US Army battalion commander noted that his area of Baghdad "had a lot of retail areas but no real industries and the only way people are going to come to a retail area is if they feel secure." As security improved, partially because of the employment of population and resource control measures, the retail areas rebounded. BG090.

Bibliography

Primary Sources

Interviews

Command and General Staff College (CGSC) Scholars Program 2011. Scholars Program *Counterinsurgency Research Study 2011*. Research Study, Fort Leavenworth, KS: Ike Skelton Chair in Counterinsurgency, 2011. This study included interviews of counterinsurgency practitioners and policy professionals from the United States and United Kingdom. All interviews are held with the Ike Skelton Chair in Counterinsurgency, CGSC Fort Leavenworth, KS.

Boston, Massachusetts

BF010, Former Army Officer. Interview by Richard Johnson and Aaron Kaufman, 11 March 2011.

BF020, Civilian Advisor to MNF-I. Interview by Richard Johnson and Aaron Kaufman, 11 March 2011.

BF030, Battery Commander. Interview by Richard Johnson and Aaron Kaufman, 12 March 2011.

BF040, Battery Commander. Interview by Richard Johnson and Aaron Kaufman, 14 March 2011.

Fort Bliss, Texas

BB010, Battalion Commander. Interview by Mark Battjes and Nathan Springer, 2 March 2011.

BB020, Battalion Commander. Interview by Mark Battjes and Nathan Springer, 2 March 2011.

BB030, Brigade Commander. Interview by Mark Battjes and Nathan Springer, 3 March 2011.

Fort Bragg, North Carolina

BC010, Field Grade Officer. Interview by Robert Green and Aaron Kaufman, 1 March 2011.

BC020, Brigade Commander. Interview by Robert Green and Aaron Kaufman, 2 March 2011.

BC030, Battalion Commander. Interview by Benjamin Boardman and Richard Johnson, 1 March 2011.

BC040, Battalion Commander. Interview by Benjamin

Boardman and Richard Johnson, 2 March 2011.

BC050, Battalion Commander. Interview by Benjamin Boardman and Richard Johnson, 2 March 2011.

BC060, Battalion Commander. Interview by Benjamin Boardman and Richard Johnson, 3 March 2011.

Fort Irwin, California

BE010, Transition Team Leader. Interview by Mark Battjes and Thomas Walton, 7 March 2011.

BE020, Transition Team Member. Interview by Mark Battjes and Thomas Walton, 7 March 2011.

BE030, Company Commander. Interview by Mark Battjes and Thomas Walton, 8 March 2011.

BE040, Transition Team Leader. Interview by Mark Battjes and Thomas Walton, 9 March 2011.

BE050, Battery Commander. Interview by Robert Green and Aaron Kaufman, 8 March 2011.

BE060, Brigade Commander. Interview by Mark Battjes and Thomas Walton, 9 March 2011.

BE070, Field Grade Officer. Interview by Robert Green and Aaron Kaufman, 9 March 2011.

BE080, Battalion Commander. Interview by Robert Green and Aaron Kaufman, 7 March 2011.

BE090, Battalion Commander. Interview by Robert Green and Aaron Kaufman, 7 March 2011.

Fort Knox, Kentucky

BD010, Field Grade Officer. Interview by Benjamin Boardman and Dustin Mitchell, 14 March 2011.

BD020, Commander. Interview by Benjamin Boardman and Dustin Mitchell, 14 March 2011.

BD030, Commander. Interview by Benjamin Boardman and Dustin Mitchell, 14 March 2011.

BD040, Commander. Interview by Benjamin Boardman and Dustin Mitchell, 15 March 2011.

BD050, Commander. Interview by Benjamin Boardman and Dustin Mitchell, 15 March 2011.

BD060, Field Grade Officer. Interview by Benjamin Boardman and Dustin Mitchell, 16 March 2011.

BD070, Field Grade Officer. Interview by Benjamin Boardman and Dustin Mitchell, 16 March 2011.

BD080, Field Grade Officer. Interview by Benjamin Boardman and Dustin Mitchell, 17 March 2011.

Fort Leavenworth, Kansas

BA010, Brigade Commander. Interview by Richard Johnson and Thomas Walton, 22 February 2011.

BA020, Battalion Commander. Interview by Mark Battjes and Benjamin Boardman, 23 February 2011.

BA030, Vietnam Veteran. Interview by Aaron Kaufman and Dustin Mitchell, 24 February 2011.

BA040, Brigade Commander. Interview by Aaron Kaufman and Dustin Mitchell, 23 February 2011.

BA050, Battalion Commander. Interview by Robert Green and Nathan Springer, 23 February 2011.

BA060, Battalion Commander. Interview by Robert Green and Nathan Springer, 23 February 2011.

BA070, Battery Commander. Interview by Richard Johnson and Thomas Walton, 24 February 2011.

BA080, Counterinsurgency Advisor. Interview by Richard Johnson and Nathan Springer, 9 March 2011.

BA090, Brigade Commander. Interview by Mark Battjes and Benjamin Boardman, 24 February 2011.

Fort Stewart, Georgia:

BG010, Battalion Commander. Interview by Nathan Springer, 14 March 2011.

BG020, Brigade Commander. Interview by Mark Battjes and Thomas Walton, 14 March 2011.

BG030, Troop Commander. Interview by Mark Battjes, Nathan Springer, and Thomas Walton, 14 March 2011.

BG040, Brigade Commander. Interview by Nathan Springer and Thomas Walton, 15 March 2011.

BG050, Battalion Commander. Interview by Mark Battjes, 15 March 2011.

BG060, Battalion Commander. Interview by Mark Battjes, 15 March 2011.

BG070, Field Grade Officer. Interview by Nathan Springer and Thomas Walton, 15 March 2011.

BG080, Battalion Commander. Interview by Mark Battjes and Thomas Walton, 16 March 2011.

BG090, Battalion Commander. Interview by Mark Battjes and Nathan Springer, 16 March 2011.

BG100, Brigade Commander. Interview by Mark Battjes and Nathan Springer, 16 March 2011.

United Kingdom

BI010, Senior British Officer. Interview by Mark Battjes, Benjamin Boardman, Robert Green, Richard Johnson, Aaron Kaufman, Dustin Mitchell, and Nathan Springer, 29 March 2011.

BI020, Battle Group Commander. Interview by Aaron Kaufman and Thomas Walton, 31 March 2011.

BI030, Field Grade Officer. Interview by Robert Green and Thomas Walton, 29 March 2011.

BI040, Field Grade Officer. Interview by Mark Battjes and Dustin Mitchell, 1 April 2011.

BI050, Dhofar Veterans Panel. Interview by Mark Battjes, Benjamin Boardman, Robert Green, Richard Johnson, Aaron Kaufman, Dustin Mitchell, Nathan Springer, and Thomas Walton, 28 March 2011.

BI060, Dhofar Veterans Panel. Interview by Interview by Mark Battjes, Benjamin Boardman, Robert Green, Richard Johnson, Aaron Kaufman, Dustin Mitchell, Nathan Springer, and Thomas Walton, 2 April 2011.

BI070, Retired General Officer. Interview by Interview by Mark Battjes, Benjamin Boardman, Robert Green, Richard Johnson, Aaron Kaufman, Dustin Mitchell, Nathan Springer, and Thomas Walton, 30 March 2011.

BI080, Retired General Officer. Interview by Benjamin Boardman, Robert Green, Nathan Springer, and Thomas Walton, 3 April 2011.

BI090, Retired General Officer. Interview by Benjamin Boardman, Robert Green, Nathan Springer, and Thomas Walton, 4 April 2011.

BI100, Senior Army Officer. Interview by Mark Battjes, Richard Johnson, Aaron Kaufman, and Dustin Mitchell, 4 April 2011.

BI110, Battalion Commander. Interview by Mark Battjes, Richard Johnson, and Dustin Mitchell, 8 April 2011.

BI120, Retired Army Officer. Interview by Benjamin Boardman, Robert Green, Nathan Springer, and Thomas Walton, 8 April 2011.

BI130, Platoon Commander. Interview by Benjamin Boardman and Richard Johnson, 5 April 2011.

BI140, Afghan Army Advisor. Interview by Benjamin Boardman and Richard Johnson, 5 April 2011.

BI150, Company Sergeant Major. Interview by Aaron Kaufman and Dustin Mitchell, 5 April 2011.

BI160, Company 2nd In Command. Interview by Aaron Kaufman and Dustin Mitchell, 5 April 2011.

BI170, Afghan Army Advisor. Interview by Aaron Kaufman and Dustin Mitchell, 5 April 2011.

BI190, Senior Non-Commissioned Officer. Interview by Mark Battjes and Thomas Walton, 5 April 2011.

BI200, Platoon Commander. Interview by Aaron Kaufman and Dustin Mitchell, 7 April 2011.

BI210, Company 2nd In Command. Interview by Mark Battjes and Thomas Walton, 7 April 2011.

BI220, Field Grade Officer. Interview by Aaron Kaufman and Dustin Mitchell, 7 April 2011.

BI230, Company Commander. Interview by Robert Green and Nathan Springer, 7 April 2011.

BI240, Company Grade Officer. Interview by Benjamin Boardman and Richard Johnson, 7 April 2011.

BI250, Battalion Commander. Interview by Benjamin Boardman and Richard Johnson, 7 April 2011.

BI260, Non-Commissioned Officer. Interview by Robert Green and Nathan Springer, 7 April 2011.

BI270, Company Grade Officer. Interview by Mark Battjes and Thomas Walton, 7 April 2011.

BI280, Commander's Panel. Interview by Richard Johnson, 1 April 2011.

BI290, Battery Commander. Interview by Richard Johnson, 1 April 2011.

BI300, Company Commander. Interview by Richard Johnson, 2 April 2011.

BI310, Company Commander. Interview by Benjamin Boardman and Nathan Springer, 31 March 2011.

BI320, Field Grade Officer. Interview by Benjamin Boardman and Dustin Mitchell, 29 March 2011.

BI330, Dhofar Veteran. Interview by Robert Green, 28 March 2011.

Washington, DC

BH010, Senior Policy Official. Interview by Mark Battjes, Benjamin Boardman, Robert Green, Richard Johnson, Aaron Kaufman, Dustin Mitchell, Nathan Springer, and Thomas Walton, 21 March 2011.

BH020, Brigade Commander. Interview by Mark Battjes, Benjamin Boardman, Robert Green, Richard Johnson, Aaron Kaufman, Dustin Mitchell, Nathan Springer, and Thomas Walton, 21 March 2011.

BH030, Iraq Veterans Panel. Interview by Mark Battjes, Robert Green, Aaron Kaufman, and Dustin Mitchell, 22 March 2011.

BH040, Afghanistan Veterans Panel. Interview by Richard Johnson, Aaron Kaufman, Nathan Springer, and Thomas Walton, 24 March 2011.

BH050, Historian. Interview by Mark Battjes, Robert Green, Richard Johnson, Aaron Kaufman, and Dustin Mitchell, 22 March 2011.

BH060, Vietnam Political and Military Analyst. Interview by Mark Battjes, Benjamin Boardman, Robert Green, and Dustin Mitchell, 24 March 2011.

BH070, Iraqi Mayor. Interview by Mark Battjes and Robert Green, 25 March 2011.

Official Reports and Memoranda

Bureau of Insular Affairs, United States. *Fourth Annual Report of the Philippine Commission, 1903, Part 1.* Washington, DC: Government Printing Office, 1904.

———. *Sixth Annual Report of the Philippine Commission, 1905, Part 1.* Washington, DC: Government Printing Office, 1906.

———. *Sixth Annual Report of the Philippine Commission, 1905, Part 3.* Washington, DC: Government Printing Office, 1906.

———. *Seventh Annual Report of the Philippine Commission, 1906, Part 1.* Washington, DC: Government Printing Office, 1907.

———. *Ninth Annual Report of the Philippine Commission, 1908, Part 1.* Washington, DC: US War Department, 1909.

Bureau of Intelligence and Research, US Department of State. "Research Memorandum RFE-58, *Strategic Hamlets*." 1 July 1963. Texas Tech University Vietnam Archive, Lubbock, TX.

Central Intelligence Agency. "Memorandum for the Secretary of Defense." 13 July 1962. Texas Tech University Vietnam Archive, Lubbock, TX.

Donnell, John C. and Gerald C. Hickey. *The Vietnamese "Strategic Hamlets": A Preliminary Report.* Santa Monica, CA: RAND Corporation, 1962.

Elliot, David W. P. and W. A. Stewart. *Pacification and the Viet Cong System in Dinh Tuong: 1966-1967.* Santa Monica, CA: RAND Corporation, 1969.

Forrestal, Michael V. "Memorandum for the President." 11 December 1963. Douglas Pike Collection: Unit 1. Texas Tech University Vietnam Archive, Lubbock, TX.

Headquarters, 2d Brigade, 25th Infantry Division. "Combat Operations After Action Report, Operation TOAN THANG, Phase II." 10 March 1969. Bud Harton Collection. Texas Tech University Vietnam Archive, Lubbock, TX.

Headquarters, 3d Brigade, 25th Infantry Division. "TOAN-THANG Phase II Execution, 1 Ooctober 68–30 November 68." 31 March 1969. Bud Harton Collection. Texas Tech University Vietnam Archive, Lubbock, TX.

Headquarters, 25th Infantry Division. "Operational Report on Lessons Learned for Period Ending 30 April 1966." Bud Harton Collection. Texas Tech University Vietnam Archive, Lubbock, TX.

———. "Operational Report for Quarterly Period Ending 30 April 1967." 19 May 1967. Bud Harton Collection. Texas Tech University Vietnam Archive, Lubbock, TX.

———. "Operational Report for Quarterly Period Ending 31 July 1967." 19 August 1967. Bud Harton Collection. Texas Tech University Vietnam Archive, Lubbock, TX.

———. "Operational Report - Lessons Learned, Period Ending 31 October 1967." 5 March 1968, Bud Harton Collection. Texas Tech University Vietnam Archive, Lubbock, TX.

———."Operational Report - Lessons Learned, Period Ending 31 January 1968." 15 May 1968. Bud Harton Collection. Texas Tech University Vietnam Archive, Lubbock, TX.

———."Operational Report - Lessons Learned, Period Ending 30 April 1968." 31 July 1968. Bud Harton Collection. Texas Tech University Vietnam Archive, Lubbock, TX.

———."Operational Report - Lessons Learned, Period Ending 31 July 1968." 27 January 1969. Bud Harton Collection. Texas Tech University Vietnam Archive, Lubbock, TX.

———. "Operational Report Period Ending 31 January 1969." 1 February 1969. 1st Battalion, 8th Artillery, 25th Infantry Association Collection. Texas Tech University Vietnam Archive, Lubbock, TX.

———. "Operational Report - Lessons Learned, Period Ending 31 July 1969." 18 December 1969. Bud Harton Collection. Texas Tech University Vietnam Archive, Lubbock, TX.

———."Operational Report - Lessons Learned, Period Ending 30 April 1970." Bud Harton Collection. Texas Tech University Vietnam Archive, Lubbock, TX.

———."Operational Report - Lessons Learned, Period Ending 31 October 1970." 30 April 1971. Bud Harton Collection. Texas Tech University Vietnam Archive, Lubbock, TX.

Hosmer, Stephen T., and Sibylle O. Crane. "Counterinsurgency, A Symposium 16-20 April 1962." *RAND Corporation Reports.* Washington DC: RAND, 1962.

II Field Force Vietnam. "Combat Operations After Action Report, Tet Offensive." Bud Harton Collection. Texas Tech University Vietnam Archive, Lubbock, TX.

Military History Institute of Vietnam. *Victory in Vietnam: The Official History of the People's Army of Vietnam, 1954–1975*, translated by Pribbenow, Merle L. Lawrence, KS: University Press of Kansas, 2002.

Ministry of Defence, United Kingdom. "Operation TELIC Lessons Learned Compendium." http://www.mod.uk/NR/rdonlyres/F0282A90-99E5-415E-B3BC-97EAD7D7873A/0/operation_telic_lessons_compendium.pdf (accessed 1 May 2011).

Pearce, R. Michael. *Evolution of a Vietnamese Village - Part I*. Santa Monica, CA: RAND Corporation, 1965.

———. *Evolution of a Vietnamese Village - Part II*. Santa Monica, CA: RAND Corporation, 1966.

Tran Dinh Tho. *Pacification*. Washington, DC: Center for Military History, 1980.

War Department, United States. *Report of the Lieutenant General Commanding the Army, 1900, Part 3*. Washington DC: Government Printing Office, 1900.

———. *Report of the Lieutenant General Commanding the Army, 1901, Part 5*. Washington, DC: Government Printing Office, 1901.

Zasloff, Joseph T. "Rural Resettlement in South Viet Nam: The Agroville Program," *Pacific Affairs* 35, no. 4 (Winter 1962-1963): 327-340.

Personal Accounts

Anderson, Joseph and Gary Volesky. "A Synchronized Approach to Population Control." *Military Review* (July-August 2007): 145-147.

Bradford, Alfred S. *Some Even Volunteered*. Westport, CT: Praeger Publishers, 1994.

Chiarelli, Peter and Patrick Michaelis. "The Requirements for Full-Spectrum Operations." *Military Review* (July-August 2005): 4-17.

Colby, William. *Lost Victory: A Firsthand Account of America's Sixteen-Year Involvement in Vietnam*. Chicago: Contemporary Books, 1989.

Collier, Craig. "Now That We're Leaving Iraq, What Did We Learn?" *Military Review* (September-October 2010): 88-93.

Feith, Douglas J. *War and Decision*. New York: Harper Collins Publishers, 2008.

Giap, Vo Nguyen. "Inside the Vietminh." In *The Guerrilla Selections from the Marine Corps Gazette*, edited by T. N. Green, 147-77. New York: Praeger, 1962.

———. *The Military Art of People's War*, edited by Russel Stetler. New York: Monthly Review Press, 1970.

Gibson, Chris. "Battlefield Victories and Strategic Success: The Path Forward in Iraq." *Military Review* (September-October 2006): 47-59.

Kalaw, Teodoro M. *Aide-de-camp to Freedom*, translated by Katigbak, Maria Kalaw Manila: Teodoro M. Kalaw Society, Inc., 1965.

Komer, Robert. *Bureaucracy at War: US Performance in the Vietnam Conflict*. Boulder, CO: Westview Press, 1986.

Kuehl, Dale. "Testing Galula in Ameriyah, The People are the Key." *Military Review* (March-April 2009): 72-80.

O'Donnell, John B. "The Strategic Hamlet Program in Kien Hoa Province, South Vietnam: A Case Study of Counter-Insurgency." Paper presented at the conference on Southeast Asian Tribes, Minorities and Central Governments, Princeton, New Jersey, 11 May 1965. Texas Tech University Vietnam Archive, Lubbock, TX.

Quezon, Manuel Luis. *The Good Fight*. New York: D. Appleton-Century Company, Incorporated, 1946.

Sassaman, Nathan with Joe Layden. *Warrior King*. New York: St. Martin's Press, 2008.

Smith, Neil and Sean MacFarland. "Anbar Awakens: The Tipping Point." *Military Review* (March-April 2008): 41-53.

Westmoreland, William C. "A Military War of Attrition." In *The Lessons of Vietnam*, edited by Thompson, W. Scott and Donaldson Frizzel, 57-71. New York: Crane, Russak and Company, 1977.

Documents, Letters, and Captured Enemy Material

Bell, J. Franklin. Telegraphic Circulars and General Orders. In Robert D. Ramsey III, *A Masterpiece of Counterguerrilla Warfare: BG J. Franklin Bell in the Philippines, 1901-1902*. Fort Leavenworth, KS: Combat Studies Institute Press, 2007.

Coalition Provisional Authority. "Order No. 1, De'Ba'athification of Iraqi Society." 16 May 2003.

———."Order No. 2, "Dissolution of Entities." 23 May 2003.

———."Regulation No. 1." 16 May 2003. http://www.iraqcoalition.org/regulations/ 20030516_CPAREG_1_The_Coalition_Provisional_Authority_.pdf (accessed 1 May 2011).

———."Order No. 7." 9 June 2003. http://www.iraqcoalition.org/regulations/ 20030610_CPAORD_7_Penal_Code.pdf (accessed 1 May 2011).

———. "Order No. 3, (Revised) (Amended)." 31 December 2003. http://www.iraqcoalition.org/regulations/20031231_CPAORD3_REV__AMD_.pdf (accessed 1 May 2011).

Current Affairs Committee C69. "Directive No. 78/CTNT, An Order to Continued to Take Advantage of our Success, Develop the Overall Attack, and Accomplish the 1969 Spring Plan." 14 May 1969. Texas Tech University Vietnam Archive, Lubbock, TX.

Durbrow, Elbridge. "Cablegram from Elbridge Durbrow, United States Ambassador in Saigon, to Secretary of State Christian A. Herter, 16 September 1960." In *The Pentagon Papers* as published by *The New York Times*, 115-18. New York: Bantam Books, Inc., 1971.

"Experiences of Struggle with and Elimination of Strategic Hamlets of Villagers." October-November 1962. Texas Tech University Vietnam Archive, Lubbock, TX.

Government of Vietnam. "Discussion Paper–From Strategic Hamlets to Self Defense Village." Texas Tech University Vietnam Archive, Lubbock, TX.

Hilsman, Roger. "The Situation and Short-Term Prospects in South Vietnam." In *The Pentagon Papers* as published by *The New York Times*, 155-57. New York: Bantam Books, Inc., 1971.

Iraqi Governing Council. "Transitional Administrative Law." 8 March 2004. http://www.constitution.org/cons/iraq/TAL.html (accessed 1 May 2011).

Komer, Robert. *Impact of Pacification on Insurgency in South Vietnam*. Santa Monica, CA: RAND Corporation, 1970.

Malvar, Miguel. "Provisions and Instructions Issued by the Superior Commander of Southern Luzon for Observation by this Department." 28 April 1901. In Taylor, John R.M. *The Philippine Insurrection Against the United States: A Compilation of Documents* (Fort Leavenworth, KS: Combined Arms Research Library Microfilm).

———. "The Reason for My Change of Attitude." 16 April 1902. In Taylor, John R.M. *The Philippine Insurrection Against the United States: A Compilation of Documents* (Fort Leavenworth, KS: Combined Arms Research Library Microfilm).

Nam Bo Regional Committee. "Letter from the Regional Committee to All Members of Cells." March 28, 1960. Douglas Pike Collection: Unit 5. Texas Tech University Vietnam Archive, Lubbock, TX.

National Liberation Front. "Anti-Strategic Hamlet Program." VC Document 93, Douglas Pike Collection: Unit 1. Texas Tech University Vietnam Archive, Lubbock, TX.

———. "Measures Against Village Merging and People Concentration." Texas Tech University Vietnam Archive, Lubbock, TX.

Office of Rural Affairs, US Operations Mission Saigon. "Notes on Strategic Hamlets." 15 August 1963. Douglas Pike Collection: Unit 2. Texas Tech University Vietnam Archive, Lubbock, TX.

Political Department, People's Liberation Army. "Outline of the Reorientation of Forthcoming Missions in 1970 (For Elementary and Intermediate Cadre)." 14 January 1970. Texas Tech University Vietnam Archive, Lubbock, TX.

Standing Committee of A. 26. "Matters to be Grasped when Performing the Ideological Task in the Party Body." In *Viet-Nam Documents and Research Notes*, '*Decisive Victory*': *Step by Step, Bit by Bit*. Texas Tech University Vietnam Archive, Lubbock, TX.

———. "Study of Directive 81 of 5 [Nam] Truong [COSVN]

Opening of Phase H." In *Viet-Nam Documents and Research Notes*, *'Decisive Victory': Step by Step, Bit by Bit*. Texas Tech University Vietnam Archive, Lubbock, TX.

Transitional National Assembly. "Iraqi Constitution." http://www.uniraq.org/documents/ iraqi_constitution.pdf (accessed 1 May 2011).

United Nations Security Council. "Resolution 1483." 22 May 2003. http://www.un.org/ Docs /sc/unsc_resolutions03.html (accessed 1 May 2011).

———."Resolution 1511." 16 October 2003. http://www.un.org/Docs/sc/ unsc_resolutions03.html (accessed 1 May 2011).

———."Resolution 1546." 8 June 2004. http://www.un.org/Docs/sc/ unsc_resolutions04.html (accessed 1 May 2011).

———."Resolution 1637." 8 November 2005. http://www.un.org/Docs/sc/ unsc_resolutions05.htm (accessed 1 May 2011).

———."Resolution 1723." 28 November 2006. http://www.un.org/Docs/sc/ unsc_resolutions06.htm (accessed 1 May 2011).

———."Resolution 1790." 18 December 2007. http://www.un.org/Docs/sc/ unsc_resolutions07.htm (accessed 1 May 2011).

"Viet Cong Loss of Population Control Evidence from Captured Documents." 1968. Texas Tech University Vietnam Archive, Lubbock, TX.

Vietnamese Communist Party. "A Party Account of the Situation in the Nam Bo Region of South Vietnam from 1954-1960." Douglas Pike Collection: Unit 6. Texas Tech University Vietnam Archive, Lubbock, TX.

Doctrinal References

Adjutant General's Office, U. S. War Department. *General Orders Number 100*, Washington, DC: War Department, 1863.

Army, Department of the. Field Manual 27-10, *The Law of Land Warfare*. Washington, DC: Department of the Army, 1956.

———. Field Manual 31-16, *Counterguerrilla Operations*. Washington, DC: Department of the Army, 1963.

———. Field Manual -3-24, *Counterinsurgency.* Washington DC: Department of the Army, 2006.

———. Field Manual 3-24.2, *Tactics in Counterinsurgency*. Washington DC: Department of the Army, 2009.

Civil Operations Rural Development Support. *The Vietnamese Village 1970 Handbook for Advisors*. 2 May 1970. Combined Arms Research Library, Fort Leavenworth, KS.

Defense, Department of. *DoD GEN-25, Handbook for US Forces in Vietnam*. 1966. Combined Arms Research Library, Fort Leavenworth, KS.

Military Assistance Command, Civil Operations Rural Development Support. *Territorial Security in Vietnam*. 1 January 1971. Combined Arms Research Library, Fort Leavenworth, KS.

Military Assistance Command, Vietnam, United States. *Handbook for Military Support of Pacification*. February 1968. Combined Arms Research Library, Fort Leavenworth, KS.

Philippine Constabulary. *Manual for the Philippine Constabulary, 1911*. Manila: Bureau of Printing: 1911.

Secondary Sources

Afsar, Shahid and Chris Samples. "The Taliban: An Organizational Analysis." *Military Review* (May-June 2008): 58-73.

Al-Jabouri, Najim Abed and Sterling Jensen. "The Iraqi and AQI Roles in the Sunni Awakening." *Prism* 2, no. 1 (2010): 3-18.

Andrade, Dale. "Westmoreland Was Right: Learning the Wrong Lessons from the Vietnam War." *Small Wars and Insurgencies* 19, no. 2 (June 2008): 145-181.

Armstrong, Karen. *A History of God* (New York: Ballantine Books, 1993.

Azjen, Icek. "The Theory of Planned Behavior." *Organizational Behavior and Human Decision Processes* 50 (1991): 179-211.

Baker, Jay B. "Tal Afar 2005: Laying the Counterinsurgency Framework." *Army* (June 2009): 61-67.

Beckett, Ian. "The British Counter-insurgency Campaign in Dhofar, 1965-1975." In *Counterinsurgency in Modern Warfare*, edited by Marston, Daniel and Carter Malkasian, 175-190. Oxford: Osprey Publishing, 2010.

Bergerud, Eric. *The Dynamics of Defeat: The Vietnam War in Hau Nghia Province*. Boulder, CO: Westview Press, Inc., 1991.

———. *Red Thunder, Tropic Lightning*. Boulder, CO: Westview Press, Inc., 1993.

Birtle, Andrew J. *US Army Counterinsurgency and Contingency Operations Doctrine 1860-1941*. Washington, DC: Center of Military History, United States Army, 2003.

Burton, Brian and John Nagl. "Learning As We Go: The US Army Adapts to COIN in Iraq, July 2004-December 2006." *Small Wars and Insurgencies* 19, no. 3 (September 2008): 303-327.

Clausewitz, Carl von. *On War*. Edited and translated by Howard, Michael and Peter Paret. Princeton, NJ:: Princeton University Press, 1976.

Fontenot, Gregory, E. J. Degan, and David Tohn. *On Point, The United States Army in Operation IRAQI FREEDOM*. Fort Leavenworth, KS: Combat Studies Institute Press, 2004.

Galula, David. *Counterinsurgency Warfare: Theory and Practice*. Saint Petersburg, FL: Glenwood Press, 1964.

———. *Pacification in Algeria, 1956-1958*. Santa Monica, CA: Rand Corporation, 2006.

Gentile, Gian. "A Strategy of Tactics: Population Centric COIN and the Army." *Parameters* (Autumn 2009): 5-17.

Gompert, David C. and John Gordon IV. *War by Other Means*. Santa Monica, CA: RAND Corporation, 2008.

Gordon, Michael R. and Bernard E. Trainor. *Cobra II*. New York: Pantheon Books, 2006.

Greem, T.N. *The Guerilla: Selections from the Marine Corps Gazzette*. New York: Praeger, 2005.

Gywnn, Major General Sir Charles W. *Imperial Policing*. London: MacMillian and CO. Ltd., 1934.

Hoffman, Frank. "Neo-Classical Counter-Insurgency?" *Parameters*, Summer 2007: 77-87.

———. *Conflict in the 21st Century: The Rise of Hybrid Wars*. Arlington, VA: The Potomac Institute for Policy Studies, 2007.

Howard, Michael. *Clausewitz: A Very Short Introduction*. Oxford: Oxford University Press, 2002.

———. *War in European History*. Oxford: Oxford University Press, 1976.

Hunt, Richard. *Pacification: The American Struggle for Vietnam's Hearts and Minds.* Boulder, CO: Westview Press, 1995.

Iron, Richard. "Britain's Longest War: Northern Ireland 1967-2007." In *Counterinsurgency in Modern Warfare,* edited by Marston, Daniel and Carter Malkasian, 157-174. Oxford: Osprey Publishing, 2010.

Joes, Anthony James. "Counterinsurgency in the Philippines, 1898-1954." In *Counterinsurgency in Modern Warfare,* edited by Marston, Daniel and Carter Malkasian, 39-56. Oxford: Osprey Publishing, 2010.

Kagan, Kimberly. "Enforcing the Law: The Baghdad Security Plan Begins." *Iraq Report.* (10 February-5 March 2007):1-19.

Kilcullen, David. *The Accidental Guerrilla : Fighting Small Wars in the Midst of a Big One.* New York: Oxford University Press., 2009.

Kitson, Frank. *Low Intensity Operations: Subversion, Insurgency, Peacekeeping.* London: Archon Books, 1971.

———. *Bunch of Five.* London: Faber and Faber, 1977.

Krepinevich, Andrew F. Jr. *The Army and Vietnam.* Baltimore, MD: Johns Hopkins University Press, 1986.

Linn, Brian. *The Philippine War, 1899-1902.* Lawrence, KS: University of Kansas Press, 2000.

Mackinlay, John. *The Insurgent Archipelago : From Mao to Bin Laden.* New York.: Columbia University Press, 2009.

Mackinlay, John and Alison Al-Baddawy. *Rethinking Counterinsurgency.* Santa Monica, CA: 2008.

Malkasian, Carter. "Counterinsurgency in Iraq." In *Counterinsurgency in Modern Warfare*, edited by Marston, Daniel and Carter Malkasian, 287-310. Oxford: Osprey Publishing, 2010.

Malkasian, Carter. "The Role of Perceptions and Political reform in Counterinsurgency: The Case of Western Iraq, 2004-2005." *Small Wars and Insurgencies* 17, no 3 (September 2006): 367-394.

Mansfield, Don. "The Irish Republican Army and Northern Ireland." In *Insurgency in the Modern World*, edited by O'Neill, Bard, 44-85. Boulder, CO: Westview Press, 1980.

Mao, Tse-Tung. *On Guerrilla Warfare.* New York: Praeger, 1961.

Markel, Wade. "Draining the Swamp: The British Strategy of Population Control." *Parameters* (Spring 2006): 35-48.

Marston, Daniel. "Adaptation in the Field: The British Army's Difficult Campaign in Iraq." *Security Challenges* 6, no. 1 (Autumn 2010): 71-84.

———. "Lost and Found in the Jungle." In *Big Wars and Small Wars*, edited by Hew Strachan, 96-114. London: Routledge, 2006.

———. "Realizing the Extent of Our Errors and Forging the Road Ahead: Afghanistan 2001-2010." In *Counterinsurgency in Modern Warfare*, edited by Marston, Daniel and Carter Malkasian, 251-286. Oxford: Osprey Publishing, 2010.

Marston, Daniel, and Carter Malkasian, eds. *Counterinsurgency in Modern Warfare.* Oxford: Osprey Publishing, 2008.

May, Glenn Anthony. *Battle for Batangas: A Philippine Province at War.* New Haven, CT: Yale University Press, 1991.

McCoy, Alfred W. *Policing America's Empire.* Madison, WI: The University of Wisconsin Press, 2009.

McCuen, John J. *The Art of Counter-Revolutionary War.* Harrisburg, PA: Stackpole Books, 1966.

Metz, Steven. "New Challenges and Old Concepts: Understanding the 21st Century Insurgency." *Parameters* (Winter 2007-2008): 20-32.

Miers, Richard. *Shoot to Kill.* London: Faber and Faber, 1959.

Moyar, Mark. *Triumph Forsaken: The Vietnam War, 1954-1965.* New York: Cambridge University Press, 2006.

O'Neill, Bard. "Revolutionary War in Oman." In *Insurgency in the Modern World*, edited by O'Neill, Bard, 213-234. Boulder, CO: Westview Press, 1980.

———. *Insurgency and Terrorism: From Revolution to Apocalypse.* 2nd ed. Washington, DC: Potomac Books, Inc., 2005.

O'Neill, Mark. *Confronting the Hydra.* Sydney, Australia: Lowy Institute, 2009.

Paget, Julian. *Counterinsurgency Operations.* New York: Walker and Company, 1967.

Paret, Peter. *French Revolutionary Warfare from Indochina to Algeria: The Analysis of a Political and Military Doctrine*. New York: Frederick A. Praeger, 1964.

Race, Jeffrey. *War Comes to Long An*. California: UC Press, 1972.

Ricks, Thomas E. *The Gamble*. New York: The Penguin Press, 2009.

Rubin, Barnett and Ahmed Rashid. "The Great Game to the Great Bargain." *Foreign Affairs* 87, no. 6 (November-December 2008): 30-44.

Russel, James A. *Innovation, Transformation, and War: Counterinsurgency Operations in Anbar and Ninewah, Iraq, 2005-2007*. Stanford, CA: Stanford Security Studies, 2011.

Scott, James C. "Revolution in the Revolution: Peasants and Commissars." *Theory and Society* 7, no. 1/2 (January-March, 1979): 97-134.

Semple, Michael and Fotini Christia. "How to Flip the Taliban." *Foreign Affairs* (July-August 2009).

Shy, John, and Thomas Collier. "Revolutionary war." In *Makers of Modern Strategy : Military Thought from Machiavelli to the Nuclear Age*, edited by Peter Paret, 815-862. Princeton, NJ: Princeton University Press., 1986.

Stubbs, Richard. "From Search and Destroy to Hearts and Minds: The Evolution of British Strategy in Malaya 1948-60." In *Counterinsurgency in Modern Warfare*, edited by Marston, Daniel and Carter Malkasian, 101-118. Oxford: Osprey Publishing, 2010.

Thompson, Robert. *Defeating Communist Insurgency*. London: Chatto and Windus, 1967.

Thompson, W. Scott and Donaldson Frizzell. *The Lessons of Vietnam*. New York: Crane, Russak and Company, 1977.

Thornton, Rod. "Getting It Wrong: The Crucial Mistakes Made in the Early Stages of the British Army's Deployment to Northern Ireland." *Journal of Strategic Studies* 30, no. 1 (February 2007): 73-107.

Trinquier, Roger. *Modern Warfare: A French View of Counterinsurgency*. Westport, Connecticut: Praego, 1964.

Ucko, David. *The New Counterinsurgency Era: Transforming the US Military for Modern Wars.* Washington DC: Georgetown University Press, 2009.

Weber, Max. "Politics as a Vocation." In *From Max Weber: Essays in Sociology*, translated and edited by Gerth, H.H. and C. Wright Mills, 77-128. New York: Oxford University Press, 1946.

West, Bing. *No True Glory: A Frontline Account of the Battle for Fallujah.* New York: Bantam Books, 2005.

———. *The Strongest Tribe*. New York: Random House, 2009.

Willbanks, James. *Abandoning Vietnam.* Lawrence, KS: University of Kansas Press, 2004.

Wolf, Charles Jr. *Insurgency and Counterinsurgency: New Myths and Old Realities.* Santa Monica, CA: RAND Corporation, 1965.

Wright, Donald P., and Timothy Reese. *On Point II.* Fort Leavenworth, KS: Combat Studies Institute, 2008.

www.ingramcontent.com/pod-product-compliance
Lightning Source LLC
Chambersburg PA
CBHW050549160426
43199CB00015B/2589